Introduction to Neural Networks with C#

Second Edition

Heaton Research

Introduction to Neural Networks for C#

Second Edition

by Jeff Heaton

Heaton Research, Inc.
St. Louis

Introduction to Neural Networks for C#

Second Edition, First printing

Publisher: Heaton Research, Inc

Author: Jeff Heaton

Editor: WordsRU.com

Cover Art: Carrie Spear

ISBN: 1-60439-009-3, Second Edition, Softcover

V

SOFTWARE LICENSE AGREEMENT: TERMS AND CONDITIONS

The media and/or any online materials accompanying this book that are available now or in the future contain programs and/or text files (the "Software") to be used in connection with the book. Heaton Research, Inc. hereby grants to you a license to use and distribute software programs that make use of the compiled binary form of this book's source code. You may not redistribute the source code contained in this book, without the written permission of Heaton Research, Inc. Your purchase, acceptance, or use of the Software will constitute your acceptance of such terms.

The Software compilation is the property of Heaton Research, Inc. unless otherwise indicated and is protected by copyright to Heaton Research, Inc. or other copyright owner(s) as indicated in the media files (the "Owner(s)"). You are hereby granted a license to use and distribute the Software for your personal, noncommercial use only. You may not reproduce, sell, distribute, publish, circulate, or commercially exploit the Software, or any portion thereof, without the written consent of Heaton Research, Inc. and the specific copyright owner(s) of any component software included on this media.

In the event that the Software or components include specific license requirements or end-user agreements, statements of condition, disclaimers, limitations or warranties ("End-User License"), those End-User Licenses supersede the terms and conditions herein as to that particular Software component. Your purchase, acceptance, or use of the Software will constitute your acceptance of such End-User Licenses.

By purchase, use or acceptance of the Software you further agree to comply with all export laws and regulations of the United States as such laws and regulations may exist from time to time.

SOFTWARE SUPPORT

Components of the supplemental Software and any offers associated with them may be supported by the specific Owner(s) of that material but they are not supported by Heaton Research, Inc.. Information regarding any available support may be obtained from the Owner(s) using the information provided in the appropriate README files or listed elsewhere on the media.

Should the manufacturer(s) or other Owner(s) cease to offer support or decline to honor any offer, Heaton Research, Inc. bears no responsibility. This notice concerning support for the Software is provided for your information only. Heaton Research, Inc. is not the agent or principal of the Owner(s), and Heaton Research, Inc. is in no way responsible for providing any support for the Software, nor is it liable or responsible for any support provided, or not provided, by the Owner(s).

WARRANTY

Heaton Research, Inc. warrants the enclosed media to be free of physical defects for a period of ninety (90) days after purchase. The Software is not available from Heaton Research, Inc. in any other form or media than that enclosed herein or posted to www.heatonresearch.com. If you discover a defect in the media during this warranty period, you may obtain a replacement of identical format at no charge by sending the defective media, postage prepaid, with proof of purchase to:

```
Heaton Research, Inc.
Customer Support Department
1734 Clarkson Rd #107
Chesterfield, MO 63017-4976

Web: www.heatonresearch.com
E-Mail: support@heatonresearch.com
```

After the 90-day period, you can obtain replacement media of identical format by sending us the defective disk, proof of purchase, and a check or money order for $10, payable to Heaton Research, Inc..

DISCLAIMER

Heaton Research, Inc. makes no warranty or representation, either expressed or implied, with respect to the Software or its contents, quality, performance, merchantability, or fitness for a particular purpose. In no event will Heaton Research, Inc., its distributors, or dealers be liable to you or any other party for direct, indirect, special, incidental, consequential, or other damages arising out of the use of or inability to use the Software or its contents even if advised of the possibility of such damage. In the event that the Software includes an online update feature, Heaton Research, Inc. further disclaims any obligation to provide this feature for any specific duration other than the initial posting.

The exclusion of implied warranties is not permitted by some states. Therefore, the above exclusion may not apply to you. This warranty provides you with specific legal rights; there may be other rights that you may have that vary from state to state. The pricing of the book with the Software by Heaton Research, Inc. reflects the allocation of risk and limitations on liability contained in this agreement of Terms and Conditions.

SHAREWARE DISTRIBUTION

This Software may contain various programs that are distributed as shareware. Copyright laws apply to both shareware and ordinary commercial software, and the copyright Owner(s) retains all rights. If you try a shareware program and continue using it, you are expected to register it. Individual programs differ on details of trial periods, registration, and payment. Please observe the requirements stated in appropriate files.

VII

*This book is dedicated to my neurons,
without whose constant support
this book would not have been possible.*

Acknowledgments

There are several people who I would like to acknowledge. I would like to thank Mary McKinnis for editing the first edition of this book. I would like to thank all of the readers of the first edition who sent in suggestions.

I would like to thank WordsRU.com for providing editing resources. I would like to thank Kerrin for editing the book.

I would like to thank my sister Carrie Spear for layout and formatting suggestions.

Contents at a Glance

Contents

XIX

Table of Figures

Table of Listings

Table of Tables

Table of Equations

INTRODUCTION

This book provides an introduction to neural network programming using C#. It focuses on the feedforward neural network, but also covers Hopfield neural networks, as well as self-organizing maps.

Chapter 1 provides an overview of neural networks. You will be introduced to the mathematical underpinnings of neural networks and how to calculate their values manually. You will also see how neural networks use weights and thresholds to determine their output.

Matrix math plays a central role in neural network processing. Chapter 2 introduces matrix operations and demonstrates how to implement them in C#. The mathematical concepts of matrix operations used later in this book are discussed. Additionally, C# classes are provided which accomplish each of the required matrix operations.

One of the most basic neural networks is the Hopfield neural network. Chapter 3 demonstrates how to use a Hopfield Neural Network. You will be shown how to construct a Hopfield neural network and how to train it to recognize patterns.

Chapter 4 introduces the concept of machine learning. To train a neural network, the weights and thresholds are adjusted until the network produces the desired output. There are many different ways training can be accomplished. This chapter introduces the different training methods.

Chapter 5 introduces perhaps the most common neural network architecture, the feedforward backpropagation neural network. This type of neural network is the central focus of this book. In this chapter, you will see how to construct a feedforward neural network and how to train it using backpropagation.

Backpropagation may not always be the optimal training algorithm. Chapter 6 expands upon backpropagation by showing how to train a network using a genetic algorithm. A genetic algorithm creates a population of neural networks and only allows the best networks to "mate" and produce offspring.

Simulated annealing can also be a very effective means of training a feedforward neural network. Chapter 7 continues the discussion of training methods by introducing simulated annealing. Simulated annealing simulates the heating and cooling of a metal to produce an optimal solution.

Neural networks may contain unnecessary neurons. Chapter 8 explains how to prune a neural network to its optimal size. Pruning allows unnecessary neurons to be removed from the neural network without adversely affecting the error rate of the network. The neural network will process information more quickly with fewer neurons.

Prediction is another popular use for neural networks. Chapter 9 introduces temporal neural networks, which attempt to predict the future. Prediction networks can be applied to many different problems, such as the prediction of sunspot cycles, weather, and the financial markets.

Chapter 10 builds upon chapter 9 by demonstrating how to apply temporal neural networks to the financial markets. The resulting neural network attempts to predict the direction of the S & P 500.

Another neural network architecture is the self-organizing map (SOM). SOM's are often used to group input into categories and are generally trained with an unsupervised training algorithm. An SOM uses a winner-takes-all strategy, in which the output is provided by the winning neuron—output is not produced by each of the neurons. Chapter 11 provides an introduction to SOMs and demonstrates how to use them.

Handwriting recognition is a popular use for SOMs. Chapter 12 continues where chapter 11 leaves off, by demonstrating how to use an SOM to read handwritten characters. The neural network must be provided with a sample of the handwriting that it is to analyze. This handwriting is categorized using the 26 characters of the Latin alphabet. The neural network is then able to recognize new characters.

Chapter 13 introduces bot programming and explains how to use a neural network to help identify data. Bots are computer programs that perform repetitive tasks. An HTTP bot is a special type of bot that uses the web much like a human uses it. The neural network is trained to recognize the specific types of data for which the bot is searching.

The book ends with chapter 14, which discusses the future of neural networks, quantum computing, and how it applies to neural networks. The Encog neural network framework is also introduced.

A Historical Perspective on Neural Networks

Neural networks have been used with computers since the 1950s. Through the years, many different neural network architectures have been presented. Following is an overview of the history of neural networks and how this history has led to the neural networks of today. We will begin this exploration with the perceptron.

Perceptron

The perceptron is one of the earliest neural networks. Invented at the Cornell Aeronautical Laboratory in 1957 by Frank Rosenblatt, the perceptron was an attempt to understand human memory, learning, and cognitive processes. In 1960, Rosenblatt demonstrated the Mark I perceptron. The Mark I was the first machine that could "learn" to identify optical patterns.

The perceptron progressed through the biological neural studies of researchers such as D.O. Hebb, Warren McCulloch, and Walter Pitts. McCulloch and Pitts were the first to describe biological neural networks, and are credited with coining the phrase "neural network." They developed a simplified model of the neuron, called the MP neuron, centered on the idea that a nerve will fire only if its threshold value is exceeded. The MP neuron functioned as a sort of scanning device that read predefined input and output associations to determine the final output. The MP neuron was incapable of learning, as it had fixed thresholds; instead, it was a hard-wired logic device that was configured manually.

Because the MP neuron did not have the ability to learn, it was very limited in comparison to the infinitely more flexible and adaptive human nervous system upon which it was modeled. Rosenblatt determined that a learning network model could improve its responses by adjusting the weights on its connections between neurons. This was taken into consideration when Rosenblatt designed the perceptron.

The perceptron showed early promise for neural networks and machine learning, but had one significant shortcoming. The perceptron was unable to learn to recognize input that was not "linearly separable." This would prove to be huge obstacle that would take some time to overcome.

CHAPTER 1: OVERVIEW OF NEURAL NETWORKS

- Understanding Biological Neural Networks
- How an Artificial Neural Network is Constructed
- Appropriate Uses for Neural Networks

Computers can perform many operations considerably faster than a human being. However, faster is not always better for problem solving. There are many tasks for which the computer falls considerably short of its human counterpart. There are numerous examples of this. For instance, given two pictures, a preschool child can easily tell the difference between a cat and a dog. Yet, this same simple task is extremely difficult for today's computers.

The goal of this book is to teach the reader how to construct neural networks using the C# programming language. As with any technology, it is just as important to know when not to use neural networks as it is to understand when they should be used. This chapter provides an introduction to the appropriate uses of neural networks, and explains which programming requirements are conducive to their use.

This chapter begins with a brief introduction to the structure of neural networks. This discussion provides an overview of neural network architecture, and explains how a typical neural network is constructed. Following this introduction is a discussion of how a neural network is trained. Finally, an overview is provided of the ultimate task, validating a trained neural network.

How is a Biological Neural Network Constructed?

The term neural network, as it is normally used, is actually a misnomer. Computers attempt to simulate biological neural networks by implementing artificial neural networks. However, most publications use the term "neural network," rather than "artificial neural network" (ANN). This book follows suit. Unless the term "neural network" is explicitly prefixed with the terms "biological" or "artificial" you can assume that the term "artificial neural network" is intended. To explore this distinction, you will first be shown the structure of a biological neural network.

To construct a computer capable of "human-like thought," researchers have used the only working model they have available—the human brain. However, the human brain as a whole is far too complex to model. Rather, the individual cells that make up the human brain are studied. At the most basic level, the human brain is composed primarily of neuron cells. They are the basic building blocks of the human brain. Artificial neural networks attempt to simulate the behavior of these cells.

A neuron cell, as seen in Figure 1.1, accepts signals from dendrites. When a neuron accepts a signal, that neuron may fire. When a neuron fires, a signal is transmitted over the neuron's axon. Ultimately, the signal will leave the neuron as it travels to the axon terminals. The signal is then transmitted to other neurons or nerves.

Figure 1.1: A neuron cell.

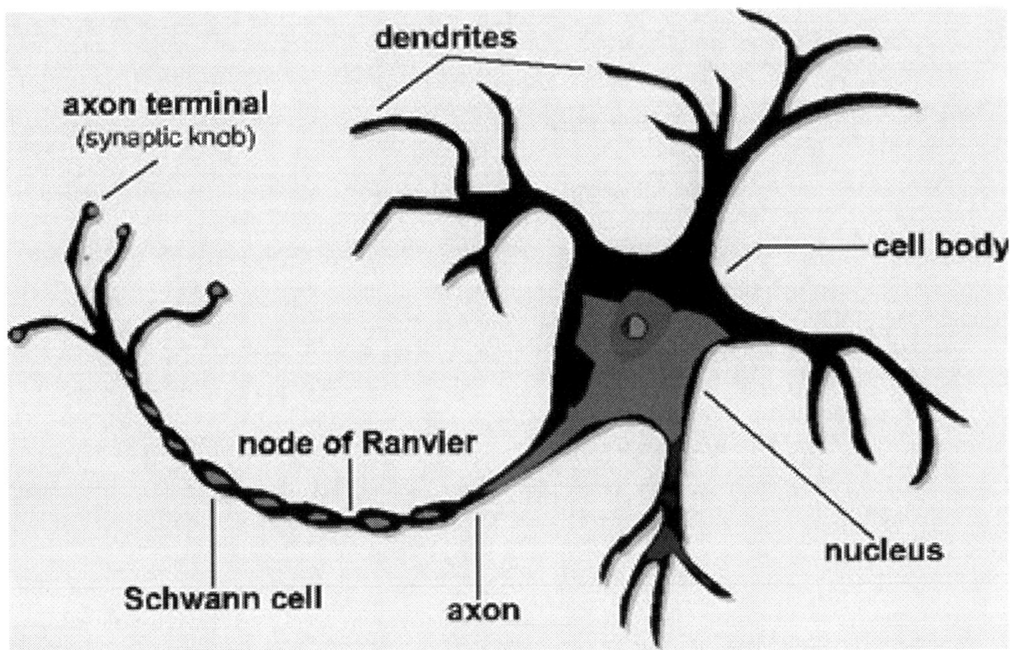

This signal, transmitted by the neuron, is an analog signal. Most modern computers are digital machines, and thus, require a digital signal. A digital computer processes information as either off or on, using the binary digits zero and one, respectively. The presence of an electric signal is indicated with a value of one, whereas the absence of an electrical signal is indicated with a value of zero. Figure 1.2 shows a digital signal.

Figure 1.2: A digital signal.

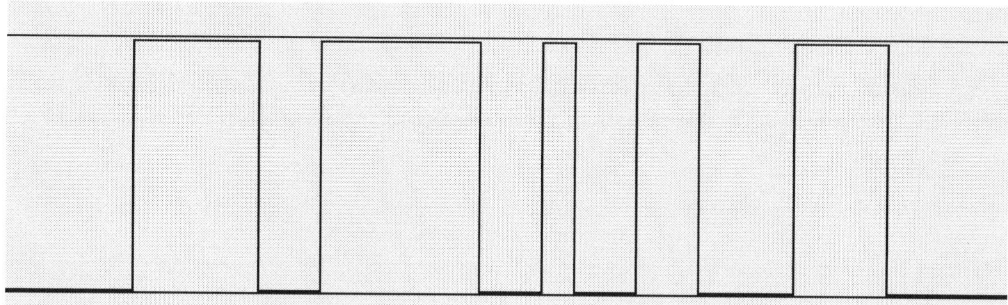

Some of the early computers were analog, rather than digital. An analog computer uses a much wider range of values than zero and one. This wider range is achieved by increasing or decreasing the voltage of the signal. Figure 1.3 shows an analog signal. Though analog computers are useful for certain simulation activities, they are not suited to processing the large volumes of data that digital computers are typically required to process. Thus, nearly every computer in use today is digital.

Figure 1.3: Sound recorder showing an analog file.

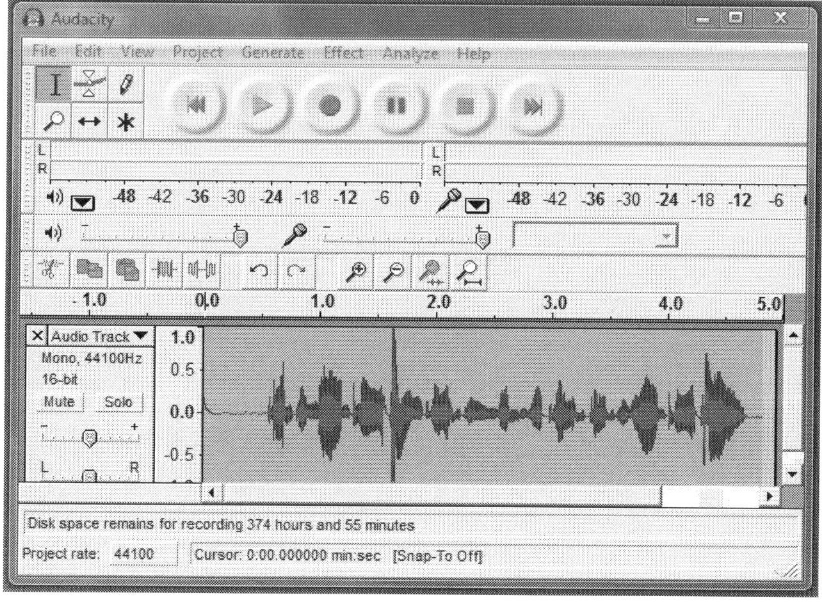

Biological neural networks are analog. As you will see in the next section, simulating analog neural networks on a digital computer can present some challenges. Neurons accept an analog signal through their dendrites, as seen in Figure 1.1. Because this signal is analog, the voltage of each signal will vary. If the voltage is within a certain range, the neuron will fire. When a neuron fires, a new analog signal is transmitted from the firing neuron to other neurons. This signal is conducted over the firing neuron's axon. The regions of input and output are called synapses. Later, in chapter 5, The Feedforward Backpropagation Neural Network example will demonstrate that the synapses are the interface between a program and a neural network.

A neuron makes a decision by firing or not firing. The decisions being made are extremely low-level decisions. It requires a large number of decisions to be made by many neurons just to read this sentence. Higher-level decisions are the result of the collective input and output of many neurons.

Decisions can be represented graphically by charting the input and output of neurons. Figure 1.4 illustrates the input and output of a particular neuron. As you will be shown in chapter 5, there are different types of neurons, all of which have differently shaped output graphs. Looking at the graph shown in Figure 1.4, it can be seen that the neuron in this example will fire at any input greater than 0.5 volts.

Figure 1.4: Activation levels of a neuron.

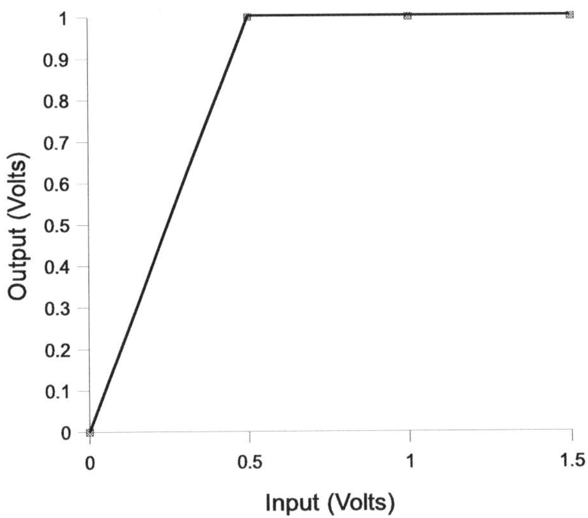

A biological neuron is capable of making basic decisions. Artificial neural networks are based on this model. Following is an explanation of how this model is simulated using a digital computer.

Solving Problems with Neural Networks

A significant goal of this book is to show you how to construct neural networks and to teach you when to use them. As a programmer of neural networks, you must understand which problems are well suited for neural network solutions and which are not. An effective neural network programmer also knows which neural network structure, if any, is most applicable to a given problem. This section begins by first focusing on those problems that are not conducive to a neural network solution.

Problems Not Suited to a Neural Network Solution

Programs that are easily written out as flowcharts are examples of problems for which neural networks are not appropriate. If your program consists of well-defined steps, normal programming techniques will suffice.

Another criterion to consider is whether the logic of your program is likely to change. One of the primary features of neural networks is their ability to learn. If the algorithm used to solve your problem is an unchanging business rule, there is no reason to use a neural network. In fact, it might be detrimental to your application if the neural network attempts to find a better solution, and begins to diverge from the desired process and produces unexpected results.

Finally, neural networks are often not suitable for problems in which you must know exactly how the solution was derived. A neural network can be very useful for solving the problem for which it was trained, but the neural network cannot explain its reasoning. The neural network knows something because it was trained to know it. The neural network cannot explain how it followed a series of steps to derive the answer.

Problems Suited to a Neural Network

Although there are many problems for which neural networks are not well suited, there are also many problems for which a neural network solution is quite useful. In addition, neural networks can often solve problems with fewer lines of code than a traditional programming algorithm. It is important to understand which problems call for a neural network approach.

Neural networks are particularly useful for solving problems that cannot be expressed as a series of steps, such as recognizing patterns, classification, series prediction, and data mining.

Pattern recognition is perhaps the most common use for neural networks. For this type of problem, the neural network is presented a pattern. This could be an image, a sound, or any other data. The neural network then attempts to determine if the input data matches a pattern that it has been trained to recognize. Chapter 3, Using a Hopfield Neural Network, provides an example of a simple neural network that recognizes input patterns.

Classification is a process that is closely related to pattern recognition. A neural network trained for classification is designed to take input samples and classify them into groups. These groups may be fuzzy, lacking clearly defined boundaries. Alternatively, these groups may have quite rigid boundaries. Chapter 12, OCR and the Self-Organizing Map, introduces an example program capable of optical character recognition (OCR). This program takes handwriting samples and classifies them by letter (e.g., the letter "A" or "B").

Training Neural Networks

The individual neurons that make up a neural network are interconnected through their synapses. These connections allow the neurons to signal each other as information is processed. Not all connections are equal. Each connection is assigned a connection weight. If there is no connection between two neurons, then their connection weight is zero. These weights are what determine the output of the neural network; therefore, it can be said that the connection weights form the memory of the neural network.

Training is the process by which these connection weights are assigned. Most training algorithms begin by assigning random numbers to a weights matrix. Then, the validity of the neural network is examined. Next, the weights are adjusted based on how well the neural network performed and the validity of the results. This process is repeated until the validation error is within an acceptable limit. There are many ways to train neural networks. Neural network training methods generally fall into the categories of supervised, unsupervised, and various hybrid approaches.

Supervised training is accomplished by giving the neural network a set of sample data along with the anticipated outputs from each of these samples. Supervised training is the most common form of neural network training. As supervised training proceeds, the neural network is taken through a number of iterations, or epochs, until the output of the neural network matches the anticipated output, with a reasonably small rate of error. Each epoch is one pass through the training samples.

Unsupervised training is similar to supervised training, except that no anticipated outputs are provided. Unsupervised training usually occurs when the neural network is being used to classify inputs into several groups. The training involves many epochs, just as in supervised training. As the training progresses, the classification groups are "discovered" by the neural network. Unsupervised training is covered in chapter 11, Using a Self-Organizing Map.

There are several hybrid methods that combine aspects of both supervised and unsupervised training. One such method is called reinforcement training. In this method, a neural network is provided with sample data that does not contain anticipated outputs, as is done with unsupervised training. However, for each output, the neural network is told whether the output was right or wrong given the input.

It is very important to understand how to properly train a neural network. This book explores several methods of neural network training, including backpropagation, simulated annealing, and genetic algorithms. Chapters 4 through 7 are dedicated to the training of neural networks. Once the neural network is trained, it must be validated to see if it is ready for use.

Validating Neural Networks

The final step, validating a neural network, is very important because it allows you to determine if additional training is required. To correctly validate a neural network, validation data must be set aside that is completely separate from the training data.

As an example, consider a classification network that must group elements into three different classification groups. You are provided with 10,000 sample elements. For this sample data, the group that each element should be classified into is known. For such a system, you would randomly divide the sample data into two groups of 5,000 elements each. The first group would form the training set. Once the network was properly trained, the second group of 5,000 elements would be used to validate the neural network.

It is very important that a separate group of data always be maintained for validation. First, training a neural network with a given sample set and also using this same set to predict the anticipated error of the neural network for a new arbitrary set will surely lead to bad results. The error achieved using the training set will almost always be substantially lower than the error on a new set of sample data. The integrity of the validation data must always be maintained.

This brings up an important question. What happens if the neural network that you have just finished training performs poorly on the validation data set? If this is the case, then you must examine possible causes. It could mean that the initial random weights were not appropriate. Rerunning the training with new initial weights could correct this. While an improper set of initial random weights could be the cause, a more likely possibility is that the training data was not properly chosen.

If the validation is performing poorly, it is likely that there was data present in the validation set that was not available in the training data. The way this situation should be rectified is to try a different random approach to separating the data into training and validation sets. If this fails, you must combine the training and validation sets into one large training set. New data must then be acquired to serve as the validation data.

In some situations it may be impossible to gather additional data to use as either training or validation data. If this is the case, then you are left with no other choice but to combine all or part of the validation set with the training set. While this approach will forgo the security of a good validation, if additional data cannot be acquired this may be your only alternative.

Problems Commonly Solved With Neural Networks

There are many different problems that can be solved with a neural network. However, neural networks are commonly used to address particular types of problems. The following four types of problem are frequently solved with neural networks:

- Classification
- Prediction
- Pattern recognition
- Optimization

These problems will be discussed briefly in the following sections. Many of the example programs throughout this book will address one of these four problems.

Classification

Classification is the process of classifying input into groups. For example, an insurance company may want to classify insurance applications into different risk categories, or an online organization may want its email system to classify incoming mail into groups of spam and non-spam messages.

Often, the neural network is trained by presenting it with a sample group of data and instructions as to which group each data element belongs. This allows the neural network to learn the characteristics that may indicate group membership.

Prediction

Prediction is another common application for neural networks. Given a time-based series of input data, a neural network will predict future values. The accuracy of the guess will be dependent upon many factors, such as the quantity and relevancy of the input data. For example, neural networks are commonly applied to problems involving predicting movements in financial markets.

This book will demonstrate several examples of prediction. Chapter 9, Predictive Neural Networks, provides an introductory explanation of how to use a neural network to make predictions. Chapter 10 shows a basic neural approach to analyzing the S&P 500.

Pattern Recognition

Pattern recognition is one of the most common uses for neural networks. Pattern recognition is a form of classification. Pattern recognition is simply the ability to recognize a pattern. The pattern must be recognized even when it is distorted. Consider the following everyday use of pattern recognition.

Every person who holds a driver's license should be able to accurately identify a traffic light. This is an extremely critical pattern recognition procedure carried out by countless drivers every day. However, not every traffic light looks the same, and the appearance of a particular traffic light can be altered depending on the time of day or the season. In addition, many variations of the traffic light exist. Still, recognizing a traffic light is not a hard task for a human driver.

How hard is it to write a computer program that accepts an image and tells you if it is a traffic light? Without the use of neural networks, this could be a very complex task. Figure 1.5 illustrates several different traffic lights. Most common programming algorithms are quickly exhausted when presented with a complex pattern recognition problem.

Figure 1.5: Different Traffic Lights

Later in this book, an example will be provided of a neural network that reads handwriting. This neural network accomplishes the task by recognizing patterns in the individual letters drawn.

Optimization

Another common use for neural networks is optimization. Optimization can be applied to many different problems for which an optimal solution is sought. The neural network may not always find the optimal solution; rather, it seeks to find an acceptable solution. Optimization problems include circuit board assembly, resource allocation, and many others.

Perhaps one of the most well-known optimization problems is the traveling sales-man problem (TSP). A salesman must visit a set number of cities. He would like to visit all cities and travel the fewest number of miles possible. With only a few cities, this is not a complex problem. However, with a large number of cities, brute force methods of calculation do not work nearly as well as a neural network approach.

Using a Simple Neural Network

Following is an example of a very simple neural network. Though the network is simple, it includes nearly all of the elements of the more complex neural networks that will be covered later in this book.

First, consider an artificial neuron, as shown in Figure 1.6.

Figure 1.6: Artificial neuron.

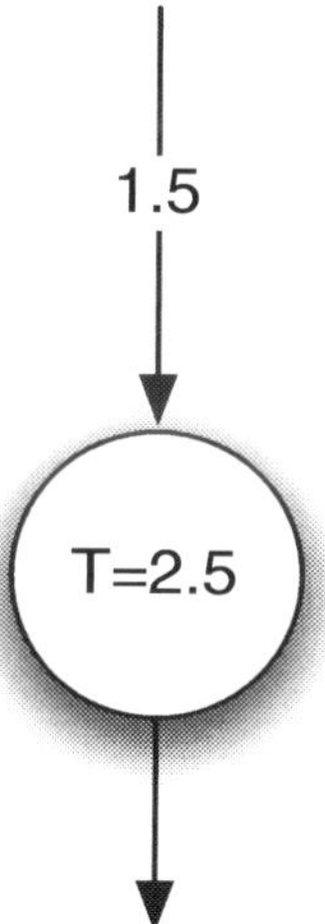

There are two attributes associated with this neuron: the threshold and the weight. The weight is 1.5 and the threshold is 2.5. An incoming signal will be amplified, or de-amplified, by the weight as it crosses the incoming synapse. If the weighted input exceeds the threshold, then the neuron will fire.

Consider a value of one (**true**) presented as the input to the neuron. The value of one will be multiplied by the weight value of 1.5. This results in a value of 1.5. The value of 1.5 is below the threshold of 2.5, so the neuron will not fire. This neuron will never fire with Boolean input values. Not all neurons accept only boolean values. However, the neurons in this section only accept the boolean values of one (**true**) and zero (**false**).

A Neural Network for the And Operator

The neuron shown in Figure 1.6 is not terribly useful. However, most neurons are not terribly useful—at least not independently. Neurons are used with other neurons to form networks. We will now look at a neural network that acts as an **AND** gate. Table 1.1 shows the truth table for the **AND** logical operation.

Table 1.1: The AND Logical Operation

A	B	A AND B
0	0	0
0	1	0
1	0	0
1	1	1

A simple neural network can be created that recognizes the **AND** logical operation. There will be three neurons in total. This network will contain two inputs and one output. A neural network that recognizes the **AND** logical operation is shown in Figure 1.7.

Figure 1.7: A neural network that recognizes the AND logical operation.

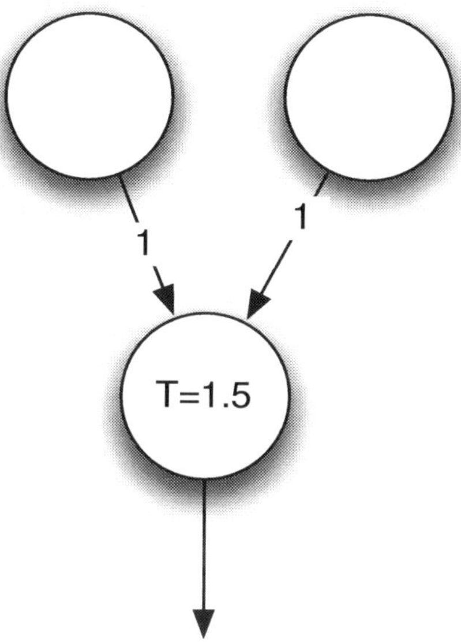

There are two inputs to the network shown in Figure 1.7. Each neuron has a weight of one. The threshold is 1.5. Therefore, a neuron will only fire if both inputs are **true**. If either input is false, the sum of the two inputs will not exceed the threshold of 1.5.

Consider inputs of **true** and **false**. The true input will send a value of one to the output neuron. This is below the threshold of 1.5. Likewise, consider inputs of **true** and **true**. Each input neuron will send a value of one. These two inputs are summed by the output neuron, resulting in two. The value of two is greater than 1.5, therefore, the neuron will fire.

A Neural Network for the Or Operation

Neural networks can be created to recognize other logical operations as well. Consider the **OR** logical operation. The truth table for the **OR** logical operation is shown in Table 1.2. The **OR** logical operation is **true** if either input is **true**.

Table 1.2: The OR Logical Operation

A	B	A OR B
0	0	0
0	1	1
1	0	1
1	1	1

The neural network that will recognize the **OR** operation is shown in Figure 1.8.

Figure 1.8: A neural network that recognizes the OR logical operation.

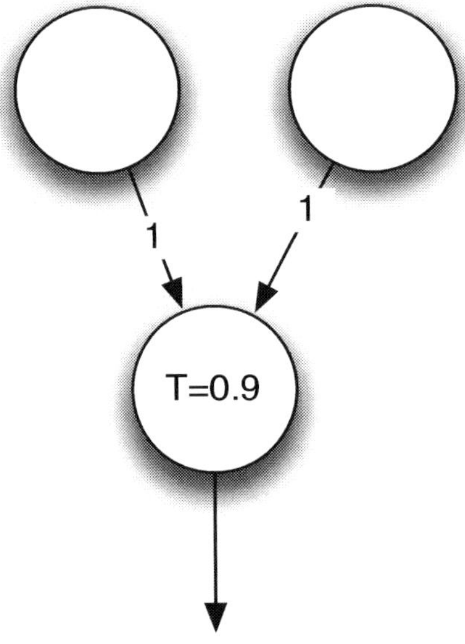

The **OR** neural network looks very similar to the **AND** neural network. The biggest difference is the threshold value. Because the threshold is lower, only one of the inputs needs to have a value of **true** for the output neuron to fire.

A Neural Network for the XOR Operation

Next we will consider a neural network for the exclusive or (**XOR**) logical operation. The **XOR** truth table is shown in Table 1.3.

Table 1.3: The XOR Logical Operation

A	B	A XOR B
0	0	0
0	1	1
1	0	1
1	1	0

The **XOR** logical operation requires a slightly more complex neural network than the **AND** and **OR** operators. The neural networks presented so far have had only two layers— an input layer and an output layer. More complex neural networks also include one or more hidden layers. The XOR operator requires a hidden layer. As a result, the XOR neural network often becomes a sort of "Hello World" application for neural networks. You will see the XOR operator again in this book as different types of neural network are introduced and trained.

Figure 1.9 shows a three-layer neural network that can be used to recognize the XOR operator.

Figure 1.9: A neural network that recognizes the XOR logical operation.

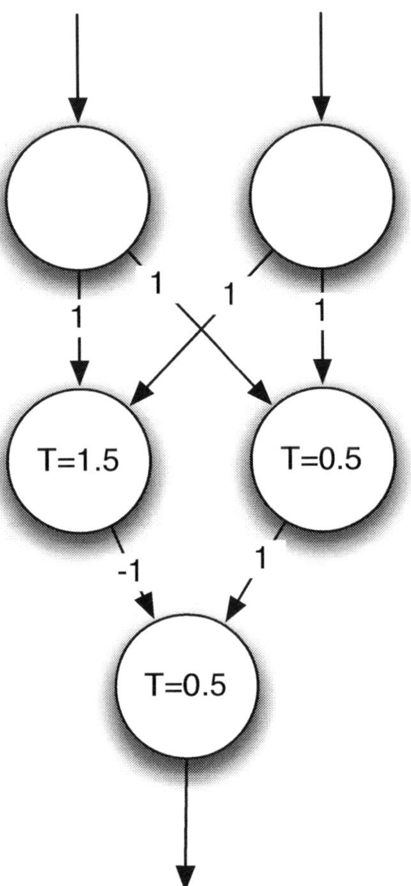

Consider the case in which the values of **true** and **true** are presented to this neural network. Both neurons in the hidden layer receive the value of two. This is above the thresholds of both of the hidden layer neurons, so they will both fire. However, the first hidden neuron has a weight of -1, so its contribution to the output neuron is -1. The second neuron has a weight of 1, so its contribution to the output neuron is 1. The sum of 1 and -1 is zero. Zero is below the threshold of the output neuron, so the output neuron does not fire. This is consistent with the **XOR** operation, because it will produce **false** if both inputs are **true**.

Now consider if the values of **false** and **true** are presented to the neural network. The input to the first hidden layer neuron will be 1, from the second input neuron. This is lower than the threshold of 1.5, so it will not fire. The input to the second hidden layer neuron will also be 1, from the second input neuron. This is over the 0.5

threshold, so it will fire. The input to the output neuron will be zero from the left hidden neuron and 1 from the right hidden neuron. This is greater than 0.5, so the output neuron will fire. This is consistent with the **XOR** operation, because it will produce **true** if one of the input neurons is **true** and the other **false**.

Of course, the neural networks shown in the preceding sections are very simple. However, they illustrate all of the key points for more complex neural networks. Future chapters will introduce additional types of neural networks; however, neural networks will almost always feature weights and thresholds.

Chapter Summary

Computers can process information considerably faster than human beings. Yet, a computer is incapable of performing many of the same tasks that a human can easily perform. For processes that cannot easily be broken into a finite number of steps, a neural network can be an ideal solution.

The term neural network typically refers to an artificial neural network. An artificial neural network attempts to simulate the biological neural networks contained in the brains of all animals. Artificial neural networks were first introduced in the 1950's and through the years of their development have experienced numerous setbacks; they have yet to deliver on the promise of simulating human thought.

Neural networks are constructed of neurons that form layers. Input is presented to the layers of neurons. If the input to a neuron is within the range that the neuron has been trained for, then the neuron will fire. When a neuron fires, a signal is sent to the layers of neurons to which the firing neuron is connected. The connections between neurons are called synapses. C# can be used to construct such a network.

Neural networks must be trained and validated. A training set is usually split in half to provide both a training and validation set. Training the neural network consists of running the neural network over the training data until the neural network learns to recognize the training set with a sufficiently low error rate. Validation occurs when the neural network's results are checked.

Just because a neural network can process the training data with a low rate of error, does not mean the neural network is trained and ready for use. Before the neural network is placed into production use, it must be validated. Validation involves presenting the validation set to the neural network and comparing the actual results produced by the neural network with the anticipated results.

The neural network is ready to be placed into production if, at the end of the validation process, the results from the validation run meet a satisfactory error level. If the results are not satisfactory, then the neural network will have to be retrained before it can be placed into production.

Neural networks are comprised of many neurons. Their threshold and weight values are combined into weight matrixes. A weight matrix is stored in a regular mathematical matrix. Chapter 2 will introduce several C# classes designed to store matrix values and perform matrix mathematics. The neural networks in this book will be built upon these matrix classes.

Vocabulary

Activation Level

Analog Computer

Artificial Intelligence

Artificial Neural Network

Axon

Binary

Biological Neural Network

Classification

Dendrite

Digital Computer

Fire

Hidden Layer

Input Layer

Layer

Matrix

Neural Network

Neuron

Output Layer

Pattern Recognition

Prediction

Supervised Training

Signal

Synapse

Thresholds

Training

Truth Table

Unsupervised Training

Weight Matrix

Validation

XOR

Questions for Review

1.   What types of problems are neural networks better able to address than traditional programming practices?

2.   Shown below is a simple neural network for an operator. Write the truth table for this neural network. What operator is this?

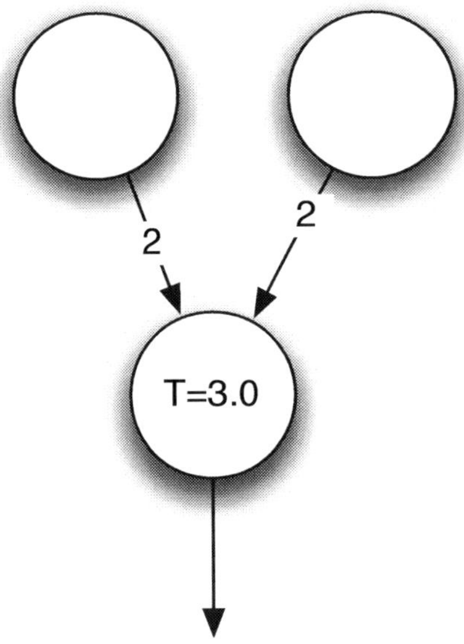

3.   Explain the purpose of a classification neural network. What sort of "real world" problem might a classification neural network be used for?

4.   What is the purpose of a threshold value?

5.   Explain the difference between supervised and unsupervised training.

Chapter 2: Matrix Operations

- Understanding Weight Matrixes
- Using the Matrix Classes
- Using Matrixes with Neural Networks
- Working with Bipolar Operations

Matrix mathematics are used to both train neural networks and calculate their outputs. Other mathematical operations are used as well; however, neural network programming is based primarily on matrix operations. This chapter will review the matrix operations that are of particular use to neural networks. Several classes will be developed to encapsulate the matrix operations used by the neural networks covered in this book. You will learn how to construct these matrix classes and how to use them. Future chapters will explain how to use the matrix classes with several different types of neural networks.

The Weight Matrix

In the last chapter, you learned that neural networks make use of two types of values: weights and thresholds. Weights define the interactions between the neurons. Thresholds define what it will take to get a neuron to fire. The weighted connections between neurons can be thought of as a matrix. For example, consider the connections between the following two layers of the neural network shown in Figure 2.1.

Figure 2.1: A two neuron layer connected to a three neuron layer.

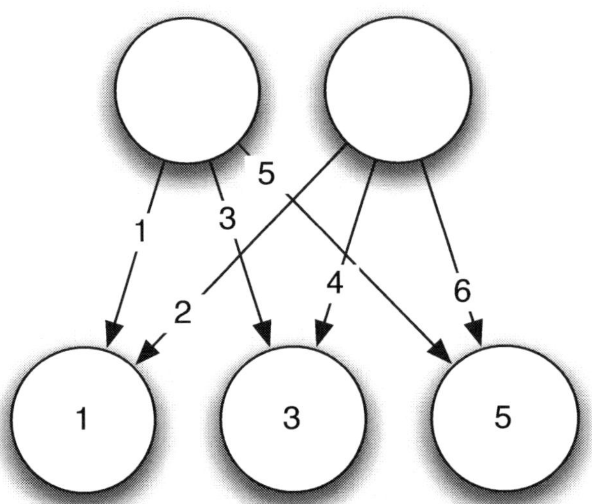

You can see the weights in Figure 2.1. The weights are attached to the lines drawn between the neurons. Each of the two neurons in the first layer is connected to each of the three neurons in the second layer. There are a total of six connections. These connections can be represented as a 3x2 weight matrix, as described in Equation 2.1.

Equation 2.1: A Weight Matrix

$$\begin{bmatrix} 1 & 2 \\ 3 & 4 \\ 5 & 6 \end{bmatrix}$$

The weight matrix can be defined in C# as follows:

```
Matrix weightMatrix = new Matrix(3,2);
```

The threshold variable is not multidimensional, like the weight matrix. There is one threshold value per neuron. Each neuron in the second layer has an individual threshold value. These values can be stored in an array of C# **double** variables. The following code shows how the entire memory of the two layers can be defined.

```
Matrix weightMatrix = new Matrix(3,2);
double[] thresholds = new double[2];
```

These declarations include both the 3x2 matrix and the two threshold values for the second layer. There is no need to store threshold values for the first layer, since it is not connected to another layer. Weight matrix and threshold values are only stored for the connections between two layers, not for each layer.

The preferred method for storing these values is to combine the thresholds with the weights in a combined matrix. The above matrix has three rows and two columns. The thresholds can be thought of as the fourth row of the weight matrix, which can be defined as follows:

```
Matrix weightMatrix = new Matrix(4,2);
```

The combined threshold and weight matrix is described in Equation 2.2. In this equation, the variable **w represents** the cells used to store weights and the variable **t** represents the cells used to hold thresholds.

Equation 2.2: A Threshold and Weight Matrix

$$\begin{bmatrix} w & w \\ w & w \\ w & w \\ t & t \end{bmatrix}$$

Combining the thresholds and weights in one matrix has several advantages. This matrix now represents the entire memory of this layer of the neural network and you only have to deal with a single structure. Further, since many of the same mathematical operations performed on the weight matrix are also performed on the threshold values, having them contained in a single matrix allows these operations to be performed more efficiently.

Matrix Classes

This chapter presents several classes that can be used to create and manipulate matrixes. These matrix classes will be used throughout this book. These classes are summarized in Table 2.1.

Table 2.1: Matrix Classes

Class	Purpose
BiPolarUtil	A utility class to convert between Boolean and bipolar numbers.
Matrix	Holds a matrix.
MatrixMath	Performs mathematical operations on a matrix.

The next three sections will examine each of these classes.

The BiPolarUtil Class

The **BiPolarUtil** class is used to switch between a bipolar number and a **bool** value. A **bool** value is either **true** or **false**. A bipolar number is either 1 or -1. Using this class, the **bool** value of **false** is expressed as a -1 bipolar value and the **bool** value of **true** is expressed as a 1 bipolar value. The **BiPolarUtil** class is a collection of **static** methods. The signatures for these methods are shown here.

```
public static double Bipolar2double(bool b)
public static double[] Bipolar2double(bool[] b)
public static double[,] Bipolar2double(bool[,] b)
public static bool Double2bipolar(double d)
public static bool[] Double2bipolar(double[] d)
public static bool[,] Double2bipolar(double[,] d)
public static double NormalizeBinary(double d)
public static double ToBinary(double d)
public static double ToBiPolar(double d)
public static double ToNormalizedBinary(double d)
```

Table 2.2 summarizes the functions provided by the **BiPolarUtil** class.

Table 2.2: The BiPolarUtil Class

Method	Purpose
Bipolar2double	Converts a Boolean bipolar to a double. For example, true is converted to 1.
Double2bipolar	Converts a double value to a bipolar Boolean. For example, -1 is converted to false.

The above two methods are overloaded, so you can convert a single value, a single dimensional array, or a two dimensional array. Bipolar values are particularly useful for Hopfield neural networks. Hopfield neural networks will be discussed in the next chapter.

The Matrix Class

The **Matrix** class is used to construct two dimensional matrixes. The values contained in the matrixes are stored as C# **double** variables. The **Matrix** class provides the fundamental operations of numerical linear algebra. For operations involving two or more matrixes, the **MatrixMath** class is used. The **MatrixMath** class is discussed in the next section.

The signatures for the **Matrix** class methods are shown here.

```
public double[] ToPackedArray()
public static Matrix CreateColumnMatrix(double[] input) public
static Matrix CreateRowMatrix(double[] input)
public void Add(int row, int col, double value)
public void Clear() public Matrix Clone()
public bool Equals(Matrix matrix)
public bool Equals(Matrix matrix, int precision)
public int FromPackedArray(double[] array, int index)
public Matrix GetCol(int col)
public Matrix GetRow(int row) public bool IsVector()
public bool IsZero()
public void Ramdomize(double min, double max)
public double Sum()
```

The methods provided by the **Matrix** class are summarized in Table 2.3.

Table 2.3: Methods of the Matrix Class

Method	Purpose
CreateColumnMatrix	Static method which creates a matrix with a single column.
CreateRowMatrix	Static method which creates a matrix with a single row.
Add	Adds the specified value to every cell in the matrix.
Clear	Sets every cell in a matrix to zero.
Clone	Creates an exact copy of a matrix.
Equals	Determines if two matrixes are equal to each other.
GetCol	Gets one column of a matrix object as a new matrix object.
GetRow	Gets one row of a matrix object as a new matrix object.
IsVector	Determines if a matrix is a vector. A vector matrix has either a single row or a single column.
IsZero	Determines if every cell in a matrix object is zero.
Set	Sets the value of a cell.
Sum	Returns the sum of every cell in a matrix object.

ToPackedArray   Converts a two dimensional matrix array into a one dimensional array of C# double variables.

The **Matrix** class also contains a number of properties. The signatures for these properties are shown here.

```
public double this[int row, int col] public int Cols
public int Rows
public int Size
```

These properties are summarized in Table 2.4.

Table 2.4: Properties of the Matrix Class

Method	Purpose
Cols	Get the number of columns in the matrix.
Rows	Get the number of rows in the matrix.
Size	Get the number of cells in the matrix.
This	Allows index access to the matrix, for example matrix[3,2].

The **Matrix** class will be used to construct the weight matrixes for all neural networks presented in this book.

The MatrixMath Class

Most mathematical operations on a **Matrix** class are accomplished using the **MatrixMath** class. All methods in the **MatrixMath** class are **static**. Further, they always return a new matrix and do not modify the matrixes passed to them. The signatures for the **MatrixMath** methods are shown here.

```
public static Matrix Add(Matrix a, Matrix b)
public static void Copy(Matrix source, Matrix target)
public static Matrix DeleteCol(Matrix matrix, int deleted)
public static Matrix DeleteRow(Matrix matrix, int deleted)
public static Matrix Divide(Matrix a, double b)
public static double DotProduct(Matrix a, Matrix b)
public static Matrix Identity(int size)
public static Matrix Multiply(Matrix a, double b)
public static Matrix Multiply(Matrix a, Matrix b)
public static Matrix Subtract(Matrix a, Matrix b)
public static Matrix Transpose(Matrix input)
public static double VectorLength(Matrix input)
```

These methods are summarized in Table 2.5.

Table 2.5: The MatrixMath Class

Method	Purpose
Add	Adds two matrixes and produces a third matrix.
Divide	Divides one matrix by a scalar and produces a second matrix.
DotProduct	Calculates the dot product of a matrix.
Identity	Creates an identity matrix of a specified size.
Multiply	Multiplies one matrix by another and produces a third matrix.
Subtract	Subtracts one matrix from another and produces a third matrix.
Transpose	Transposes a matrix and produces a new matrix.
VectorLength	Calculates the squared length of a vector.

These are the primary mathematical operations that neural networks need to perform. Each of these operations will be discussed at length later in this chapter.

Many C# neural network implementations build matrix operations directly into their neural network classes. The result being many nested **for** loops inside the neural network class. For example, the following code allows a neural network to learn.

```csharp
public void Learn(double learnRate, double momentum) {

  if (layer.HasMatrix() ) {
    for (int i1 = 0; i1 < layer.NeuronCount; i1++) {
      for (int i2 = 0; i2 < layer.Next.NeuronCount; i2++) {
matrixDelta[i1][i2] = (learnRate * accMatrixDelta[i1][i2])
+ (momentum * matrixDelta[i1][i2]);
        layer.GetMatrix().SetMatrix(i1,i2,layer.GetMatrix().
GetMatrix(i1,i2) + matrixDelta[i1][i2]);
        accMatrixDelta[i1][i2] = 0;
      }
    }
  }
}
```

The above code performs several matrix operations; however, it is not completely obvious which matrix operations are being performed. By encapsulating the matrix operations inside several matrix classes, the above code can be simplified. Further, you will be able to tell, at a glance, which matrix operations are being performed. The following code accomplishes the same as the code above; however, it uses matrix classes.

```
public void Learn(double learnRate, double momentum)
{
  if (this.layer.HasMatrix()) {

    Matrix m1 = MatrixMath.Multiply( accMatrixDelta, learnRate );
    Matrix m2 = MatrixMath.Multiply( matrixDelta, momentum);
    matrixDelta = MatrixMath.Add(m1, m2);
    layer.SetMatrix(MatrixMath.Add(layer.
GetMatrix(),matrixDelta));
    accMatrixDelta.Clear();
  }
}
```

As you can see, several matrixes are constructed and then the **MatrixMath** class is used to perform operations upon them.

Constructing a Matrix

There are several ways to construct a Matrix object. To construct an empty matrix, use the following code:

```
Matrix matrix = new Matrix(3,2);
```

This will construct an empty matrix of three rows and two columns, which contains only zeros. This matrix is described in Equation 2.3.

Equation 2.3: An Empty Matrix

$$\begin{bmatrix} 0 & 0 & 0 \\ 0 & 0 & 0 \\ 0 & 0 & 0 \end{bmatrix}$$

You can also construct a matrix using a two dimensional array, which allows you to initialize the cells of the matrix in the declaration. The following code creates an initialized 3x2 matrix.

```
double[,] matrixData = {
  {1.0,2.0,3.0,4.0},
  {5.0,6.0,7.0,8.0}
};

Matrix matrix = new Matrix(matrixData);
```

This matrix is described in Equation 2.4.

Equation 2.4: An Initialized Matrix

$$\begin{bmatrix} 1.0 & 2.0 & 3.0 & 4.0 \\ 5.0 & 6.0 & 7.0 & 8.0 \end{bmatrix}$$

Matrixes can also be created using a single dimensional array. A single dimensional array can be used to create a row or a column matrix. Row and column matrixes contain either a single row or a single column, respectively. These matrixes are also called vectors. The following code can be used to create a row matrix.

```
double[] matrixData = {1.0,2.0,3.0,4.0};
Matrix matrix = Matrix.CreateRowMatrix(matrixData);
```

This will create a matrix that contains a single row. This matrix is described in Equation 2.5.

Equation 2.5: A Row Matrix/Vector

$$\begin{bmatrix} 1.0 & 2.0 & 3.0 & 4.0 \end{bmatrix}$$

It is also possible to create a column matrix. This matrix takes a single dimensional array, just as before; however, this time a matrix with a single column is created. The code to do this is shown here.

```
double matrixData[] = {1.0,2.0,3.0,4.0};
Matrix matrix = Matrix.CreateColumnMatrix(matrixData);
```

This matrix is described in Equation 2.6.

Equation 2.6: A Column Matrix/Vector

$$\begin{bmatrix} 1.0 \\ 2.0 \\ 3.0 \\ 4.0 \end{bmatrix}$$

In the next section you will see how mathematical operations can be performed on one or more matrixes.

Matrix Operations

This section will review some of the matrix operations that are provided by the **MatrixMath** class. Each matrix operation will be explained, as well as the code that is used to perform the operation. You can try some of the matrix operations online at the following URL.

http://www.heatonresearch.com/examples/math/matrix

Matrix Addition

Matrix addition is a relatively simple procedure. The corresponding cells of two matrixes of exactly the same size are summed. The results are returned in a new matrix of equal size. Equation 2.7 describes the process of matrix addition.

Equation 2.7: Matrix Addition

$$\begin{bmatrix} 1 & 2 \\ 3 & 4 \end{bmatrix} + \begin{bmatrix} 4 & 5 \\ 6 & 7 \end{bmatrix} = \begin{bmatrix} 5 & 7 \\ 9 & 11 \end{bmatrix}$$

The signature for the **Add** method of the **MatrixMath** class is shown here.

```
public static Matrix Add(Matrix a, Matrix b)
```

To add two matrixes they must have the same number of rows and columns. First check the rows, if they do not match, then throw an error.

```
if (a.Rows != b.Rows)
{
  throw new MatrixError(
    "To add the matrixes they must have the same number of rows
and columns.  Matrix a has "
    + a.Rows
    + " rows and matrix b has "
    + b.Rows + " rows.");
}
```

Next, check the columns, if they do not match then throw an error.

```
if (a.Cols != b.Cols)
{
  throw new MatrixError(
    "To add the matrixes they must have the same number of rows and
columns.  Matrix a has "
      + a.Cols
```

```
    + " cols and matrix b has "
    + b.Cols + " cols.");
}
```

Allocate a new 2D array to hold the newly created matrix. The new matrix will contain the result of the addition.

```
double[,] result = new double[a.Rows, a.Cols];
```

Loop over every row and column in the matrix.

```
for (int resultRow = 0; resultRow < a.Rows; resultRow++)
{
  for (int resultCol = 0; resultCol < a.Cols; resultCol++)
  {
```

Add the each cell in the two matrixes and store the result in the newly created matrix stored in the **result** variable.

```
    result[resultRow, resultCol] = a[resultRow, resultCol]
    + b[resultRow, resultCol];
  }
}
```

Construct a new **Matrix** from the result variable.

```
return new Matrix(result);
```

This new matrix is returned.

Matrix Division by a Scalar

A matrix can be divided by a single number, or scalar. For example, to divide a matrix by the number 10, each cell in the matrix would be divided by 10. Equation 2.8 describes the process of dividing a matrix by a scalar.

Equation 2.8: Matrix Division by a Scalar

$$\begin{bmatrix} 2 & 4 \\ 6 & 8 \end{bmatrix} / 2 = \begin{bmatrix} 1 & 2 \\ 3 & 4 \end{bmatrix}$$

The signature for the matrix **Divide** function is shown here.

```
public static Matrix Divide(Matrix a, double b)
```

First, allocate a new array to hold the result of the division.

```
double[,] result = new double[a.Rows, a.Cols];
```

Loop over every cell in the matrix that is to be divided by the scalar.

```
for (int row = 0; row < a.Rows; row++)
{
  for (int col = 0; col < a.Cols; col++)
  {
```

Divide every cell by the specified scalar. The result of the division is placed in the **result** array.

```
    result[row, col] = a[row, col] / b;
  }
}
```

Finally, a new matrix is created to hold the result.

```
return new Matrix(result);
```

This new matrix is returned to the caller.

Compute the Dot Product

The dot product can be computed from two vector matrixes. A vector matrix contains either a single row or a single column. To determine the dot product of two matrixes, they must have the same number of cells. It is not necessary that the cells in the two matrixes be oriented the same way. It is only necessary that they have the same number of cells.

The dot product is a scalar, a single number, not another matrix. To calculate the dot product, each cell, taken in order and beginning at the top-left side of the matrix, is multiplied by the corresponding cell in the other matrix. The results of these multiplication operations are then summed. Equation 2.9 describes the process of computing the dot product.

Equation 2.9: Dot Product

$$[1 \quad 2 \quad 3 \quad 4] * \begin{bmatrix} 5 \\ 6 \\ 7 \\ 8 \end{bmatrix} = (1*5) + (2*6) + (3*7) + (4*8) = 5 + 12 + 21 + 32 = 70$$

The signature for the **DotProduct** method is shown here.

```
public static double DotProduct(Matrix a, Matrix b)
```

To take the dot product of two matrixes one, or both, must be a vector. If this is not the case, then **throw** an error.

```
if (!a.IsVector() || !b.IsVector())
{
  throw new MatrixError(
"To take the dot product, both matrixes must be vectors.");
}
```

Convert both matrixes into flat arrays.

```
Double[] aArray = a.ToPackedArray();
Double[] bArray = b.ToPackedArray();
```

If both matrixes are not of the same length, then the dot product cannot be taken. If this is the case, throw an exception.

```
if (aArray.Length != bArray.Length)
{
  throw new MatrixError(
    "To take the dot product, both matrixes must be of the same
length.");
}
```

Setup an **result** variable and calculate the length. The **result** variable will hold the addition of each array element.

```
double result = 0;
int length = aArray.Length;
```

Loop over each element in the arrays.

```
for (int i = 0; i < length; i++)
{
```

Add up the product of each of the two arrays.

```
  result += aArray[i] * bArray[i];
}
```

Finally, return the result.

```
return result;
```

The dot product is returned to the calling method.

Matrix Multiplication and the Identity Matrix

Matrix multiplication can only be performed if two matrixes have compatible dimensions. Compatible dimensions mean that the number of columns of the first matrix must be equal to the number of rows of the second matrix. This means that it is legal to multiply a 2x3 matrix by a 3x2 matrix. However, it is not legal to multiply a 2x3 matrix by a 2x6 matrix!

Next, we will see how to multiply two matrixes. Equation 2.10 describes how a 2x3 matrix is multiplied by a 3x2 matrix.

Equation 2.10: Matrix Multiplication

$$\begin{bmatrix} 1 & 4 \\ 2 & 5 \\ 3 & 6 \end{bmatrix} * \begin{bmatrix} 7 & 8 & 9 \\ 10 & 11 & 12 \end{bmatrix} = \begin{bmatrix} (1*7)+(4*10) & (1*8)+(4*11) & (1*9)+(4*12) \\ (2*7)+(5*10) & (2*8)+(5*11) & (2*9)+(5*12) \\ (3*7)+(6*10) & (3*8)+(6*11) & (3*9)+(6*12) \end{bmatrix} = \begin{bmatrix} 47 & 52 & 57 \\ 64 & 71 & 78 \\ 81 & 90 & 99 \end{bmatrix}$$

It is also important to note that matrix multiplication is not commutative. The result of 2*6 is the same as 6*2. This is because multiplication is commutative when dealing with scalars—not so with matrixes. The result of multiplying a 1x3 matrix by a 3x2 matrix is not at all the same as multiplying a 3x2 matrix by a 1x3 matrix. In fact, it is not even valid to multiply a 3x2 matrix by a 1x3. Recall in Equation 2.10 we multiplied a 2x3 matrix by a 3x2 matrix. Equation 2.11 illustrates the results of multiplying a 3x2 matrix by a 2x3 matrix. This operation produces a completely different result than Equation 2.10.

Equation 2.11: Non-Commutative Matrix Multiplication

$$\begin{bmatrix} 7 & 8 & 9 \\ 10 & 11 & 12 \end{bmatrix} * \begin{bmatrix} 1 & 4 \\ 2 & 5 \\ 3 & 6 \end{bmatrix} = \begin{bmatrix} (7*1)+(8*2)+(9*3) & (7*4)+(8*5)+(9*6) \\ (10*1)+(11*2)+(12*3) & (10*4)+(11*5)+(12*6) \end{bmatrix} = \begin{bmatrix} 50 & 122 \\ 68 & 167 \end{bmatrix}$$

An identity matrix is a matrix that when multiplied by another matrix produces the same matrix. Think of this as multiplying a number by 1. Equation 2.12 describes the identity matrix.

Equation 2.12: Identity Matrix

$$\begin{bmatrix} 1 & 0 & 0 \\ 0 & 1 & 0 \\ 0 & 0 & 1 \end{bmatrix}$$

An identity matrix is always perfectly square. A matrix that is not square does not have an identity matrix. As you can see from Equation 2.12, the identity matrix is created by starting with a matrix that has only zero values. The cells in the diagonal from the northwest corner to the southeast corner are then set to one.

Equation 2.13 describes an identity matrix being multiplied by another matrix.

Equation 2.13: Multiply by an Identity Matrix

$$\begin{bmatrix} 1 & 2 & 3 \\ 4 & 5 & 6 \\ 7 & 8 & 9 \end{bmatrix} * \begin{bmatrix} 1 & 0 & 0 \\ 0 & 1 & 0 \\ 0 & 0 & 1 \end{bmatrix} = \begin{bmatrix} (1*1)+(2*0)+(3*0) & (1*0)+(2*1)+(3*0) & (1*0)+(2*0)+(3*1) \\ (4*1)+(5*0)+(6*0) & (4*0)+(5*1)+(6*0) & (4*0)+(5*0)+(6*1) \\ (7*1)+(8*0)+(9*0) & (7*0)+(8*1)+(9*0) & (7*0)+(8*0)+(9*1) \end{bmatrix} = \begin{bmatrix} 1 & 2 & 3 \\ 4 & 5 & 6 \\ 7 & 8 & 9 \end{bmatrix}$$

The resulting matrix in Equation 2.13 is the same as the matrix that was multiplied by the identity matrix.

The signature for the **Identity** method is shown here.

```
public static Matrix Identity(int size)
```

To take the identity the size must be greater than one. If this is not the case then throw an exception.

```
if (size < 1)
{
  throw new MatrixError("Identity matrix must be at least of size
1.");
}
```

Create a new matrix to hold the identify. Identity matrixes are always square.

```
Matrix result = new Matrix(size, size);
```

Loop across the diagonal of the matrix.

```
for (int i = 0; i < size; i++)
{
```

Set each element of the diagonal to one.

```
  result[i, i] = 1;
}
```

The result of the identity is stored in the **result** variable.

```
return result;
```

The identity is returned to the calling method.

Matrix Multiplication by a Scalar

Matrixes can also be multiplied by a scalar. Matrix multiplication by a scalar is very simple to perform—every cell in the matrix is multiplied by the specified scalar. Equation 2.14 shows how this is done.

Equation 2.14: Matrix Multiplication by a Scalar

$$\begin{bmatrix} 1 & 2 & 3 \\ 4 & 5 & 6 \\ 7 & 8 & 9 \end{bmatrix} * 2 = \begin{bmatrix} 1*2 & 2*2 & 3*2 \\ 4*2 & 5*2 & 6*2 \\ 7*2 & 8*2 & 9*2 \end{bmatrix} = \begin{bmatrix} 2 & 4 & 6 \\ 8 & 10 & 12 \\ 14 & 16 & 18 \end{bmatrix}$$

The signature for the **Multiply** by a scalar method is shown here.

```
public static Matrix Multiply(Matrix a, double b)
```

First, create a new matrix to hold the result of the multiplication.

```
double[,] result = new double[a.Rows, a.Cols];
```

Loop over every cell in the **a** matrix.

```
for (int row = 0; row < a.Rows; row++)
{
  for (int col = 0; col < a.Cols; col++)
  {
```

Assign each cell in the **result** matrix to the product of something in the **a** matrix and the **b** scalar.

```
    result[row, col] = a[row, col] * b;
  }
}
```

Finally, create a new matrix based on the **result** variable.

```
return new Matrix(result);
```

The result of the multiplication is returned to the calling method.

Matrix Subtraction

Matrix subtraction is a relatively simple procedure, also. The two matrixes on which the subtraction operation will be performed must be exactly the same size. Each cell in the resulting matrix is the difference of the two corresponding cells from the source matrixes. Equation 2.15 describes the process of matrix subtraction.

Equation 2.15: Matrix Subtraction

$$\begin{bmatrix} 4 & 5 \\ 6 & 7 \end{bmatrix} - \begin{bmatrix} 1 & 2 \\ 3 & 4 \end{bmatrix} = \begin{bmatrix} (4-1) & (5-2) \\ (6-3) & (7-4) \end{bmatrix} = \begin{bmatrix} 3 & 3 \\ 3 & 3 \end{bmatrix}$$

The signature for the **Subtract** method of the **MatrixMath** class is shown here.

```
public static Matrix Subtract(Matrix a, Matrix b)
```

Both matrixes should have the same number of rows and columns. First check to see if they have the same number of rows. If they do not, then throw an exception.

```
if (a.Rows != b.Rows)
{
  throw new MatrixError(
```

```
"To subtract the matrixes they must have the same number of rows
and columns.  Matrix a has "
    + a.Rows
    + " rows and matrix b has "
    + b.Rows + " rows.");
}
```

Next check to see if they have the same number of columns. If they do not, then throw an exception.

```
if (a.Cols != b.Cols)
{
  throw new MatrixError(
"To subtract the matrixes they must have the same number of rows
and columns.  Matrix a has "
    + a.Cols
    + " cols and matrix b has "
    + b.Cols + " cols.");
}
```

Create a new array that is large enough to hold the results of the subtraction.

```
double[,] result = new double[a.Rows, a.Cols];
```

Loop over every cell in the matrix.

```
for (int resultRow = 0; resultRow < a.Rows; resultRow++)
{
  for (int resultCol = 0; resultCol < a.Cols; resultCol++)
  {
```

For each cell store the result of the subtraction in the **result** array.

```
    result[resultRow, resultCol] = a[resultRow, resultCol]
      - b[resultRow, resultCol];
  }
}
```

Finally, create a new matrix based on the **result** variable.

```
return new Matrix(result);
```

The result of the subtraction is returned to the calling method.

Transpose a Matrix

Matrix transposition occurs when the rows and columns of a matrix are interchanged. Equation 2.16 describes the transposition of a matrix.

Equation 2.16: Matrix Transpose

$$\begin{bmatrix} 1 & 2 \\ 3 & 4 \\ 5 & 6 \end{bmatrix} \begin{bmatrix} 1 & 3 & 5 \\ 2 & 4 & 6 \end{bmatrix}$$

The signature for the transpose method is shown here.

```
public static Matrix Transpose(Matrix input)
```

Create a new array that is large enough to hold the results of the transposition.

```
double[,] inverseMatrix = new double[input.Cols,
   input.Rows];
```

Loop over every cell in the matrix.

```
for (int r = 0; r < input.Rows; r++)
{
   for (int c = 0; c < input.Cols; c++)
   {
```

For each cell store the result of the transposition in the **result** array.

```
      inverseMatrix[c, r] = input[r, c];
   }
}
```

Finally, create a new matrix based on the **result** variable.

```
return new Matrix(inverseMatrix);
```

The result of the subtraction is returned to the calling method.

Vector Length

The length of a vector matrix is defined to be the square root of the squared sums of every cell in the matrix. Equation 2.17 describes how the vector length for a vector matrix is calculated.

Equation 2.17: Calculate Vector Length

$$\begin{bmatrix} x_1 & x_2 & ... & x_n \end{bmatrix} = \sqrt{(x_1)^2 + (x_2)^2 + ... + (x_n)^2}$$

The **MatrixMath** class provides the **VectorLength** function which can be used to calculate this length. The signature for the **VectorLength** function is shown here.

```
public static double VectorLength(Matrix input)
```

To take the vector length of a matrix, that matrix must be a vector. First check to see if the matrix is actually a vector. If the matrix is not a vector, then throw an exception.

```
if (!input.IsVector())
{
  throw new MatrixError(
    "Can only take the vector length of a vector.");
}
```

Convert the matrix to a packed array. This allows us to view the matrix as a linear array of numbers.

```
Double[] v = input.ToPackedArray();
double rtn = 0.0;
```

Loop over every element in the packed array.

```
for (int i = 0; i < v.Length; i++)
{
```

Take the square of each each array element. Sum these values into the **rtn** variable.

```
  rtn += Math.Pow(v[i], 2);
}
```

Finally, return the square root of this sum.

```
return Math.Sqrt(rtn);
```

This square root will be returned to the calling method. The length of a vector will be particularly important for the self-organizing maps that will be presented in chapter 8.

Bipolar Operations

In binary format, **true** is represented with the number one and **false** is represented with zero. Bipolar notation is another way to represent binary states. In bipolar notation **true** is represented by one and **false** is represented by negative one.

Equation 2.18 describes how a Boolean number is converted into a bipolar number.

Equation 2.18: Boolean to Bipolar

$$f(x)=2x-1$$

Equation 2.19 does the opposite. This equation shows how to convert a bipolar number into a **boolean** number.

Equation 2.19: Bipolar to Boolean

$$f(x)=\frac{(x+1)}{2}$$

Neural networks that operate on **bool** numbers will usually require these **bool** values to be expressed as bipolar numbers. To assist with this conversion, the **BiPolarUtil** class is provided. Table 2.2 summarized the functions provided by the **BiPolarUtil** class.

The following code uses the **BiPolarUtil** class to construct a bipolar matrix.

```
bool booleanData2[,] = {
   new bool[2] {true,false},
   new bool[2] {false,true}
};
```

```
Matrix matrix2 = new Matrix(BiPolarUtil.
Bipolar2double(booleanData2));
```

This code will produce the matrix described in Equation 2.20.

Equation 2.20: A Bipolar Matrix

$$\begin{bmatrix} 1 & -1 \\ -1 & 1 \end{bmatrix}$$

This will be particularly useful in the next chapter in which a Hopfield neural network is presented. A Hopfield neural network makes use of bipolar matrixes.

Chapter Summary

Matrix mathematics is very important to neural networks. C# does not include built-in support for matrixes; thus, three matrix classes have been presented here. These matrix classes are used to both create matrixes and perform various mathematical operations on them.

Bipolar notation is a special way of representing binary values. In bipolar notation, the binary value of **true** is represented with a one, and the binary value of **false** is represented with a negative one. Most neural networks that work with binary values will make use of bipolar notation. The Hopfield neural network, which will be introduced in chapter 3, makes use of bipolar numbers.

This book will make use of the matrix classes presented in this chapter for all neural networks that will be introduced. This will allow you to quickly see the mathematical underpinnings of each neural network.

Vocabulary

Bipolar

Boolean

Column Matrix

Dot Product

Identity Matrix

Matrix

Row Matrix

Scalar

Vector

Weight Matrix

Questions for Review

1. What is the purpose of using bipolar numbers, as opposed to Boolean numbers?

2. Is matrix multiplication commutative?

3. What are the dimensions of a weight matrix used to connect a two neuron layer to a three neuron layer?

4. Perform the following multiplication.

$$\begin{bmatrix} 3 & 2 \\ 1 & 3 \\ 1 & 4 \end{bmatrix} * \begin{bmatrix} 1 & 2 & 3 \\ 4 & 5 & 6 \end{bmatrix} = ?$$

5. Perform the following dot product.

$$\begin{bmatrix} 6 & 2 & 7 & 4 \end{bmatrix} \cdot \begin{bmatrix} 6 \\ 6 \\ 7 \\ 9 \end{bmatrix} = ?$$

Chapter 3: Using a Hopfield Neural Network

- Understanding the Hopfield Neural Network
- Recognizing Patterns
- Using Autoassociation
- Constructing a Neural Network Application

Neural networks have long been the mainstay of artificial intelligence (AI) programming. As programmers, we can create programs that do fairly amazing things. However, ordinary programs can only automate repetitive tasks, such as balancing checkbooks or calculating the value of an investment portfolio. While a program can easily maintain a large collection of images, it cannot tell us what is illustrated in any of those images. Programs are inherently unintelligent and uncreative.

Neural networks attempt to give computer programs human-like intelligence. They are usually designed and trained to recognize specific patterns in data. This chapter will teach you the basic layout of a neural network by introducing the Hopfield neural network.

The Hopfield Neural Network

The Hopfield neural network is perhaps the simplest type of neural network. The Hopfield neural network is a fully connected single layer, autoassociative network. This means it has a single layer in which each neuron is connected to every other neuron. Autoassociative means that if the neural network recognizes a pattern, it will return that pattern.

In this chapter we will examine a Hopfield neural network with just four neurons. It is small enough to be easily understood, yet it can recognize a few patterns. A Hopfield network, with connections, is shown in Figure 3.1.

Figure 3.1: A Hopfield neural network with 12 connections.

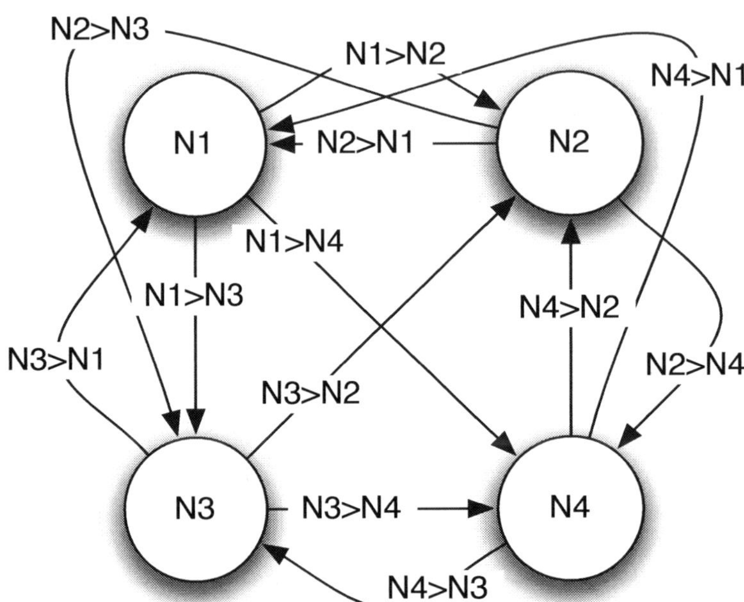

We will build an example program that creates the Hopfield network shown in Figure 3.1. Since every neuron in a Hopfield neural network is connected to every other neuron, you might assume a four-neuron network contains 42 or 16 connections. However, 16 connections would require that every neuron be connected to itself, as well as to every other neuron. This is not the case in a Hopfield neural network, so the actual number of connections is 12.

As we develop an example neural network program, we will store the connections in a matrix. Since each neuron in a Hopfield neural network is by definition connected to every other neuron, a two dimensional matrix works well. All neural network examples in this book will use some form of matrix to store their weights.

Table 3.1 shows the layout of the matrix.

Table 3.1: Connections in a Hopfield Neural Network

	Neuron 1 (N1)	Neuron 2 (N2)	Neuron 3 (N3)	Neuron 4 (N4)
Neuron 1(N1)	(n/a)	N2->N1	N3->N1	N4->N1
Neuron 2(N2)	N1->N2	(n/a)	N3->N2	N3->N2
Neuron 3(N3)	N1->N3	N2->N3	(n/a)	N4->N3
Neuron 4(N4)	N1->N4	N2->N4	N3->N4	(n/a)

This matrix is called the weight matrix, and contains the weights associated with each connection. This matrix is the "memory" of the neural network, and will allow the neural network to recall certain patterns when they are presented. Many of the neural networks in this book will also contain threshold values, in addition to the weights. However, the Hopfield neural network contains only weights.

For example, the values shown in Table 3.2 show the correct weight values to use to enable a network to recall the patterns **0101** and **1010**. The method used to create a network with the values contained in Table 3.2 will be covered shortly. First, you will be shown how the values in Table 3.2 are used by the network to recall **0101** and **1010**.

Table 3.2: Weights Used to Recall 0101 and 1010

	Neuron 1 (N1)	Neuron 2 (N2)	Neuron 3 (N3)	Neuron 4 (N4)
Neuron 1 (N1)	0	-1	1	-1
Neuron 2 (N2)	-1	0	-1	1
Neuron 3 (N3)	1	-1	0	-1
Neuron 4 (N4)	-1	1	-1	0

Recalling Patterns

You will now be shown exactly how a neural network is used to recall patterns. We will begin by presenting **0101** to the Hopfield network. To do this, we present each input neuron, which in this case are also the output neurons, with the pattern. Each neuron will activate based upon the input pattern. For example, when Neuron 1 is presented with **0101**, its activation will result in the sum of all weights that have a 1 in the input pattern. For example, we can see from Table 3.2 that Neuron 1 has connections to the other neurons with the following weights:

0   -1   1   -1

We must now compare those weights with the input pattern of **0101**:

```
0    1      0      1

0    -1     1      -1
```

We will sum only the weights corresponding to the positions that contain a 1 in the input pattern. Therefore, the activation of the first neuron is −1 + −1, or −2. The results of the activation of each neuron are shown below.

$$N1 = -1 + -1 = -2$$
$$N2 = 0 + 1 = 1$$
$$N3 = -1 + -1 = -2$$
$$N4 = 1 + 0 = 1$$

Therefore, the output neurons, which are also the input neurons, will report the above activation results. The final output vector will then be −2, 1, −2, 1. These values are meaningless without an activation function. We said earlier that a threshold establishes when a neuron will fire. A threshold is a type of activation function. An activation function determines the range of values that will cause the neuron, in this case the output neuron, to fire. A threshold is a simple activation function that fires when the input is above a certain value.

The activation function used for a Hopfield network is any value greater than zero, so the following neurons will fire. This establishes the threshold for the network.

```
N1 activation result is -2; will not fire (0)
N2 activation result is 1; will fire (1)
N3 activation result is -2; will not fire (0)
N4 activation result is 1; will fire (1)
```

As you can see, we assign a binary value of 1 to all neurons that fired, and a binary value of 0 to all neurons that did not fire. The final binary output from the Hopfield network will be **0101**. This is the same as the input pattern. An autoassociative neural network, such as a Hopfield network, will echo a pattern back if the pattern is recognized. The pattern was successfully recognized. Now that you have seen how a connection weight matrix can cause a neural network to recall certain patterns, you will be shown how the connection weight matrix was derived.

Deriving the Weight Matrix

You are probably wondering how the weight matrix shown in Table 3.2 was derived. This section will explain how to create a weight matrix that can recall any number of patterns. First you should start with a blank connection weight matrix, as described in Equation 3.1.

Equation 3.1: A Blank Matrix

$$\begin{bmatrix} 0 & 0 & 0 & 0 \\ 0 & 0 & 0 & 0 \\ 0 & 0 & 0 & 0 \\ 0 & 0 & 0 & 0 \end{bmatrix}$$

We will first train this neural network to accept the value **0101**. To do this, we must first calculate a matrix just for **0101**, which is called **0101**'s contribution matrix. The contribution matrix will then be added to the connection weight matrix. As additional contribution matrixes are added to the connection weight matrix, the connection weight is said to learn each of the new patterns.

We begin by calculating the contribution matrix of **0101**. There are three steps involved in this process. First, we must calculate the bipolar values of **0101**. Bipolar representation simply means that we are representing a binary string with −1's and 1's, rather than 0's and 1's. Next, we transpose and multiply the bipolar equivalent of **0101** by itself. Finally, we set all the values from the northwest diagonal to zero, because neurons do not have connections to themselves in a Hopfield network. Let's take the steps one at a time and see how this is done. We will start with the bipolar conversion.

Step 1: Convert 0101 to its bipolar equivalent.

We convert the input, because the binary representation has one minor flaw. Zero is NOT the inverse of 1. Rather −1 is the mathematical inverse of 1. Equation 3.2 can be used to convert the input string from binary to bipolar.

Equation 3.2: Binary to Bipolar

$$f(x) = 2x - 1$$

Conversely, Equation 3.3 can be used to convert from bipolar to binary.

Equation 3.3: Bipolar to Binary

$$f(x) = \frac{(x+1)}{2}$$

To convert 0101 to its bipolar equivalent, we convert all of the zeros to –1's, as follows:

0 = -1

1 = 1

0 = -1

1 = 1

The final result is the array –1, 1, –1, 1. This array will be used in step 2 to begin building the contribution matrix for 0101.

Step 2: Multiply –1, 1, –1, 1 by its inverse.

For this step, we will consider –1, 1, –1, 1 to be a matrix:

Equation 3.4: Input Matrix

$$\begin{bmatrix} -1 \\ 1 \\ -1 \\ 1 \end{bmatrix}$$

Taking the inverse of this matrix we have:

Equation 3.5: Inverse Matrix

$$\begin{bmatrix} -1 & 1 & -1 & 1 \end{bmatrix}$$

We must now multiply these two matrixes. Matrix multiplication was covered in chapter 2. It is a relatively easy procedure in which the rows and columns are multiplied against each other, resulting in the following:

-1 X -1 = 1   1 X -1 = -1   -1 X -1 = 1   1 X -1 = -1

-1 X 1 = -1   1 X 1 = 1   -1 X 1 = -1   1 X 1 = 1

-1 X -1 = 1   1 X -1 = -1   -1 X -1 = 1   1 X -1 = -1

-1 X 1 = -1   1 X 1 = 1   -1 X 1 = -1   1 X 1 = 1

Condensed, the above results in the following matrix:

Equation 3.6: Resulting Matrix

$$\begin{bmatrix} 1 & -1 & 1 & -1 \\ -1 & 1 & -1 & 1 \\ 1 & -1 & 1 & -1 \\ -1 & 1 & -1 & 1 \end{bmatrix}$$

Now that we have successfully multiplied the matrix by its inverse, we are ready for step 3.

Step 3: Set the northwest diagonal to zero.

Mathematically speaking, we are now going to subtract the identity matrix from the matrix we derived in step 2. The net result is that the cells in the northwest diagonal get set to zero. The real reason we do this is that neurons do not have connections to themselves in Hopfield networks. Thus, positions **[0][0]**, **[1][1]**, **[2][2]**, and **[3][3]** in our two dimensional array, or matrix, get set to zero. This results in the final contribution matrix for the bit pattern **0101**.

Equation 3.7: Contribution Matrix

$$\begin{bmatrix} 0 & -1 & 1 & -1 \\ -1 & 0 & -1 & 1 \\ 1 & -1 & 0 & -1 \\ -1 & 1 & -1 & 0 \end{bmatrix}$$

This contribution matrix can now be added to the connection weight matrix. If we only want this network to recognize **0101**, then this contribution matrix becomes our connection weight matrix. If we also want to recognize **1001**, then we would calculate both contribution matrixes and add the results to create the connection weight matrix.

If this process seems a bit confusing, you might try looking at the next section in which we actually develop a program that builds connection weight matrixes. The process is explained using C# terminology.

Before we end the discussion of determining the weight matrix, one small side effect should be mentioned. We went through several steps to determine the correct weight matrix for **0101**. Any time you create a Hopfield network that recognizes a binary pattern, the network also recognizes the inverse of that bit pattern. You can get the inverse of a bit pattern by flipping all 0's to 1's and 1's to 0's. The inverse of **0101** is **1010**. As a result, the connection weight matrix we just calculated would also recognize **1010**.

Creating a C# Hopfield Neural Network

The **Hopfield** neural network is implemented using two classes. The first class, called **HopfieldNetwork** is the main class that performs training and pattern recognition. This class relies on the **Matrix** and **MatrixMath** classes, introduced in chapter 2, to work with the neural network's weight matrix. The second class, called **HopfieldException**, is an exception that is raised when an error occurs while processing the Hopfield network. This is usually triggered as a result of bad input.

The HopfieldNetwork Class

The **HopfieldNetwork** class is shown in Listing 3.1.

Listing 3.1: The Hopfield Neural Network (HopfieldNetwork.cs)

```
using System;
using System.Collections.Generic;
using System.Linq;
using System.Text;
using HeatonResearchNeural.Matrix;
using HeatonResearchNeural.Exception;

namespace HeatonResearchNeural.Hopfield
{


    public class HopfieldNetwork
    {


        /// <summary>
        /// The weight matrix for this neural network. A
        /// Hopfield neural network is a
        /// single layer, fully connected neural network.
        ///
        /// The inputs and outputs to/from a Hopfield neural
        /// network are always
        /// boolean values.
        /// </summary>
```

```csharp
public Matrix.Matrix LayerMatrix
{
    get
    {
        return this.weightMatrix;
    }
}


/// <summary>
/// The number of neurons.
/// </summary>
public int Size
{
    get
    {
        return this.weightMatrix.Rows;
    }
}



/// <summary>
/// The weight matrix.
/// </summary>
private Matrix.Matrix weightMatrix;

/// <summary>
/// Construct a Hopfield neural network of the
/// specified size.
/// </summary>
/// <param name="size">The number of neurons in the
/// network.</param>
public HopfieldNetwork(int size)
{
    this.weightMatrix = new Matrix.Matrix(size, size);

}


/// <summary>
/// Present a pattern to the neural network and
/// receive the result.
/// </summary>
/// <param name="pattern">The pattern to be presented
/// to the neural network.</param>
/// <returns>The output from the neural network.</returns>
public bool[] Present(bool[] pattern)
{
```

```csharp
bool[] output = new bool[pattern.Length];

// convert the input pattern into a matrix with a
// single row.
// also convert the boolean values to
// bipolar(-1=false, 1=true)
Matrix.Matrix inputMatrix =
      Matrix.Matrix.CreateRowMatrix(BiPolarUtil
         .Bipolar2double(pattern));

// Process each value in the pattern
for (int col = 0; col < pattern.Length; col++)
{
    Matrix.Matrix columnMatrix =
       this.weightMatrix.GetCol(col);
    columnMatrix = MatrixMath.Transpose(columnMatrix);

    // The output for this input element is the
    // dot product of the
    // input matrix and one column from the weight
    // matrix.
    double dotProduct =
       MatrixMath.DotProduct(inputMatrix,
            columnMatrix);

    // Convert the dot product to either true
    // or false.
    if (dotProduct > 0)
    {
        output[col] = true;
    }
    else
    {
        output[col] = false;
    }
}

return output;
}


/// <summary>
/// Train the neural network for the specified pattern.
/// The neural network
/// can be trained for more than one pattern. To do this
```

```csharp
/// simply call the
/// train method more than once.
/// </summary>
/// <param name="pattern">The pattern to train on.</param>
public void Train(bool[] pattern)
{
    if (pattern.Length != this.weightMatrix.Rows)
    {
        throw new NeuralNetworkError(
          "Can't train a pattern of size "
                + pattern.Length +
          " on a hopfield network of size "
                + this.weightMatrix.Rows);
    }


    // Create a row matrix from the input, convert
    // boolean to bipolar
    Matrix.Matrix m2 =
          Matrix.Matrix.CreateRowMatrix(BiPolarUtil
            .Bipolar2double(pattern));
    // Transpose the matrix and multiply by the
    // original input matrix
    Matrix.Matrix m1 = MatrixMath.Transpose(m2);
    Matrix.Matrix m3 = MatrixMath.Multiply(m1, m2);

    // matrix 3 should be square by now, so
    // create an identity
    // matrix of the same size.
    Matrix.Matrix identity = MatrixMath.Identity(m3.Rows);

    // subtract the identity matrix
    Matrix.Matrix m4 = MatrixMath.Subtract(m3, identity);

    // now add the calculated matrix, for this
    // pattern, to the
    // existing weight matrix.
    this.weightMatrix =
          MatrixMath.Add(this.weightMatrix, m4);


}
    }
}
```

To make use of the Hopfield neural network, you should instantiate an instance of this class. The constructor takes one integer parameter that specifies the size of the neural network. Once the **HopfieldNetwork** class has been instantiated, you can call the provided properties and methods to use the neural network. The next two tables will summarize these properties and methods. These properties are summarized in Table 3.3.

Table 3.3: Summary of HopfieldNetwork Properties

Property Name	Purpose
Matrix	Accesses the neural network's weight matrix.
Size	Gets the size of the neural network.

Table 3.4 shows a summary of the **HopfieldNetwork** methods.

Table 3.4: Summary of HopfieldNetwork Methods

Method Name	Purpose
Present	Presents a pattern to the neural network.
Train	Trains the neural network on a pattern.

The **Matrix** and **Size** properties are both very simple accessor properties and will not be covered further. Most of the work is done with the **Present** and **Train** methods. These methods will be covered in the next two sections.

Recalling Patterns with the C# Hopfield Network

To recall a pattern with the **HopfieldNetwork** class, the **Present** method should be used. The signature for this method is shown here:

```
public bool[] Present(bool[] pattern)
```

The procedure for training a Hopfield neural network was already discussed earlier in this chapter. The earlier discussion explained how to recall a pattern mathematically. Now we will see how to implement Hopfield pattern recollection in C#.

First, an array is created to hold the output from the neural network. This array is the same length as the input array.

```
bool[] output = new bool[pattern.Length];
```

Next, a **Matrix** is created to hold the bipolar form of the input array. The **Bipolar2double** method of the **BiPolarUtil** class is used to convert the **bool** array. The one-dimensional array is converted into a "row matrix." A "row matrix" is a **Matrix** that consists of a single row.

```
Matrix.Matrix inputMatrix = Matrix.Matrix.CreateRowMatrix(
     BiPolarUtil.Bipolar2double(pattern));
```

We must now loop through each item in the input array. Each item in the input array will be applied to the weight matrix to produce an output.

```
for (int col = 0; col < pattern.Length; col++)
{
```

Each column in the weight matrix represents the weights associated with the connections between the neuron and the other neurons. Therefore, we must extract the column that corresponds to each of the input array values.

```
Matrix.Matrix columnMatrix = this.weightMatrix.GetCol(col);
```

```
Matrix columnMatrix = this.weightMatrix.GetCol(col);
```

We must now determine the dot product of that column and the input array. However, before that can be done we must transpose the column from the weight matrix. This will properly orient the values in the column so the dot product computation can be performed.

```
columnMatrix = MatrixMath.Transpose(columnMatrix);
```

Next, the dot product is calculated.

```
double dotProduct = MatrixMath.DotProduct(inputMatrix,
columnMatrix);
```

If the dot product is above zero, then the output will be **true**; otherwise the output will be **false**.

```
  if (dotProduct > 0)
  {
    output[col] = true;
  }
  else
  {
    output[col] = false;
  }
}
```

Zero is the threshold. A value above the threshold will cause the output neuron to fire; at or below the threshold and the output neuron will not fire. It is important to note that since the Hopfield network has a single layer, the input and output neurons are the same. Thresholds will be expanded upon in the next chapter when we deal with the feedforward neural network.

Finally, the **output** array is returned.

```
return output;
```

The next section will explain how the C# Hopfield network is trained.

Training the Hopfield Network

The **Train** method is used to train instances of the **HopfieldNetwork** class. The signature for this method is shown here:

```
public void Train(bool[] pattern)
```

The length of the pattern must be the same as the size of the neural network. If it is not, then an exception is thrown.

```
if (pattern.Length != this.weightMatrix.Rows)
{
  throw new NeuralNetworkError("Can't train a pattern of size "
  + pattern.Length + " on a hopfield network of size "
  + this.weightMatrix.Rows);
}
```

If the **pattern** is the proper length, a matrix is created that contains a single row. This row will contain the bipolar representation of the input pattern.

```
Matrix.Matrix m2 = Matrix.Matrix.CreateRowMatrix(
  BiPolarUtil.Bipolar2double(pattern));
```

The row matrix is then transposed into a column matrix.

```
Matrix.Matrix m1 = MatrixMath.Transpose(m2);
```

Finally, the row is multiplied by the column.

```
Matrix.Matrix m3 = MatrixMath.Multiply(m1, m2);
```

Multiplying the row by the column results in a square matrix. This matrix will have a diagonal of ones running from its northwest corner to its southwest corner. The ones must be converted to zeros. To do this, an identity matrix of the same size is created.

```
Matrix.Matrix identity = MatrixMath.Identity(m3.Rows);
```

The identity matrix is nothing more than a matrix containing a diagonal of ones, which can be subtracted from the pervious matrix to set the diagonal to zero.

```
Matrix.Matrix m4 = MatrixMath.Subtract(m3, identity);
```

The new matrix is now added to the old weight matrix.

```
this.weightMatrix = MatrixMath.Add(this.weightMatrix, m4);
```

This produces a weight matrix that will likely recognize the new pattern, as well as the old patterns.

Simple Hopfield Example

Now you will see how to make use of the **HopfieldNetwork** class that was created in the last section. The first example implements a simple console application that demonstrates basic pattern recognition. The second example graphically displays the weight matrix using a C# application. Finally, the third example uses a C# application to illustrate how a Hopfield neural network can be used to recognize a grid pattern.

The first example, which is a simple console application, is shown in Listing 3.2.

Listing 3.2: Simple Console Example (ConsoleHopfield.cs)

```
using System;
using System.Collections.Generic;
using System.Linq;
using System.Text;

using HeatonResearchNeural.Hopfield;

namespace Chapter03Console
{

    /// <summary>
    /// Chapter 3: Using a Hopfield Neural Network
    ///
    /// ConsoleHopfield: Simple console application that shows
    /// how to
    /// use a Hopfield Neural Network.
    /// </summary>
    public class ConsoleHopfield
    {
        /// <summary>
        /// Convert a boolean array to the form [T,T,F,F]
        /// </summary>
        /// <param name="b">A boolen array.</param>
        /// <returns>The boolen array in string form.</returns>
        public static String FormatBoolean(bool[] b)
        {
            StringBuilder result = new StringBuilder();
```

```csharp
        result.Append('[');
        for (int i = 0; i < b.Length; i++)
        {
            if (b[i])
            {
                result.Append("T");
            }
            else
            {
                result.Append("F");
            }
            if (i != b.Length - 1)
            {
                result.Append(",");
            }
        }
        result.Append(']');
        return (result.ToString());
    }


    /// <summary>
    /// A simple main method to test the Hopfield neural
    /// network.
    /// </summary>
    /// <param name="args">Not used</param>
    static void Main(string[] args)
    {

        // Create the neural network.
        HopfieldNetwork network = new HopfieldNetwork(4);
        // This pattern will be trained
        bool[] pattern1 = { true, true, false, false };
        // This pattern will be presented
        bool[] pattern2 = { true, false, false, false };
        bool[] result;

        // train the neural network with pattern1
        Console.WriteLine("Training Hopfield network with: "
                + FormatBoolean(pattern1));
        network.Train(pattern1);
        // present pattern1 and see it recognized
        result = network.Present(pattern1);
        Console.WriteLine("Presenting pattern:"
                + FormatBoolean(pattern1)
                    + ", and got " + FormatBoolean(result));
        // Present pattern2, which is similar to pattern 1.
```

```
            // Pattern 1
            // should be recalled.
            result = network.Present(pattern2);
            Console.WriteLine("Presenting pattern:"
                    + FormatBoolean(pattern2)
                    + ", and got " + FormatBoolean(result));


        }
    }
}
```

There are two methods provided in Listing 3.2. The first method, named **FormatBoolean**, is used to format Boolean arrays as follows:

```
[T,T,F,F]
```

This method allows the program to easily display both input and output for the neural network. The **FormatBoolean** function is relatively simple. It loops through each element in the array and displays either a **T** or an **F** depending upon whether the array element is **true** or **false**. This can be seen in Listing 3.2.

The second method, **Main**, is used to set up the Hopfield network and use it. First, a new **HopfieldNetwork** is created with four neurons.

```
HopfieldNetwork network = new HopfieldNetwork(4);
```

Next, an input pattern named **pattern1** is created. This is the pattern that the Hopfield network will be trained on. Since there are four neurons in the network, there must also be four values in the training pattern.

```
bool[] pattern1 = { true, true, false, false };
```

A second input pattern, named **pattern2**, is then created. This pattern is slightly different than **pattern1**. This pattern will allow the network to be tested to see if it still recognizes **pattern1**, even though this pattern is slightly different.

```
bool[] pattern2 = { true, false, false, false };
```

A Boolean array named **result** is created to hold the results of presenting patterns to the network.

```
bool[] result;
```

The user is then informed that we are training the network with **pattern1**. The **FormatBoolean** method is used to display **pattern1**.

```
Console.WriteLine("Training Hopfield network with: "
+ FormatBoolean(pattern1));
```

The network is called and trained with **pattern1**.

```
network.Train(pattern1);
```

Now, **pattern1** is presented to the network to see if it will be recognized. We tell the user that we are doing this and display the **result**.

```
result = network.Present(pattern1);
Console.WriteLine("Presenting pattern:" + FormatBoolean(pattern1)
      + ", and got " + FormatBoolean(result));
```

Next, **pattern2**, which is similar to **pattern1**, is presented. The same values should be recalled for **pattern2** as were recalled for **pattern1**.

```
result = network.Present(pattern2);
Console.WriteLine("Presenting pattern:" + FormatBoolean(pattern2)
      + ", and got " + FormatBoolean(result));
```

The results are displayed to the user. The output from this program is as follows:

```
Training Hopfield network with: [T,T,F,F]
Presenting pattern:[T,T,F,F] and got [T,T,F,F]
Presenting pattern:[T,F,F,F] and got [T,T,F,F]
```

This program shows how to instantiate and use a Hopfield neural network without any bells or whistles. The next program is an application that will allow you to see the weight matrix as the network is trained.

Visualizing the Weight Matrix

This second example is essentially the same as the first; however, this example uses an application. Therefore, it has a GUI that allows the user to interact with it. The user interface for this program can be seen in Figure 3.2.

Figure 3.2: A Hopfield Application

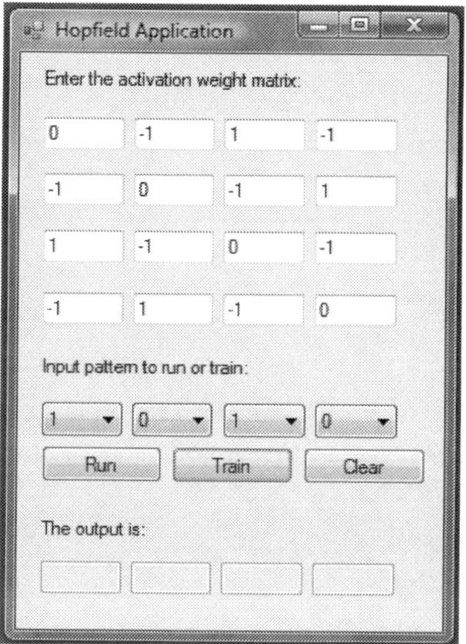

The 4x4 grid is the weight matrix. The four "0/1" fields allow you to input four-part patterns into the neural network. This pattern can then be presented to the network to be recognized or to be used for training.

The Hopfield application is shown in Listing 3.3.

Listing 3.3: Visual Hopfield Application (HopfieldApp.cs)

```
using System;
using System.Collections.Generic;
using System.Linq;
using System.Windows.Forms;

namespace Chapter03App
{
    static class HopfieldApp
    {
        /// <summary>
        /// The main entry point for the application.
        /// </summary>
        [STAThread]
        static void Main()
        {
            Application.EnableVisualStyles();
```

```
Application.SetCompatibleTextRenderingDefault(false);
Application.Run(new HopfieldForm());
    }
  }
}
```

To use the application, follow these steps:

1.   Notice the activation weight matrix is empty (contains all zeros). This neural network has no knowledge. Let's teach it to recognize the pattern 1001. Enter 1001 under the "Input pattern to run or train:" prompt. Click the "Train" button. Notice the weight matrix adjusts to absorb the new knowledge.

2.   Now test it. Enter the pattern 1001 under the "Input pattern to run or train:" prompt. (It should still be there from your training.) Now click "Run." The output will be "1001." This is an autoassociative network, therefore it echos the input if it recognizes it.

3.   Let's test it some more. Enter the pattern 1000 and click "Run." The output will now be "1001." The neural network did not recognize "1000;" the closest thing it knew was "1001." It figured you made an error typing and attempted a correction!

4.   Now, notice a side effect. Enter "0110," which is the binary inverse of what the network was trained with ("1001"). Hopfield networks ALWAYS get trained for a pattern's binary inverse. So, if you enter "0110," the network will recognize it.

5.   Likewise, if you enter "0100," the neural network will output "0110" thinking that is what you meant.

6.   One final test—let's try "1111," which is totally off base and not at all close to anything the neural network knows. The neural network responds with "0000." It did not try to correct you. It has no idea what you mean!

7.   Play with it some more. It can be taught multiple patterns. As you train new patterns, it builds upon the matrix already in memory. Pressing "Clear," clears out the memory.

The Hopfield network works exactly the same way it did in the first example. Patterns are presented to a four-neuron Hopfield neural network for training and recognition. All of the extra code shown in Listing 3.3 simply connects the Hopfield network to a GUI using the C#'s forms technology.

Hopfield Pattern Recognition Application

Hopfield networks can be much larger than four neurons. For the third example, we will examine a 64-neuron Hopfield network. This network is connected to an 8x8 grid, which an application allows you to draw upon. As you draw patterns, you can either train the network with them or present them for recognition.

The user interface for the application can be seen in Figure 3.3.

Figure 3.3: A pattern recognition Hopfield application.

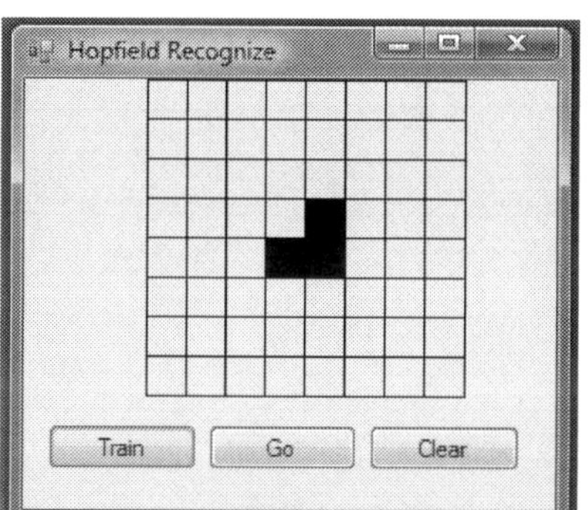

The source code for this example is provided in Listing 3.4.

Listing 3.4: Hopfield Pattern Recognition (HopfieldPattern.cs)

```csharp
using System;
using System.Collections.Generic;
using System.Linq;
using System.Windows.Forms;

namespace Chapter03Pattern
{
    static class HopfieldPattern
    {
        /// <summary>
        /// The main entry point for the application.
        /// </summary>
        [STAThread]
        static void Main()
        {
            Application.EnableVisualStyles();
```

```
            Application.SetCompatibleTextRenderingDefault(false);
            Application.Run(new HopfieldRecForm());
        }
    }
}
```

To make use of the application, draw some sort of pattern on the grid and click "Train." Now draw another pattern and also click "Train." Finally, draw a pattern similar to one of the two previous patterns in the same location, and click "Go." The network will attempt to recognize what you drew. You can also click "Clear" to clear the grid. Clicking "Clear Matrix" will clear the training matrix.

The following sections explain how the main methods of this program were constructed.

Drawing the Grid

The grid is drawn using the application's **Paint** event. The signature for this method is shown here:

```
private void HopfieldRecForm_Paint(object sender, PaintEventArgs e)
```

First, obtain a **Graphics** object to paint to the form.

```
Graphics g = e.Graphics;
```

The grid size is defined by several constants. Unless you change these, the grid itself will be 8x8 and the cells will be 20 pixels square. This means that the buttons will take up more space than the grid; therefore, it looks better if the grid is centered. A **margin** is calculated to center the grid.

The margin is the actual width minus the grid's width, divided by two.

```
this.margin = (this.Width - (HopfieldRecForm.CELL_WIDTH *
    HopfieldRecForm.GRID_X)) / 2;
```

Next, the index variable is created. This variable holds the current position in the **grid bool** array. Even though the grid appears visually as an 8x8 matrix, it must be presented to the neural network as a flat 64-part Boolean pattern.

```
int index = 0;
```

Create a black **SolidBrush** and a black **Pen** object. These will be used to draw a grid.

```
SolidBrush brush = new SolidBrush(Color.Black);
Pen pen = new Pen(Color.Black);
```

Two loops are then established to loop through the **x** and **y** coordinates of the grid.

```
for (int y = 0; y < HopfieldRecForm.GRID_Y; y++)
{
  for (int x = 0; x < HopfieldRecForm.GRID_X; x++)
  {
```

If the grid element for this cell is **true**, then draw a rectangle and fill it in.

```
    if (this.grid[index++])
    {
      g.FillRectangle(brush, this.margin + (x *
        HopfieldRecForm.CELL_WIDTH), y
        * HopfieldRecForm.CELL_HEIGHT,
        HopfieldRecForm.CELL_WIDTH,
        HopfieldRecForm.CELL_HEIGHT);
    }
```

If the grid element for this cell is **false**, then draw an empty rectangle.

```
    {
      g.DrawRectangle(pen, this.margin + (x *
        HopfieldRecForm.CELL_WIDTH), y
        * HopfieldRecForm.CELL_HEIGHT,
        HopfieldRecForm.CELL_WIDTH,
        HopfieldRecForm.CELL_HEIGHT);
    }
```

The **Paint** method is called by C# whenever the grid needs to be redrawn. Additionally, other methods will force the **Paint** method to be called using the **Invalidate** method.

Toggling Grid Positions

The **MouseDown** method is called by C# whenever the mouse has been pressed. The signature for the **MouseDown** event is shown here:

```
private void HopfieldRecForm_MouseDown(object sender,
     MouseEventArgs e)
```

First, the **x** and **y** coordinates are calculated in terms of the grid position, and not the pixel coordinates that are passed to the **MouseDown** event.

```
int x = ((e.X - this.margin) / HopfieldRecForm.CELL_WIDTH);
int y = e.Y / HopfieldRecForm.CELL_HEIGHT;
```

These coordinates must fall on the grid. If the click was outside of the grid, then the click will be ignored.

```
if (((x >= 0) && (x < HopfieldRecForm.GRID_X)) && ((y >= 0)
    && (y < HopfieldRecForm.GRID_Y)))
{
```

The **index** into the one-dimensional grid array is calculated, then it is toggled using the Boolean **!** operator.

```
int index = (y * HopfieldRecForm.GRID_X) + x;
this.grid[index] = !this.grid[index];
}
```

Finally, the application repaints the grid.

```
this.Invalidate();
```

Thus, the grid can be drawn by tracking when the mouse is released.

Training and Presenting Patterns

The "Train" and "Go" buttons allow you to train and recognize patterns respectively. The **btnTrain_Click** method is called whenever the "Train" button is clicked. The **btnTrain_Click** method is shown here:

```
private void btnTrain_Click(object sender, EventArgs e) {
  this.hopfield.Train(this.grid);
}
```

As you can see this method simply hands off to the **Train** method provided by the **HopfieldNetwork** class.

When the "Go" button is clicked, the **Click** event is called. This method is shown here.

```
private void btnGo_Click(object sender, EventArgs e)
{
  this.grid = this.hopfield.Present(this.grid);
  this.Invalidate();
}
```

As you can see this method simply hands off to the **Present** method provided by the **HopfieldNetwork** class. The window is then redrawn to show the output from the neural network.

Chapter Summary

Neural networks are one of the most commonly used concepts in Artificial Intelligence. Neural networks are particularly useful for recognizing patterns. They are able to recognize something even when it is distorted.

A neural network may have input, output, and hidden layers. The input and output layers are the only required layers. The input and output layers may be the same neurons. Neural networks are typically presented input patterns that will produce some output pattern.

If a neural network mimics the input pattern it was presented with, then that network is said to be autoassociative. For example, if a neural network is presented with the pattern "0110," and the output is also "0110," then that network is said to be autoassociative.

A neural network calculates its output based on the input pattern and the neural network's internal connection weight matrix. The values for the connection weights will determine the output from the neural network.

A Hopfield neural network is a fully connected autoassociative neural network. This means that each neuron is connected to every other neuron in the neural network. A Hopfield neural network can be trained to recognize certain patterns. Training a Hopfield neural network involves performing some basic matrix manipulations on the input pattern that is to be recognized.

This chapter explained how to construct a simple Hopfield neural network. This network was trained using a simple training algorithm. Training algorithms allow weights to be adjusted to produce the desired outputs. There are many advanced training algorithms. Chapter 4 will introduce more complex training algorithms.

Vocabulary

Activation Function

Autoassociation

Bipolar

Hopfield neural network

Single layer neural network

Questions for Review

1.   A typical Hopfield neural network contains six neurons. How many connections will this produce?

2.   Convert 1 from binary to bipolar.

3.   Convert -1 from binary to bipolar.

4.   Consider a four-neuron Hopfield neural network with the following weight matrix.

$$\begin{bmatrix} 0 & 1 & -1 & -1 \\ 1 & 0 & -1 & -1 \\ -1 & -1 & 0 & 1 \\ -1 & -1 & 1 & 0 \end{bmatrix}$$

What output will an input of 1101 produce?

5.   Consider a four-neuron Hopfield network. Produce a weight matrix that will recognize the pattern 1100.

CHAPTER 4: HOW A MACHINE LEARNS

- Understanding Layers
- Supervised Training
- Unsupervised Training
- Error Calculation
- Understanding Hebb's Rule and the Delta Rule

There are many different ways that a neural network can learn; however, every learning algorithm involves the modification of the weight matrix, which holds the weights for the connections between the neurons. In this chapter, we will examine some of the more popular methods used to adjust these weights. In chapter 5, "The Feedforward Backpropagation Neural Network," we will follow up this discussion with an introduction to the backpropagation method of training. Backpropagation is one of the most common neural network training methods used today.

Learning Methods

Training is a very important process for a neural network. There are two forms of training that can be employed, supervised and unsupervised. Supervised training involves providing the neural network with training sets and the anticipated output. In unsupervised training, the neural network is also provided with training sets, but not with anticipated outputs. In this book, we will examine both supervised and unsupervised training. This chapter will provide a brief introduction to each approach. They will then be covered in much greater detail in later chapters.

Unsupervised Training

What does it mean to train a neural network without supervision? As previously mentioned, the neural network is provided with training sets, which are collections of defined input values. The unsupervised neural network is not provided with anticipated outputs.

Unsupervised training is typically used to train classification neural networks. A classification neural network receives input patterns, which are presented to the input neurons. These input patterns are then processed, causing a single neuron on the output layer to fire. This firing neuron provides the classification for the pattern and identifies to which group the pattern belongs.

Another common application for unsupervised training is data mining. In this case, you have a large amount of data to be searched, but you may not know exactly what you are looking for. You want the neural network to classify this data into several groups. You do not want to dictate to the neural network ahead of time which input pattern should be classified into which group. As the neural network trains, the input patterns fall into groups with other inputs having similar characteristics. This allows you to see which input patterns share similarities.

Unsupervised training is also a very common training technique for self-organizing maps (SOM), also called Kohonen neural networks. In chapter 11, we will discuss how to construct an SOM and introduce the general process for training them without supervision.

In chapter 12, "OCR and the Self-Organizing Map," you will be shown a practical application of an SOM. The example program presented in chapter 12, which is designed to read handwriting, learns through the use of an unsupervised training method. The input patterns presented to the SOM are dot images of handwritten characters and there are 26 output neurons, which correspond to the 26 letters of the English alphabet. As the SOM is trained, the weights are adjusted so input patterns can then be classified into these 26 groups. As will be demonstrated in chapter 12, this technique results in a relatively effective method for character recognition.

As you can see, unsupervised training can be applied to a number of situations. It will be covered in much greater detail in chapters 11 and 12. Figure 4.1 illustrates the flow of information through an unsupervised training algorithm.

Figure 4.1: Unsupervised training.

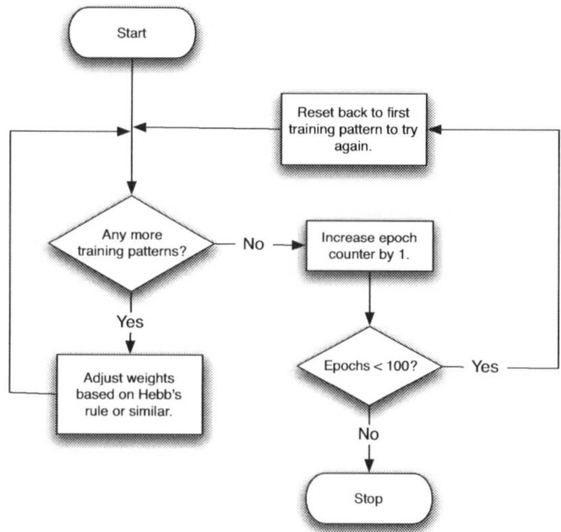

Supervised Training

The supervised training method is similar to the unsupervised training method, in that training sets are provided. Just as with unsupervised training, these training sets specify input signals to the neural network. The primary difference between supervised and unsupervised training is that in supervised training the expected outputs are provided. This allows the neural network to adjust the values in the weight matrix based on the differences between the anticipated output and the actual output.

There are several popular supervised training algorithms. One of the most common is the backpropagation algorithm. Backpropagation will be discussed in the next chapter. It is also possible to use simulated annealing or genetic algorithms to implement supervised training. Simulated annealing and genetic algorithms will be discussed in chapters 6, "Training using a Genetic Algorithm," and chapter 7, "Training using Simulated Annealing." We will now discuss how errors are calculated for both supervised and unsupervised training algorithms.

Figure 4.2 illustrates the flow of information through a supervised training algorithm.

Figure 4.2: Supervised training.

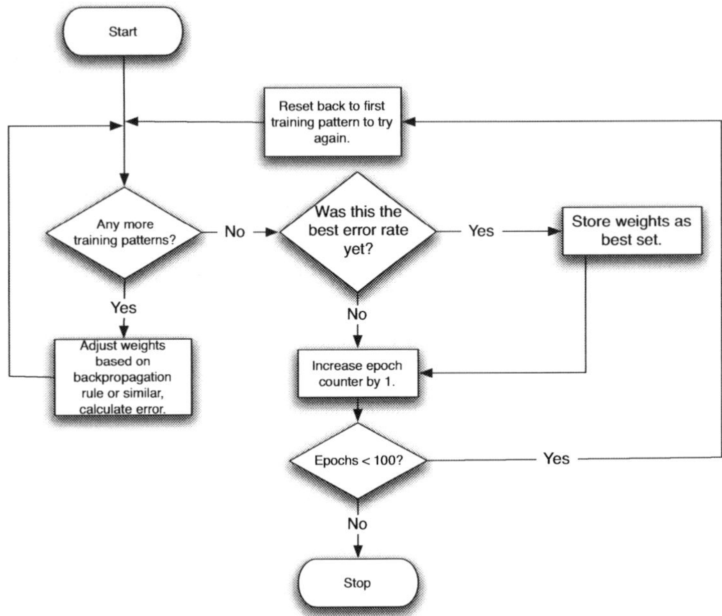

Error Calculation

Error calculation is an important aspect of any neural network. Whether the neural network is supervised or unsupervised, an error rate must be calculated. The goal of virtually all training algorithms is to minimize the rate of error. In this section, we will examine how the rate of error is calculated for a supervised neural network. We will also discuss how the rate of error is determined for an unsupervised training algorithm. We will begin this section by examining two error calculation steps used for supervised training.

Error Calculation and Supervised Training

There are two values that must be considered in determining the rate of error for supervised training. First, we must calculate the error for each element of the training set as it is processed. Second, we must calculate the average of the errors for all of the elements of the training set across each sample. For example, consider the XOR logical operator from chapter 1 that has only four items in its training set. Refer to Table 1.3 to review the XOR logical operator.

In chapter 1, we intuitively chose values for the weight matrix. This is fine for a simple neural network, such as the one that implements the XOR operator. However, this is not practical for more complex neural networks. Typically, the process involves creating a random weight matrix and then testing each row in the training set. An output error is then calculated for each element of the training set. Finally, after all of the elements of the training set have been processed, the root mean square (RMS) error is determined for all of them.

Output Error

The output error is simply an error calculation that is performed to determine how different a neural network's output is from the ideal output. This value is rarely used for any purpose other than as a steppingstone in the calculation of the root mean square (RMS) error for the entire training set. Once all of the elements of a training set have been run through the network, the RMS error can be calculated. This error acts as the global rate of error for the entire neural network.

We will create a generic error calculation class that will be used in all of the neural networks in this book. This class is named **ErrorCalculation**. This class works by calculating the output error for each member of the training set. This error is allowed to grow until all of the elements of the training set have been presented. Then, the RMS error is calculated. The calculation of the RMS error is covered in the next section. The **ErrorCalculation** class is shown in Listing 4.1.

Listing 4.1: The ErrorCalculation Class (ErrorCalculation.cs)

```csharp
using System;
using System.Collections.Generic;
using System.Linq;
using System.Text;

namespace HeatonResearchNeural.Util
{
    public class ErrorCalculation
    {
        /// <summary>
        /// The current error level.
        /// </summary>
        private double globalError;

        /// <summary>
        /// The size of a training set.
        /// </summary>
        private int setSize;

        /// <summary>
        /// Returns the root mean square error for a
```

```csharp
        /// complete training set.
        /// </summary>
        /// <returns>The current error for the
        /// neural network.</returns>
        public double CalculateRMS()
        {
            double err = Math.Sqrt(this.globalError /
                    (this.setSize));
            return err;


        }


        /// <summary>
        /// Reset the error accumulation to zero.
        /// </summary>
        public void Reset()
        {
            this.globalError = 0;
            this.setSize = 0;
        }


        /// <summary>
        /// Called to update for each number that
        /// should be checked.
        /// </summary>
        /// <param name="actual">The actual number.</param>
        /// <param name="ideal">The ideal number.</param>
        public void UpdateError(double[] actual, double[] ideal)
        {
            for (int i = 0; i < actual.Length; i++)
            {
                double delta = ideal[i] - actual[i];
                this.globalError += delta * delta;
                this.setSize += ideal.Length;
            }
        }
    }
}
```

First, we will see how to use the **ErrorCalculation** class. When an error is to be calculated, there will usually be two arrays, the **ideal** array and the **actual** array. The **ideal** array contains the values that we hope the neural network will produce. An **ideal** array is shown here:

```csharp
double[][] ideal = {
   new double[4] {1,2,3,4},
   new double[4] {5,6,7,8},
```

```
new double[4] {9,10,11,12},
new double[4] {13,14,15,16} };
```

This **ideal** array contains four sets, which are the rows of the array. Each row contains four numbers. The neural network that this array would be used to train would, therefore, have four output neurons. The columns correspond to the output neurons. The rows are the individual elements of the training set.

The actual output of the neural network is stored in an **actual** array. If we were training a neural network, we would have an array of input values that would result in the actual output values. A hypothetical **actual** array is provided here for use with the above **ideal** array.

```
double[][] actual = {
  new double[4] {1,2,3,5},
  new double[4] {5,6,7,8},
  new double[4] {9,10,11,12},
  new double[4] {13,14,15,16} };
```

As you can see, the **actual** array is fairly close to the **ideal** array. An **ErrorCalculation** object is now instantiated named **error**.

```
ErrorCalculation error = new ErrorCalculation();
```

The output for each element in the training set must now be compared to the ideal output. We loop through all four rows in the arrays.

```
for(int i=0;i<ideal.Length;i++) {
  error.UpdateError(actual[i], ideal[i]);
}
```

The corresponding rows of the **actual** array and the **ideal** array are presented to the **error** object and the **error object is updated.**

Finally, the RMS error is calculated and printed.

```
Console.WriteLine( error.CalculateRMS());
```

The **error** object can be reused for another error calculation, if needed. Simply call the **Reset** method and the error object is ready to be used again.

This **CalculateError** class will be used frequently in this book. Any time the RMS error is needed for a neural network, this class will be used. The next section will describe how the RMS error is calculated.

Root Mean Square (RMS) Error

The RMS method is used to calculate the rate of error for a training set based on predefined ideal results. The RMS method is effective in calculating the rate of error regardless of whether the actual results are above or below the ideal results. To calculate the RMS for a series of **n** values of **x**, consider Equation 4.1.

Equation 4.1: Root Mean Square Error (RMS)

$$x_{rms} = \sqrt{\frac{1}{n}\sum_{i=1}^{n} x_i^2} = \sqrt{\frac{x_1^2 + x_2^2 + \ldots + x_n^2}{n}}$$

The values of **x** are squared and their sum is divided by **n**. Squaring the values eliminates the issue associated with some values being above the ideal values and others below, since computing the square of a value always results in a positive number.

To apply RMS to the output of a neural network, consider Equation 4.2.

Equation 4.2: RMS for a Neural Network

$$x_{rms} = \sqrt{\frac{1}{n}\sum_{i=1}^{n} \left(actual_i - ideal_i\right)^2}$$

To calculate the RMS for the arrays in the previous section, you would calculate the difference between the actual results and the ideal results, as shown in the above equation. The square of each of these would then be calculated and the results would be summed. The sum would then be divided by the number of elements, and the square root of the result of that computation would provide the rate of error.

To implement this in C#, the **UpdateError** method is called to compare the output produced for each element of the training set with the ideal output values for the neural network. The signature for the **UpdateError** method is shown here:

```
public void UpdateError(double[] actual, double[] ideal)
{
```

First, we loop through all of the elements in the **actual** array.

```
for (int i = 0; i < actual.Length; i++)
{
```

We determine the difference, or **delta**, between the actual and the ideal values. It does not matter if this is a negative number; that will be handled in the next step.

```
double delta = ideal[i] - actual[i];
```

We then add the square of each **delta** to the **globalError** variable. The **setSize** variable is used to track how many elements have been processed.

```
this.globalError += delta * delta;
this.setSize += ideal.Length;
}
```

Finally, once all of the elements in the training set have been cycled through the **UpdateError** method, the **CalculateRMS** method is called to calculate the RMS error. The signature for the **CalculateRMS** method is shown here.

```
public double CalculateRMS()
{
```

We calculate the error as the square root of the **globalError** divided by the **setSize**, and return the error.

```
double err = Math.Sqrt(this.globalError / (this.setSize));
return err;
}
```

Once the **CalculateError** object has been used to calculate the rate of error, it must be reset before another training set can be processed. Otherwise, the **globalError** variable would continue to grow, rather than start from zero. To reset the **CalculateError** class, the **Reset** method should be called.

Error Calculation and Unsupervised Training

We have discussed how errors are calculated for supervised training, we must now discuss how they are calculated for unsupervised training. This may not be immediately obvious. How can an error be calculated when no ideal outputs are provided? The exact procedure by which this is done will be covered in chapter 11, "Using a Self-Organizing Map." For now, we will simply highlight the most important details of the process.

Most unsupervised neural networks are designed to classify input data. The input data is classified based on one of the output neurons. The degree to which each output neuron fires for the input data is studied in order to produce an error for unsupervised training. Ideally, we would like a single neuron to fire at a high level for each member of the training set. If this is not the case, we adjust the weights to the neuron with the greatest number of firings, that is, the winning neuron consolidates its win. This training method causes more and more neurons to fire for the different elements in the training set.

Training Algorithms

Training occurs as the neuron connection weights are modified to produce more desirable results. There are several ways that training can take place. In the following sections we will discuss two simple methods for training the connection weights of a neural network. In chapter 5, we will examine backpropagation, which is a much more complex training algorithm.

Neuron connection weights are not modified in a single pass. The process by which neuron weights are modified occurs over multiple iterations. The neural network is presented with training data and the results are then observed. Neural network learning occurs when these results change the connection weights. The exact process by which this happens is determined by the learning algorithm used.

Learning algorithms, which are commonly called learning rules, are almost always expressed as functions. A learning function provides guidance on how a weight between two neurons should be changed. Consider a weight matrix containing the weights for the connections between four neurons, such as we saw in chapter 3, "Using a Hopfield Neural Network." This is expressed as an array of doubles.

```
double weights[,] = new double[4,4];
```

This matrix is used to store the weights between four neurons. Since C# array indexes begin with zero, we shall refer to these neurons as neurons zero through three. Using the above array, the weight between neuron two and neuron three would be contained in the location **weights[2,3]**. Therefore, we would like a learning function that will return the new weight between neurons "i" and "j," such that

```
weights[i,j] += TrainingFunction(...)
```

The hypothetical method **TrainingFunction** calculates the change (delta) that must occur between the two neurons in order for learning to take place. We never discard the previous weight value altogether; rather, we compute a delta value that is used to modify the original weight. It takes more than a single modification for the neural network to learn. Once the weights of the neural network have been modified, the network is again presented with the training data and the process continues. These iterations continue until the neural network's error rate has dropped to an acceptable level.

Another common input to the learning rule is the error. The error is the degree to which the actual output of the neural network differs from the anticipated output. If such an error is provided to the training function, then the method is called supervised training. In supervised training, the neural network is constantly adjusting the weights to attempt to better align the actual results with the anticipated outputs that were provided.

Conversely, if no error was provided to the training function, then we are using an unsupervised training algorithm. Recall, in unsupervised training, the neural network is not told what the "correct" output is. Unsupervised training leaves the neural network to determine this for itself. Often, unsupervised training is used to allow the neural network to group the input data. The programmer does not know ahead of time exactly what the groupings will be.

We will now examine two common training algorithms. The first, Hebb's rule, is used for unsupervised training and does not take into account network error. The second, the delta rule, is used with supervised training and adjusts the weights so that the input to the neural network will more accurately produce the anticipated output. We will begin with Hebb's Rule.

Hebb's Rule

One of the most common learning algorithms is called Hebb's Rule. This rule was developed by Donald Hebb to assist with unsupervised training. We previously examined a hypothetical learning rule defined by the following expression:

```
weights[i,j] += TrainingFunction(...)
```

Rules for training neural networks are almost always represented as algebraic formulas. Hebb's rule is expressed in Equation 4.3.

Equation 4.3: Hebb's Rule

$$\Delta w_{ij} = \mu\, a_i a_j$$

The above equation calculates the needed change (delta) in the weight for the connection from neuron "i" to neuron "j." The Greek letter mu (μ) represents the learning rate. The activation of each neuron is given as **ai** and **aj**. This equation can easily be translated into the following C# method.

```
protected double TrainingFunction(double rate, double input,
double output)
{
  return rate * input * output;
}
```

We will now examine how this training algorithm actually works. To do this, we will consider a simple neural network with only two neurons. In this neural network, these two neurons make up both the input and output layer. There is no hidden layer. Table 4.1 summarizes some of the possible scenarios using Hebbian training. Assume that the learning rate is one.

Table 4.1: Using Hebb's Rule

Case	Neuron i Value	Neuron j Output	Hebb's Rule	Weight Delta
Case 1	+1	-1	1*1*-1	-1
Case 2	-1	+1	1*-1*1	-1
Case 3	+1	+1	1*1*1	+1

As you can see from the above table, if the activation of neuron "i" was +1 and the activation of neuron j was −1, the neuron connection weight between neuron "i" and neuron "j" would be decreased by one.

Hebb's rule is unsupervised, so we are not training the neural network for some ideal output. Rather, Hebb's rule works by reinforcing what the neural network already knows. This is sometimes summarized with the catchy phrase: "Neurons that fire together, wire together." That is, if the two neurons have similar activations, their weight is increased. If two neurons have dissimilar activations, their weight is decreased.

An example of Hebb's rule is shown in Listing 4.2.

Listing 4.2: Using Hebb's Rule (Hebb.cs)

```csharp
using System;
using System.Collections.Generic;
using System.Linq;
using System.Text;

namespace Chapter04Hebb
{


    /// <summary>
    /// Chapter 4: Machine Learning
    ///
    /// Hebb: Learn, using Hebb's rule.
    /// </summary>
    public class Hebb
    {

        /// <summary>
        /// Main method just instanciates a delta object and
        /// calls run.
        /// </summary>
        /// <param name="args">Not used</param>
        static void Main(string[] args)
```

```
{
    Hebb hebb = new Hebb();
    hebb.run();

}


/// <summary>
/// Weight for neuron 1
/// </summary>
double w1;

/// <summary>
/// Weight for neuron 2
/// </summary>
double w2;

/// <summary>
/// Learning rate
/// </summary>
double rate = 1.0;

/// <summary>
/// Current epoch #
/// </summary>
int epoch = 1;

/// <summary>
/// Simple constructor.
/// </summary>
public Hebb()
{
    this.w1 = 1;
    this.w2 = -1;
}



/// <summary>
/// Process one epoch. Here we learn from all three
/// training samples and then
/// update the weights based on error.
/// </summary>
protected void Epoch()
{
    Console.WriteLine("***Beginning Epoch #"
            + this.epoch + "***");
    PresentPattern(-1, -1);
```

```csharp
        PresentPattern(-1, 1);
        PresentPattern(1, -1);
        PresentPattern(1, 1);
        this.epoch++;
    }


    /// <summary>
    /// Present a pattern and learn from it.
    /// </summary>
    /// <param name="i1">Input to neuron 1</param>
    /// <param name="i2">Input to neuron 2</param>
    protected void PresentPattern(double i1, double i2)
    {
        double result;
        double delta;

        // run the net as is on training data
        // and get the error
        Console.Write("Presented [" + i1 + "," + i2 + "]");
        result = Recognize(i1, i2);
        Console.Write(" result=" + result);

        // adjust weight 1
        delta = TrainingFunction(this.rate, i1, result);
        this.w1 += delta;
        Console.Write(",delta w1=" + delta);

        // adjust weight 2
        delta = TrainingFunction(this.rate, i2, result);
        this.w2 += delta;
        Console.WriteLine(",delta w2=" + delta);

    }


    /// <summary>
    /// Attempt to recognize a pattern.
    /// </summary>
    /// <param name="i1">Input to neuron 1</param>
    /// <param name="i2">Input to neuron 2</param>
    /// <returns>The output from the neural network</returns>
    protected double Recognize(double i1, double i2)
    {
        double a = (this.w1 * i1) + (this.w2 * i2);
        return (a * .5);
    }
```

```
/// <summary>
/// This method loops through 10 epochs.
/// </summary>
public void run()
{
    for (int i = 0; i < 5; i++)
    {
        Epoch();
    }
}




/// <summary>
/// This functionimplements the delta rule.
/// This method will return
/// the weight adjustment for the specified input neuron.
/// </summary>
/// <param name="rate">The learning rate</param>
/// <param name="input">The input neuron we're
/// processing</param>
/// <param name="output">The output from the neural
/// network.</param>
/// <returns>The amount to adjust the weight by.</returns>
protected double TrainingFunction(double rate,
    double input,
        double output)
{
    return rate * input * output;
}
    }
}
```

The Hebb's rule example uses two input neurons and one output neuron. As a result, there are a total of two weights, one weight for each of the connections between the input neurons and the output neuron. The first weight, which is the weight between neuron one and the output neuron is initialized to one. The second weight, which is the weight between neuron two and the output neuron, is initialized to two.

Consider the output from the first epoch.

```
***Beginning Epoch #1***
Presented [-1.0,-1.0] result=0.0,delta w1=-0.0,delta w2=-0.0
Presented [-1.0,1.0] result=-1.0,delta w1=1.0,delta w2=-1.0
Presented [1.0,-1.0] result=2.0,delta w1=2.0,delta w2=-2.0
Presented [1.0,1.0] result=0.0,delta w1=0.0,delta w2=0.0
```

The above output shows how the three-neuron network responded to four different input patterns. The middle two input patterns returned the strongest results. The second pattern was strong in the negative direction, the third pattern was strong in the positive direction. Hebb's rule tends to strengthen the output in the direction it already has a tendency towards.

The above output also shows the calculated deltas for weight one (w1) and weight two (w2). The first and fourth patterns both produced outputs of zero, so neither will produce a delta for the weight, other than zero. However, the negative output for pattern two will produce a weight delta of –1, and the positive result of pattern three will produce a weight delta of 2. These delta weights will be applied and will strengthen the negative or positive tendencies of the respective neurons.

It is also important to note that this example is always applying the deltas as the patterns are presented. This is why the third pattern will always have a stronger output than the second pattern; the delta for the second pattern has already been applied by the time the third pattern is presented.

The second epoch continues in much the same way as the first.

```
***Beginning Epoch #2***
Presented [-1.0,-1.0] result=0.0,delta w1=-0.0,delta w2=-0.0
Presented [-1.0,1.0] result=-4.0,delta w1=4.0,delta w2=-4.0
Presented [1.0,-1.0] result=8.0,delta w1=8.0,delta w2=-8.0
Presented [1.0,1.0] result=0.0,delta w1=0.0,delta w2=0.0
```

However, the deltas from the previous epoch have already been applied. New weight deltas are calculated that further enhance the positive or negative tendencies of the neurons.

Delta Rule

The delta rule is also known as the least mean squared error rule (LMS). Using this rule, the actual output of a neural network is compared against the anticipated output. Because the anticipated output is specified, using the delta rule is considered supervised training. Algebraically, the delta rule is written as follows in Equation 4.4.

Equation 4.4: The Delta Rule

$$\Delta w_{ij} = 2\mu\, x_i (ideal - actual)_j$$

The above equation calculates the needed change (delta) in weights for the connection from neuron "i" to neuron "j." The Greek letter mu (μ) represents the learning rate. The variable **ideal** represents the desired output of the "j" neuron. The variable **actual** represents the actual output of the "j" neuron. As a result, **(ideal-actual)** is the error. This equation can easily be translated into the following C# method.

```csharp
protected double TrainingFunction(double rate, double input,
        double error)
{
  return rate * input * error;
}
```

We will now examine how the delta training algorithm actually works. To see this, we will look at the example program shown in Listing 4.3.

Listing 4.3: Using the Delta Rule (Delta.cs)

```csharp
using System;
using System.Collections.Generic;
using System.Linq;
using System.Text;

namespace Chapter04Delta
{
    /// <summary>
    /// Delta: Learn, using the delta rule.
    /// </summary>
    class Delta
    {
        /// <summary>
        /// Main method just instanciates a delta object
        /// and calls run.
        /// </summary>
        /// <param name="args">Not used</param>
        static void Main(string[] args)
        {
            Delta delta = new Delta();
            delta.Run();

        }


        /// <summary>
        /// Weight for neuron 1
        /// </summary>
        double w1;


        /// <summary>
```

```csharp
/// Weight for neuron 2
/// </summary>
double w2;

/// <summary>
/// Weight for neuron 3
/// </summary>
double w3;

/// <summary>
/// Learning rate
/// </summary>
double rate = 0.5;

/// <summary>
/// Current epoch #
/// </summary>
int epoch = 1;




/// <summary>
/// Process one epoch. Here we learn from all three
/// training samples and then
/// update the weights based on error.
/// </summary>
protected void Epoch()
{
    Console.WriteLine("***Beginning Epoch #"
        + this.epoch + "***");
    PresentPattern(0, 0, 1, 0);
    PresentPattern(0, 1, 1, 0);
    PresentPattern(1, 0, 1, 0);
    PresentPattern(1, 1, 1, 1);
    this.epoch++;
}


/// <summary>
/// This method will calculate the error between
/// the anticipated output and
/// the actual output.
/// </summary>
/// <param name="actual">The actual output from
/// the neural network.</param>
/// <param name="anticipated">The anticipated
/// neuron output.</param>
```

```
/// <returns>The error.</returns>
protected double GetError(double actual,
    double anticipated)
{
    return (anticipated - actual);
}


/// <summary>
/// Present a pattern and learn from it.
/// </summary>
/// <param name="i1">Input to neuron 1</param>
/// <param name="i2">Input to neuron 2</param>
/// <param name="i3">Input to neuron 3</param>
/// <param name="anticipated">The anticipated output
/// </param>
protected void PresentPattern(double i1, double i2,
        double i3, double anticipated)
{
    double error;
    double actual;
    double delta;

    // run the net as is on training data
    // and get the error
    Console.Write("Presented [" + i1 + "," + i2 + ","
        + i3 + "]");
    actual = Recognize(i1, i2, i3);
    error = GetError(actual, anticipated);
    Console.Write(" anticipated=" + anticipated);
    Console.Write(" actual=" + actual);
    Console.WriteLine(" error=" + error);

    // adjust weight 1
    delta = TrainingFunction(this.rate, i1, error);
    this.w1 += delta;

    // adjust weight 2
    delta = TrainingFunction(this.rate, i2, error);
    this.w2 += delta;

    // adjust weight 3
    delta = TrainingFunction(this.rate, i3, error);
    this.w3 += delta;
}
```

```csharp
/// <summary>
/// Try to recognize a pattern.
/// </summary>
/// <param name="i1">Input to neuron 1</param>
/// <param name="i2">Input to neuron 2</param>
/// <param name="i3">Input to neuron 3</param>
/// <returns>The output from the neural network</returns>
protected double Recognize(double i1, double i2,
    double i3)
{
    double a = (this.w1 * i1) + (this.w2 * i2) +
    (this.w3 * i3);
    return (a * .5);
}


/// <summary>
/// This method loops through 100 epochs.
/// </summary>
public void Run()
{
    for (int i = 0; i < 100; i++)
    {
        Epoch();
    }
}


/// <summary>
/// Thisimplements the delta rule.
/// This method will return
/// the weight adjustment for the specified input neuron.
/// </summary>
/// <param name="rate">The learning rate</param>
/// <param name="input">The input neuron we're
/// processing</param>
/// <param name="error">The error between the actual
/// output and anticipated output.</param>
/// <returns>The amount to adjust the weight by.</returns>
protected double TrainingFunction(double rate,
            double input,
          double error)
{
    return rate * input * error;
}
    }
}
```

This program will train for 100 iterations. It is designed to teach the neural network to recognize three patterns. These patterns are summarized as follows:

```
For 001 output 0
For 011 output 0
For 101 output 0
For 111 output 1
```

For each epoch, you will be shown the actual and anticipated results. By epoch 100, the network will be trained. The output from epoch 100 is shown here:

```
***Beginning Epoch #100***
Presented [0.0,0.0,1.0] anticipated=0.0 actu-
al=-0.33333333131711973 error=0.33333333131711973
Presented [0.0,1.0,1.0] anticipated=0.0 actual=0.333333333558949
error=-0.333333333558949
Presented [1.0,0.0,1.0] anticipated=0.0 actual=0.33333333370649876
error=-0.33333333370649876
Presented [1.0,1.0,1.0] anticipated=1.0 actual=0.6666666655103011
error=0.33333333448969893
```

As you can see from the above display, there are only two possible outputs 0.333 and 0.666. The output of 0.333 corresponds to 0 and the output of 0.666 corresponds to 1. A neural network will never produce the exact output desired, but through rounding it gets pretty close. While the delta rule is efficient at adjusting weights, it is not the most commonly used.

In the next chapter we will examine the feedforward backpropagation network, which is one of the most commonly used neural networks. Backpropagation is a more advanced form of the delta rule.

Chapter Summary

The rate of error for a neural network is a very important statistic, which is used as a part of the training process. This chapter showed you how to calculate the output error for an individual training set element, as well as how to calculate the RMS error for the entire training set.

Training occurs when the weights of the synapse are modified to produce a more suitable output. Unsupervised training occurs when the neural network is left to determine the correct responses. Supervised training occurs when the neural network is provided with training data and anticipated outputs. Hebb's rule can be used for unsupervised training. The delta rule is used for supervised training.

In this chapter we learned how a machine learns through the modification of the weights associated with the connections between neurons. This chapter introduced the basic concepts of how a machine learns. Backpropagation is a more advanced form of the delta rule, which was introduced in this chapter. In the next chapter we will explore backpropagation and see how the neural network class implements it.

Vocabulary

Classification

Delta Rule

Epoch

Hebb's Rule

Iteration

Kohonen Neural Network

Learning Rate

Root Mean Square (RMS)

Self-Organizing Map (SOM)

Supervised Training

Unsupervised Training

Questions for Review

1. Explain the difference between supervised and unsupervised training.

2. What is the primary difference between the delta rule and Hebb's rule?

3. Consider the following four results; calculate the RMS error.

```
Training Set #1, Expected = 5, Actual = 5
Training Set #2, Expected = 2, Actual = 3
Training Set #3, Expected = 6, Actual = 5
Training Set #4, Expected = 8, Actual = 4
Trainining Set #5, Expected = 1, Actual = 2
```

4.   Use Hebb's rule to calculate the weight adjustment.

```
Two Neurons: N1 and N2
N1 to N2 Weight: 3
N1 Activation: 2
N2 Activation: 6
```

Calculate the weight delta.

5.   Use the delta rule to calculate the weight adjustment.

```
Two neurons: N1 and N2
N1 to N2 Weight: 3
N1 Activation: 2
N2 Activation: 6, Expected: 5
```

Calculate the weight delta.

CHAPTER 5: FEEDFORWARD BACKPROPAGATION NETWORKS

- Introducing the Feedforward Backpropagation Neural Network
- Understanding the Feedforward Algorithm
- Implementing the Feedforward Algorithm
- Understanding the Backpropagation Algorithm
- Implementing the Backpropagation Algorithm

In this chapter we shall examine one of the most common neural network architectures, the feedforword backpropagation neural network. This neural network architecture is very popular, because it can be applied to many different tasks. To understand this neural network architecture, we must examine how it is trained and how it processes a pattern.

The first term, "feedforward" describes how this neural network processes and recalls patterns. In a feedforward neural network, neurons are only connected foreword. Each layer of the neural network contains connections to the next layer (for example, from the input to the hidden layer), but there are no connections back. This differs from the Hopfield neural network that was examined in chapter 3. The Hopfield neural network was fully connected, and its connections are both forward and backward. Exactly how a feedforward neural network recalls a pattern will be explored later in this chapter.

The term "backpropagation" describes how this type of neural network is trained. Backpropagation is a form of supervised training. When using a supervised training method, the network must be provided with both sample inputs and anticipated outputs. The anticipated outputs are compared against the actual outputs for given input. Using the anticipated outputs, the backpropagation training algorithm then takes a calculated error and adjusts the weights of the various layers backwards from the output layer to the input layer. The exact process by which backpropagation occurs will also be discussed later in this chapter.

The backpropagation and feedforward algorithms are often used together; however, this is by no means a requirement. It would be quite permissible to create a neural network that uses the feedforward algorithm to determine its output and does not use the backpropagation training algorithm. Similarly, if you choose to create a neural network that uses backpropagation training methods, you are not necessarily limited to a feedforward algorithm to determine the output of the neural network. Though such cases are less common than the feedforward backpropagation neural network, examples can be found. In this book, we will examine only the case in which the feedforward and backpropagation algorithms are used together. We will begin this discussion by examining how a feedforward neural network functions.

A Feedforward Neural Network

A feedforward neural network is similar to the types of neural networks that we have already examined. Just like many other types of neural networks, the feedforward neural network begins with an input layer. The input layer may be connected to a hidden layer or directly to the output layer. If it is connected to a hidden layer, the hidden layer can then be connected to another hidden layer or directly to the output layer. There can be any number of hidden layers, as long as there is at least one hidden layer or output layer provided. In common use, most neural networks will have one hidden layer, and it is very rare for a neural network to have more than two hidden layers.

The Structure of a Feedforward Neural Network

Figure 5.1 illustrates a typical feedforward neural network with a single hidden layer.

Figure 5.1: A typical feedforward neural network (single hidden layer).

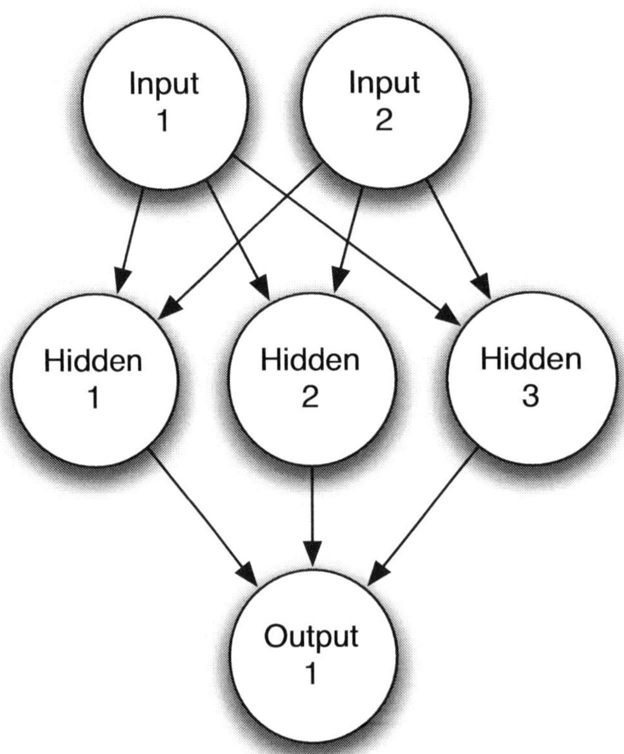

Neural networks with more than two hidden layers are uncommon.

Choosing Your Network Structure

As we saw in the previous section, there are many ways that feedforward neural networks can be constructed. You must decide how many neurons will be inside the input and output layers. You must also decide how many hidden layers you are going to have and how many neurons will be in each of them.

There are many techniques for choosing these parameters. In this section we will cover some of the general "rules of thumb" that you can use to assist you in these decisions; however, these rules will only take you so far. In nearly all cases, some experimentation will be required to determine the optimal structure for your feedforward neural network. There are many books dedicated entirely to this topic. For a thorough discussion on structuring feedforward neural networks, you should refer to the book Neural Smithing: Supervised Learning in Feedforward Artificial Neural Networks (MIT Press, 1999).

The Input Layer

The input layer is the conduit through which the external environment presents a pattern to the neural network. Once a pattern is presented to the input layer, the output layer will produce another pattern. In essence, this is all the neural network does. The input layer should represent the condition for which we are training the neural network. Every input neuron should represent some independent variable that has an influence over the output of the neural network.

It is important to remember that the inputs to the neural network are floating point numbers. These values are expressed as the primitive C# data type "double." This is not to say that you can only process numeric data with the neural network; if you wish to process a form of data that is non-numeric, you must develop a process that normalizes this data to a numeric representation. In chapter 12, "OCR and the Self-Organizing Map," I will show you how to communicate graphic information to a neural network.

The Output Layer

The output layer of the neural network is what actually presents a pattern to the external environment. The pattern presented by the output layer can be directly traced back to the input layer. The number of output neurons should be directly related to the type of work that the neural network is to perform.

To determine the number of neurons to use in your output layer, you must first consider the intended use of the neural network. If the neural network is to be used to classify items into groups, then it is often preferable to have one output neuron for each group that input items are to be assigned into. If the neural network is to perform noise reduction on a signal, then it is likely that the number of input neurons will match the number of output neurons. In this sort of neural network, you will want the patterns to leave the neural network in the same format as they entered.

For a specific example of how to choose the number of input neurons and the number of output neurons, consider a program that is used for optical character recognition (OCR), such as the program presented in the example in chapter 12, "OCR and the Self-Organizing Map." To determine the number of neurons used for the OCR example, we will first consider the input layer. The number of input neurons that we will use is the number of pixels that might represent any given character. Characters processed by this program are normalized to a universal size that is represented by a 5x7 grid. A 5x7 grid contains a total of 35 pixels. Therefore, the OCR program has 35 input neurons.

The number of output neurons used by the OCR program will vary depending on how many characters the program has been trained to recognize. The default training file that is provided with the OCR program is used to train it to recognize 26 characters. Using this file, the neural network will have 26 output neurons. Presenting a pattern to the input neurons will fire the appropriate output neuron that corresponds to the letter that the input pattern represents.

Solving the XOR Problem

Next, we will examine a simple neural network that will learn the XOR operator. The XOR operator was covered in chapter 1. You will see how to use several classes from this neural network. These classes are provided in the companion download available with the purchase of this book. Appendix A describes how to obtain this download. Later in the chapter, you will be shown how these classes were constructed.

Listing 5.1: The XOR Problem (XOR.cs)

```
using System;
using System.Collections.Generic;
using System.Linq;
using System.Text;

using HeatonResearchNeural.Feedforward;
using HeatonResearchNeural.Feedforward.Train;

namespace Chapter5XOR
{
    /// <summary>
    /// Chapter 5: The Feedforward Backpropagation Neural Network
```

```
///
/// Solve the classic XOR problem.
/// </summary>
class XOR
{
    /// <summary>
    /// Input for the XOR function.
    /// </summary>
    public static double[][] XOR_INPUT ={
        new double[2] { 0.0, 0.0 },
        new double[2] { 1.0, 0.0 },
            new double[2] { 0.0, 1.0 },
        new double[2] { 1.0, 1.0 } };

    /// <summary>
    /// Ideal output for the XOR function.
    /// </summary>
    public static double[][] XOR_IDEAL = {
        new double[1] { 0.0 },
        new double[1] { 1.0 },
        new double[1] { 1.0 },
        new double[1] { 0.0 } };

    /// <summary>
    /// Create, train and use a neural network for XOR.
    /// </summary>
    /// <param name="args">Not used</param>
    static void Main(string[] args)
    {
        FeedforwardNetwork network = new FeedforwardNetwork();
        network.AddLayer(new FeedforwardLayer(2));
        network.AddLayer(new FeedforwardLayer(3));
        network.AddLayer(new FeedforwardLayer(1));
        network.Reset();

        // train the neural network
        Train train = new HeatonResearchNeural.Feedforward.
Train.Backpropagation.Backpropagation(
network, XOR_INPUT, XOR_IDEAL,
                0.7, 0.9);

        int epoch = 1;

        do
        {
            train.Iteration();
```

```
            Console.WriteLine("Epoch #" + epoch + " Error:"
               + train.Error);
            epoch++;
       } while ((epoch < 5000) && (train.Error > 0.001));

       // test the neural network
       Console.WriteLine("Neural Network Results:");
       for (int i = 0; i < XOR_IDEAL.Length; i++)
       {
            double[] actual = network.ComputeOutputs(
               XOR_INPUT[i]);
            Console.WriteLine(XOR_INPUT[i][0] + ","
               + XOR_INPUT[i][1]
                    + ", actual=" + actual[0] + ",ideal="
                    + XOR_IDEAL[i][0]);

       }
     }
   }
}
```

The last few lines of output from this program are shown here.

```
Epoch #4997 Error:0.006073963240271441 Epoch #4998 Er-
ror:0.006073315333403568 Epoch #4999 Error:0.0060726676304029325
Neural Network Results: 0.0,0.0, actual=0.0025486129720869773,ide
al=0.0 1.0,0.0, actual=0.9929280525379659,ideal=1.0 0.0,1.0, actu
al=0.9944310234678858,ideal=1.0 1.0,1.0, actual=0.007745179145434
604,ideal=0.0
```

As you can see, the network ran through nearly 5,000 training epochs. This produced an error of just over half a percent and took only a few seconds. The results were then displayed. The neural network produced a number close to zero for the input of 0,0 and 1,1. It also produced a number close to 1 for the inputs of 1,0 and 0,1.

This program is very easy to construct. First, a two dimensional **double** array is created that holds the input for the neural network. These are the training sets for the neural network.

```
public static double[][] XOR_INPUT ={
   new double[2] { 0.0, 0.0 },
   new double[2] { 1.0, 0.0 },
   new double[2] { 0.0, 1.0 },
   new double[2] { 1.0, 1.0 } };
```

Next, a two dimensional **double** array is created that holds the ideal output for each of the training sets given above.

```
public static double[][] XOR_IDEAL = {
   new double[1] { 0.0 },
```

```
new double[1] { 1.0 },
new double[1] { 1.0 },
new double[1] { 0.0 } };
```

It may seem as though a single dimensional **double** array would suffice for this task. However, neural networks can have more than one output neuron, which would produce more than one **double** value. This neural network has only one output neuron.

A **FeedforwardNetwork** object is now created. This is the main object for the neural network. Layers will be added to this object.

```
FeedforwardNetwork network = new FeedforwardNetwork();
```

The first layer to be added will be the input layer. A **FeedforwardLayer** object is created. The value of two specifies that there will be two input neurons.

```
network.AddLayer(new FeedforwardLayer(2));
```

The second layer to be added will be a hidden layer. If no additional layers are added beyond this layer, then it will be the output layer. The first layer added is always the input layer, the last layer added is always the output layer. Any layers added between those two layers are the hidden layers. A **FeedforwardLayer** object is created to serve as the hidden layer. The value of three specifies that there will be three neurons in the hidden layer.

```
network.AddLayer(new FeedforwardLayer(3));
```

The final layer to be added will be the output layer. A **FeedforwardLayer** object is created. The value of one specifies that there will be a single output neuron.

```
network.AddLayer(new FeedforwardLayer(1));
```

Finally, the neural network is reset. This randomizes the weight and threshold values. This random neural network will now need to be trained.

```
network.Reset();
```

The backpropagation method will be used to train the neural network. To do this, a **Backpropagation** object is created.

```
Train train = new HeatonResearchNeural.Feedforward.Train.
Backpropagation.Backpropagation(
network, XOR_INPUT, XOR_IDEAL, 0.7, 0.9);
```

The training object requires several arguments to be passed to its constructor. The first argument is the network to be trained. The second argument is the **XOR_INPUT** and **XOR_IDEAL** variables, which provide the training sets and expected results. Finally, the learning rate and momentum are specified.

The learning rate specifies how fast the neural network will learn. This is usually a value around one, as it is a percent. The momentum specifies how much of an effect the previous training iteration will have on the current iteration. The momentum is also a percent, and is usually a value near one. To use no momentum in the backpropagation algorithm, you will specify a value of zero. The learning rate and momentum values will be discussed further later in this chapter.

Now that the training object is set up, the program will loop through training iterations until the error rate is small, or it performs 5,000 epochs, or iterations.

```
int epoch = 1;

do
{
   train.Iteration();
   Console.WriteLine("Epoch #" + epoch + " Error:" + train.Error);
   epoch++;
} while ((epoch < 5000) && (train.Error > 0.001));
```

To perform a training iteration, simply call the **Iteration** method on the training object. The loop will continue until the error is smaller than one-tenth of a percent, or the program has performed 5,000 training iterations.

Finally, the program will display the results produced by the neural network.

```
Console.WriteLine("Neural Network Results:");
for (int i = 0; i < XOR_IDEAL.Length; i++)
{
```

As the program loops through each of the training sets, that training set is presented to the neural network. To present a pattern to the neural network, the **ComputeOutputs** method is used. This method accepts a **double** array of input values. This array must be the same size as the number of input neurons or an exception will be thrown. This method returns an array of **double** values the same size as the number of output neurons.

```
double[] actual = network.ComputeOutputs(XOR_INPUT[i]);
```

The output from the neural network is displayed.

```
Console.WriteLine(XOR_INPUT[i][0] + "," + XOR_INPUT[i][1]
+ ", actual=" + actual[0] + ",ideal=" + XOR_IDEAL[i][0]);

   }
}
```

This is a very simple neural network. It used the default sigmoid activation function. As you will see in the next section, other activation functions can be specified.

Activation Functions

Most neural networks pass the output of their layers through activation functions. These activation functions scale the output of the neural network into proper ranges. The neural network program in the last section used the sigmoid activation function. The sigmoid activation function is the default choice for the **FeedforwardLayer** class. It is possible to use others. For example, to use the hyperbolic tangent activation function, the following lines of code would be used to create the layers.

```
network.AddLayer(new FeedforwardLayer(new ActivationTANH(),2));
network.AddLayer(new FeedforwardLayer(new ActivationTANH(),3));
network.AddLayer(new FeedforwardLayer(new ActivationTANH(),1));
```

As you can see from the above code, a new instance of **ActivationTANH** is created and passed to each layer of the network. This specifies that the hyperbolic tangent should be used, rather than the sigmoid function.

You may notice that it would be possible to use a different activation function for each layer of the neural network. While technically there is nothing stopping you from doing this, such practice would be unusual.

There are a total of three activation functions provided:

- Hyperbolic Tangent
- Sigmoid
- Linear

It is also possible to create your own activation function. There is an interface named **ActivationFunction**. Any class that implements the **ActivationFunction** interface can serve as an activation function. The three activation functions provided will be discussed in the following sections.

Using a Sigmoid Activation Function

A sigmoid activation function uses the sigmoid function to determine its activation. The sigmoid function is defined as follows:

Equation 5.1: The Sigmoid Function.

$$f(x) = \frac{1}{1 + e^{-x}}$$

The term sigmoid means curved in two directions, like the letter "S." You can see the sigmoid function in Figure 5.2.

Figure 5.2: The Sigmoid function.

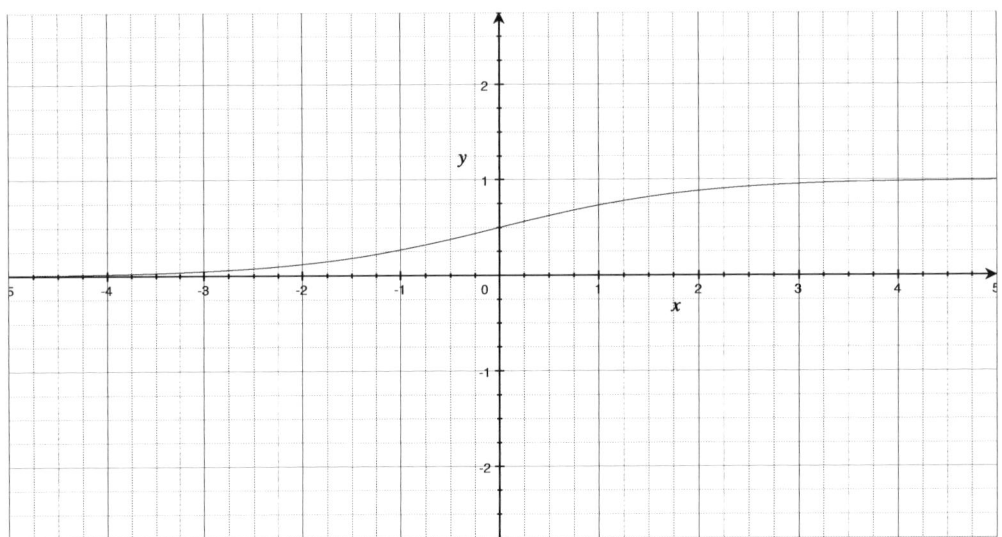

One important thing to note about the sigmoid activation function is that it only returns positive values. If you need the neural network to return negative numbers, the sigmoid function will be unsuitable. The sigmoid activation function is implemented in the **ActivationFunctionSigmoid** class. This class is shown in Listing 5.2.

Listing 5.2: The Sigmoid Activation Function Class (ActivationSigmoid.cs)

```csharp
using System;
using System.Collections.Generic;
using System.Linq;
using System.Text;

namespace HeatonResearchNeural.Activation
{
    /// <summary>
    /// ActivationSigmoid: The sigmoid activation function
    /// takes on a sigmoidal shape.  Only positive numbers are
    /// generated.  Do not use this activation function if
    /// negative number output is desired.
    /// </summary>
    [Serializable]
    public class ActivationSigmoid : ActivationFunction
    {
        /// <summary>
```

```
/// A activation function for a neural network.
/// </summary>
/// <param name="d">The input to the function.</param>
/// <returns>The ouput from the function.</returns>
public double ActivationFunction(double d)
{
    return 1.0 / (1 + Math.Exp(-1.0 * d));
}


/// <summary>
/// Performs the derivative function of the
/// activation function function on the input.
/// </summary>
/// <param name="d">The input to the function.</param>
/// <returns>The ouput from the function.</returns>
public double DerivativeFunction(double d)
{
    return d * (1.0 - d);
}
    }
}
```

As you can see, the sigmoid function is defined inside the **ActivationFunction** method. This method was defined by the **ActivationFunction** interface. If you would like to create your own activation function, it is as simple as creating a class that implements the **ActivationFunction** interface and providing an **ActivationFunction** method.

The **ActivationFunction** interface also defines a method named **DerivativeFunction** that implements the derivative of the main activation function. Certain training methods require the derivative of the activation function. **Backpropagation** is one such method. **Backpropagation** cannot be used on a neural network that uses an activation function that does not have a derivative. However, a genetic algorithm or simulated annealing could still be used. These two techniques will be covered in the next two chapters.

Using a Hyperbolic Tangent Activation Function

As previously mentioned, the sigmoid activation function does not return values less than zero. However, it is possible to "move" the sigmoid function to a region of the graph so that it does provide negative numbers. This is done using the hyperbolic tangent function. The equation for the hyperbolic activation function is shown in Equation 5.2.

Equation 5.2: The TANH function

$$f(x) = \frac{e^{2x} - 1}{e^{2x} + 1}$$

Although this looks considerably more complex than the sigmoid function, you can safely think of it as a positive and negative compatible version of the sigmoid function. The graph for the hyperbolic tangent function is provided in Figure 5.3.

Figure 5.3: The hyperbolic tangent function.

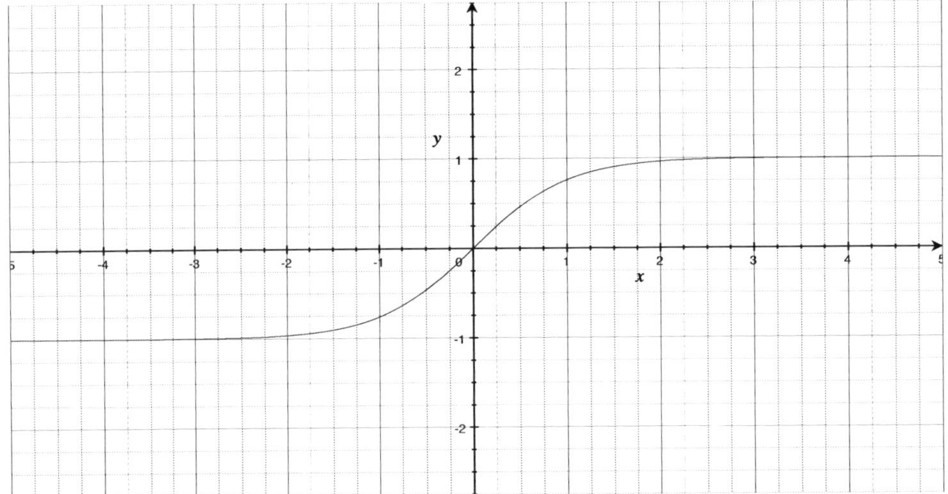

One important thing to note about the hyperbolic tangent activation function is that it returns both positive and negative values. If you need the neural network to return negative numbers, this is the activation function to use. The hyperbolic tangent activation function is implemented in the **ActivationFunctionTANH** class. This class is shown in Listing 5.3.

Listing 5.3: The Hyperbolic Tangent Function Class (ActivationTANH.cs)

```
using System;
using System.Collections.Generic;
using System.Linq;
using System.Text;

namespace HeatonResearchNeural.Activation
{
```

```
/// <summary>
/// ActivationTANH: The hyperbolic tangent activation
/// function takes the
/// curved shape of the hyperbolic tangent.  This
/// activation function produces
/// both positive and negative output.  Use this
/// activation function if
/// both negative and positive output is desired.
/// </summary>
[Serializable]
public class ActivationTANH : ActivationFunction
{

    /// <summary>
    /// A activation function for a neural network.
    /// </summary>
    /// <param name="d">The input to the function.</param>
    /// <returns>The ouput from the function.</returns>
    public double ActivationFunction(double d)
    {
        double result = (Math.Exp(d * 2.0) - 1.0)
        / (Math.Exp(d * 2.0) + 1.0);
        return result;
    }


    /// <summary>
    /// Performs the derivative function of the
    /// activation function function on the input.
    /// </summary>
    /// <param name="d">The input to the function.</param>
    /// <returns>The ouput from the function.</returns>
    public double DerivativeFunction(double d)
    {
        return (1.0 - Math.Pow(ActivationFunction(d), 2.0));
    }


}


}
```

As you can see, the hyperbolic tangent function is defined inside the **ActivationFunction** method. This method was defined by the **ActivationFunction** interface. The **DerivativeFunction** is also defined to return the result of the derivative of the hyperbolic tangent function.

Using a Linear Activation Function

The linear activation function is essentially no activation function at all. It is probably the least commonly used of the activation functions. The linear activation function does not modify a pattern before outputting it. The function for the linear layer is given in Equation 5.3.

Equation 5.3: A Linear Function

$$f(x) = x$$

The linear activation function might be useful in situations when you need the entire range of numbers to be output. Usually, you will want to think of your neurons as active or non-active. Because the hyperbolic tangent and sigmoid activation functions both have established upper and lower bounds, they tend to be used more for Boolean (on or off) type operations. The linear activation function is useful for presenting a range. A graph of the linear activation function is provided in Figure 5.4.

Figure 5.4: The linear activation function.

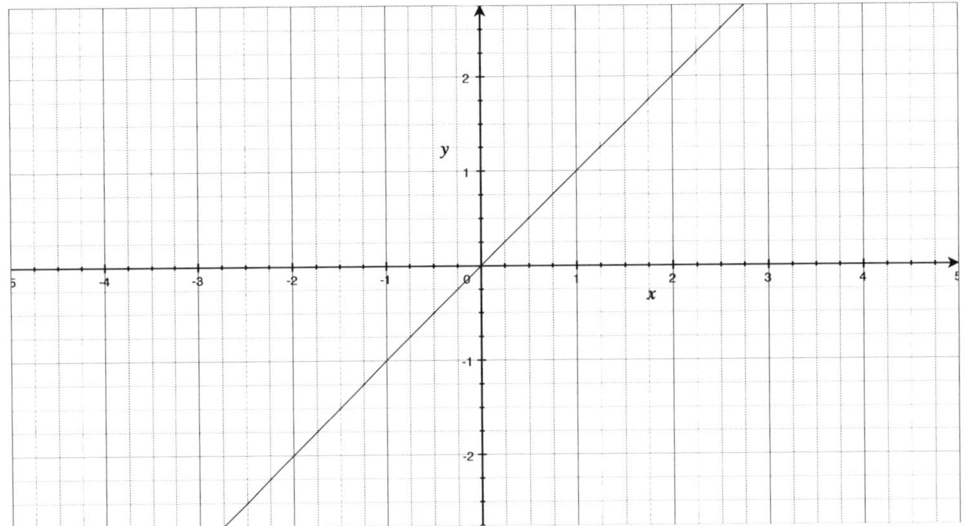

The implementation for the linear activation function is fairly simple. It is shown in Listing 5.4.

Listing 5.4: The Linear Activation Function (ActivationLinear.cs)

```csharp
using System;
using System.Collections.Generic;
using System.Linq;
using System.Text;

using HeatonResearchNeural.Exception;

namespace HeatonResearchNeural.Activation
{
    /// <summary>
    /// ActivationLinear: The Linear layer is really not an
    /// activation function
    /// at all.  The input is simply passed on, unmodified,
    /// to the output.
    /// This activation function is primarily theoretical
    /// and of little actual
    /// use.  Usually an activation function that scales
    /// between 0 and 1 or
    /// -1 and 1 should be used.
    /// </summary>
    [Serializable]
    public class ActivationLinear : ActivationFunction
    {
        /// <summary>
        /// A activation function for a neural network.
        /// </summary>
        /// <param name="d">The input to the function.</param>
        /// <returns>The ouput from the function.</returns>
        public double ActivationFunction(double d)
        {
            return d;
        }


        /// <summary>
        /// Performs the derivative function of the
        /// activation function function on the input.  There is
        /// no derivative function for the linear activation
        /// function, so this method throws an error.
        /// </summary>
        /// <param name="d">The input to the function.</param>
        /// <returns>The ouput from the function.</returns>
        public double DerivativeFunction(double d)
        {
```

```
        throw new NeuralNetworkError(
"Can't use the linear activation function where a derivative is
required.");
        }
    }
}
```

As you can see, the linear activation function does no more than return what it is given. The derivative of the linear function is 1. This is not useful for training, thus the **DerivativeFunction** for the linear activation function throws an exception. You cannot use backpropagation to train a neural network that makes use of the linear function.

The Number of Hidden Layers

There are really two decisions that must be made regarding the hidden layers: how many hidden layers to actually have in the neural network and how many neurons will be in each of these layers. We will first examine how to determine the number of hidden layers to use with the neural network.

Problems that require two hidden layers are rarely encountered. However, neural networks with two hidden layers can represent functions with any kind of shape. There is currently no theoretical reason to use neural networks with any more than two hidden layers. In fact, for many practical problems, there is no reason to use any more than one hidden layer. Table 5.1 summarizes the capabilities of neural network architectures with various hidden layers.

Table 5.1: Determining the Number of Hidden Layers

Number of Hidden Layers	Result
none	Only capable of representing linear separable functions or decisions.
1	Can approximate any function that contains a continuous mapping from one finite space to another.
2	Can represent an arbitrary decision boundary to arbitrary accuracy with rational activation functions and can approximate any smooth mapping to any accuracy.

Deciding the number of hidden neuron layers is only a small part of the problem. You must also determine how many neurons will be in each of these hidden layers. This process is covered in the next section.

The Number of Neurons in the Hidden Layers

Deciding the number of neurons in the hidden layers is a very important part of deciding your overall neural network architecture. Though these layers do not directly interact with the external environment, they have a tremendous influence on the final output. Both the number of hidden layers and the number of neurons in each of these hidden layers must be carefully considered.

Using too few neurons in the hidden layers will result in something called under-fitting. Underfitting occurs when there are too few neurons in the hidden layers to adequately detect the signals in a complicated data set.

Using too many neurons in the hidden layers can result in several problems. First, too many neurons in the hidden layers may result in overfitting. Overfitting occurs when the neural network has so much information processing capacity that the limited amount of information contained in the training set is not enough to train all of the neurons in the hidden layers. A second problem can occur even when the training data is sufficient. An inordinately large number of neurons in the hidden layers can increase the time it takes to train the network. The amount of training time can increase to the point that it is impossible to adequately train the neural network. Obviously, some compromise must be reached between too many and too few neurons in the hidden layers.

There are many rule-of-thumb methods for determining the correct number of neurons to use in the hidden layers, such as the following:

• The number of hidden neurons should be between the size of the input layer and the size of the output layer.

• The number of hidden neurons should be 2/3 the size of the input layer, plus the size of the output layer.

• The number of hidden neurons should be less than twice the size of the input layer.

These three rules provide a starting point for you to consider. Ultimately, the selection of an architecture for your neural network will come down to trial and error. But what exactly is meant by trial and error? You do not want to start throwing random numbers of layers and neurons at your network. To do so would be very time consuming. Chapter 8, "Pruning a Neural Network" will explore various ways to determine an optimal structure for a neural network.

Examining the Feedforward Process

Earlier in this chapter you saw how to present data to a neural network and train that neural network. The remainder of this chapter will focus on how these operations were performed. The neural network classes presented earlier are not overly complex. We will begin by exploring how they calculate the output of the neural network. This is called the feedforward process.

Calculating the Output Mathematically

Equation 5.4 describes how the output of a single neuron can be calculated.

Equation 5.4: Feedforward Calculations

$$output = \left(\sum_{i=0}^{n-1} x_i w_i \right) + w_n$$

The above equation takes input values named **x**, and multiplies them by the weight **w**. As you will recall from chapter 2, the last value in the weight matrix is the threshold. This threshold is **wn**.

To perform the above operation with matrix mathematics, the input is used to populate a matrix and a row is added, the elements of which are all ones. This value will be multiplied against the threshold value. For example, if the input were 0.1, 0.2, and 0.3, the following input matrix would be produced.

Equation 5.5: An Input Matrix

$$\begin{bmatrix} 0.1 & 0.2 & 0.3 & 1 \end{bmatrix}$$

The dot product would then be taken between the input matrix and the weight matrix. This number would then be fed to the activation function to produce the output from the neuron.

Calculating the Output for a Feedforward Neural Network

To obtain the output from the neural network, the **ComputeOutputs** function should be called. This function will call the layers of the neural network and determine the output. The signature for the **ComputeOutputs** function is shown here:

```
public double[] ComputeOutputs(double[] input)
```

The first thing that the **ComputeOutputs** function does is to check and see if the **input** array is of the correct size. The size of the **input** array must match the number of input neurons in the input layer.

```
if (input.Length != this.inputLayer.NeuronCount)
{
  throw new NeuralNetworkError(
  "Size mismatch: Can't compute outputs for input size="
  + input.Length + " for input layer size="
  + this.inputLayer.NeuronCount);
}
```

Next, each of the **FeedforwardLayer** objects will be looped across.

```
foreach (FeedforwardLayer layer in this.layers)
{
```

The input layer will receive the input that was provided.

```
  if (layer.IsInput())
  {
    layer.ComputeOutputs(input);
  }
```

Each of the hidden layers will receive the output from the previous layer as input.

```
  else if (layer.IsHidden())
  {
    layer.ComputeOutputs(null);
  }
}
```

Finally, the output layer's result is returned.

```
return this.outputLayer.Fire;
```

The **ComputeOutputs** method for the neural network obtains its output by calculating the output for each layer. The next section will explain how the output for a layer is calculated.

Calculating the Output for a Layer

The **FeedforwardLayer** class contains a **ComputeOutputs** method as well. This method is used to calculate the output for each of the layers. The signature for this method is shown here:

```
public double[] ComputeOutputs(double[] pattern)
```

First, the **ComputeOutputs** method checks to see whether or not a pattern was presented to it.

```
if (pattern != null)
{
```

If a **pattern** was presented, then the pattern should be copied to the **fire** instance variable.

```
for (i = 0; i < this.NeuronCount; i++)
{
  SetFire(i, pattern[i]);
}
}
```

If a **pattern** was not presented, then the **fire** instance variable will have already been set by the previous layer.

```
Matrix.Matrix inputMatrix = CreateInputMatrix(this.fire);
```

Next, an output value must be calculated to become the input value for each of the neurons in the next layer.

```
for (i = 0; i < this.next.NeuronCount; i++)
{
```

To do this, we obtain a column matrix for each of the neurons in the next layer.

```
Matrix.Matrix col = this.matrix.GetCol(i);
```

The dot product between the weight matrix column and input is then determined. This will be the value that will be presented to the next layer.

```
double sum = MatrixMath.DotProduct(col, inputMatrix);
```

The output is passed to the **ActivationFunction** and then stored in the fire instance variable of the next layer.

```
this.next.SetFire(i, this.activationFunction.
ActivationFunction(sum));

}
```

The **fire** instance variable is returned as the output for this layer.

```
return this.fire;
```

This process continues with each layer. The output from the output layer is the output from the neural network.

Examining the Backpropagation Process

You have now seen how to calculate the output for a feedforward neural network. You have seen both the mathematical equations and the C# implementation. As we examined how to calculate the final values for the network, we used the connection weights and threshold values to determine the final result. You may be wondering how these values were determined.

The values contained in the weight and threshold matrix were determined using the backpropagation algorithm. This is a very useful algorithm for training neural networks. The backpropagation algorithm works by running the neural network just as we did in our recognition example, as shown in the previous section. The main difference in the backpropagation algorithm is that we present the neural network with training data. As each item of training data is presented to the neural network, the error is calculated between the actual output of the neural network and the output that was expected (and specified in the training set). The weights and threshold are then modified, so there is a greater chance of the network returning the correct result when the network is next presented with the same input.

Backpropagation is a very common method for training multilayered feedforward networks. Backpropagation can be used with any feedforward network that uses a activation function that is differentiable. It is this derivative function that we will use during training. It is not necessary that you understand calculus or how to take the derivative of an equation to work with the material in this chapter. If you are using one of the common activation functions, you can simply get the activation function derivative from a chart.

To train the neural network, a method must be determined to calculate the error. As the neural network is trained, the network is presented with samples from the training set. The result obtained from the neural network is then compared with the anticipated result that is part of the training set. The degree to which the output from the neural network differs from this anticipated output is the error.

To train the neural network, we must try to minimize this error. To minimize the error, the neuron connection weights and thresholds must be modified. We must define a function that will calculate the rate of error of the neural network. This error function must be mathematically differentiable. Because the network uses a differentiable activation function, the activations of the output neurons can be thought of as differentiable functions of the input, weights, and thresholds. If the error function is also a differentiable function, such as the sum of square error function, the error function itself is a differentiable function of these weights. This allows us to evaluate the derivative of the error using the weights. Then, using these derivatives, we find weights and thresholds that will minimize the error function.

There are several ways to find weights that will minimize the error function. The most popular approach is to use the gradient descent method. The algorithm that evaluates the derivative of the error function is known as backpropagation, because it propagates the errors backward through the network.

The Train Interface

This book will cover three different training methods that can be used for feedforward neural networks. This chapter presents the backpropagation method. Chapter 6 will discuss using a genetic algorithm for training. Chapter 7 will discuss using simulated annealing for a neural network. All three of these training methods implement the Train interface. The **Train** interface is shown in Listing 5.5.

Listing 5.5: The Train Interface (Train.cs)

```
using System;
using System.Collections.Generic;
using System.Linq;
using System.Text;

namespace HeatonResearchNeural.Feedforward.Train
{
    public interface Train
    {
        /// <summary>
        /// Get the current best network from the training.
        /// </summary>
        FeedforwardNetwork Network
        {
            get;
        }


        /// <summary>
        /// Get the current error percent from the training.
        /// </summary>
        double Error
        {
            get;
        }


        /// <summary>
        /// Perform one iteration of training.
        /// </summary>
        void Iteration();
    }
}
```

There are two properties and one method that must be implemented to use the **Train** interface. The **Error** property will return the current error level, calculated using root mean square (RMS) for the current neural network. The **Network** property returns a trained neural network that achieves the error level reported by the **Error** property. Finally, the **Iteration** method is called to perform one training iteration. Generally, the **Iteration** method is called repeatedly until the **Error** method returns an acceptable error.

The Backpropagation C# Classes

The backpropagation algorithm is implemented in two classes. The **Backpropagation** class, which implements the **Train** interface, is the main training class used. Internally, the **Backpropagation** class uses the **BackpropagationLayer** class to hold information that the backpropagation algorithm needs for each layer of the neural network.

The **Train** interface is made up of two properties and a method. The **Backpropagation** class provides the **Iteration** to perform each iteration of the training. The **Error** property reveals the current error level of the neural network. The **Network** property contains the current best trained neural network. The **Iteration** method has the following signature:

```
public void Iteration()
{
```

The **Iteration** method begins by looping through all of the training sets that were provided.

```
for (int j = 0; j < this.input.Length; j++)
{
```

Each training set is presented to the neural network and the outputs are calculated.

```
this.network.ComputeOutputs(this.input[j]);
```

Once the outputs have been calculated, the training can begin. This is a two-step process. First, the error is calculated by comparing the output to the ideal values.

```
CalcError(this.ideal[j]);
}
```

Once all the sets have been processed, then the network learns from these errors.

```
Learn();
```

Finally, the new global error, that is, the error across all training sets, is calculated.

```
this.error = this.network.CalculateError(this.input, this.ideal);
```

It is this error that will be returned when the **Error** property is accessed.

Calculating the Error for Backpropagation

The first step in backpropagation error calculation is to call the **CalcError** method of the **BackPropagation** object. The signature for the **CalcError** method is shown here:

```
public void CalcError(double[] ideal)
{
```

First, we verify that the size of the **ideal** array corresponds to the number of output neurons. Since the **ideal** array specifies ideal values for the output neurons, it must match the size of the output layer.

```
if (ideal.Length != this.network.OutputLayer.NeuronCount)
{

  throw new NeuralNetworkError(
  "Size mismatch: Can't calcError for ideal input size="
  + ideal.Length + " for output layer size="
  + this.network.OutputLayer.NeuronCount);

}
```

The **BackPropagation** object contains a **BackpropagationLayer** object for each of the layers in the neural network. These objects should be cleared. The following code zeros out any previous errors from the **BackpropagationLayer** objects.

```
foreach (FeedforwardLayer layer in this.network.Layers)
{

  GetBackpropagationLayer(layer).ClearError();

}
```

As its name implies, the backpropagation propagates backwards through the neural network.

```
for (int i = this.network.Layers.Count - 1; i >= 0; i--)
{
```

Obtain each layer of the neural network.

```
  FeedforwardLayer layer = this.network.Layers[i];
```

Now call either of two overloaded versions of the **CalcError** method. If it is the output layer, then pass in the **ideal** for comparison. If it is not the output layer, then the **ideal** values are not needed.

```
if (layer.IsOutput())
{

  GetBackpropagationLayer(layer).CalcError(ideal);

}
```

```
else
{
  GetBackpropagationLayer(layer).CalcError();
}
```

The **BackpropagationLayer** class has two versions of the **CalcError** method. The signature for the version that operates on the output layer is shown below:

```
public void CalcError(double[] ideal)
{
```

First, calculate the error share for each neuron. Loop across all of the output neurons.

```
for (int i = 0; i < this.layer.NeuronCount; i++)
{
```

Next, set the error for this neuron. The error is simply the difference between the ideal output and the actual output.

```
  SetError(i, ideal[i] - this.layer.GetFire(i));
```

Calculate the delta for this neuron. The delta is the error multiplied by the derivative of the activation function. Bound the number, so that it does not become extremely small or large.

```
  SetErrorDelta(i, BoundNumbers.Bound(CalculateDelta(i)));
}
```

These error deltas will be used during the learning process that is covered in the next section.

All other layers in the neural network will have their errors calculated by the **CalcError** method that does not require an **ideal** array.

```
public void CalcError()
{
```

First, obtain the next layer. Since we are propagating backwards, this will be the layer that was just processed.

```
BackpropagationLayer next = this.backpropagation
                  .GetBackpropagationLayer(this.layer.Next);
```

Loop through every matrix value for connections between this layer and the next.

```
for (int i = 0; i < this.layer.Next.NeuronCount; i++)
{
  for (int j = 0; j < this.layer.NeuronCount; j++)
  {
```

The error calculation methods are called for each training set, therefore, it is necessary to accumulate the matrix deltas before the errors are cleared out. Determine this layer's contribution to the error by looking at the next layer's delta, and compare it to the outputs from this layer. Since we are propagating backwards, the next layer is actually the layer we just processed.

```
AccumulateMatrixDelta(j, i, next.GetErrorDelta(i)
                        * this.layer.GetFire(j));
```

Calculate, and add to, this layer's error by multiplying the matrix value by its delta.

```
SetError(j, GetError(j) + this.layer.LayerMatrix[j, i]
                        * next.GetErrorDelta(i));
}
```

Also, accumulate deltas that affect the threshold.

```
AccumulateThresholdDelta(i, next.GetErrorDelta(i));
}
```

For the hidden layers, calculate the delta using the derivative of the activation function.

```
if (this.layer.IsHidden())
{
  // hidden layer deltas
  for (int i = 0; i < this.layer.NeuronCount; i++)
            {
    SetErrorDelta(i, BoundNumbers.Bound(CalculateDelta(i)));
}
```

Once all of the errors have been calculated, the **Learn** method can be used to apply the deltas to the weight matrix and teach the neural network to better recognize the input pattern.

Backpropagation Learning

The learning process is relatively simple. All of the desired changes were already calculated during the error calculation. It is now simply a matter of applying these changes. The values of the learning rate and momentum parameters will affect how these changes are applied.

The **Learn** method in the **BackPropagation** object is called to begin the learning process.

```
public void Learn()
```

Loop across all of the layers. The order is not important. During error calculation, the results from one layer depended upon another. As a result, it was very important to ensure that the error propagated backwards. However, during the learning process, values are simply applied to the neural network layers one at a time.

```
foreach (FeedforwardLayer layer in this.network.Layers)
{
```

Calling the **Learn** method of each of the **BackpropagationLayer** objects causes the calculated changes to be applied.

```
  GetBackpropagationLayer(layer).Learn(this.learnRate, this.momen-
tum);
}
```

The **Learn** method provided in the **BackpropagationLayer** class is used to perform the actual modifications. The signature for the **Learn** method is shown here:

```
public void Learn(double learnRate, double momentum)
{
```

The **Learn** layer makes sure there is a matrix. If there is no matrix, then there is nothing to train.

```
if (this.layer.HasMatrix())
{
```

A matrix is then made that contains the accumulated matrix delta values that are scaled by the **learnRate**. The learning rate can be thought of as a percent. A value of one means that the deltas will be applied with no scaling.

```
Matrix.Matrix m1 = MatrixMath.Multiply(this.accMatrixDelta,
                       learnRate);
```

The previous deltas are stored in the **matrixDelta** variable. The learning from the previous iteration is applied to the current iteration scaled by the **momentum** variable. Some variants of **Backpropagation** use no momentum. To specify no momentum, use a **momentum** value of zero.

```
    Matrix.Matrix m2 = MatrixMath.Multiply(this.matrixDelta, mo-
mentum);
```

Add the two together and store the result in the **matrixDelta** variable. This will be used with the momentum for the next training iteration.

```
    this.matrixDelta = MatrixMath.Add(m1, m2);
```

Add the calculated values to the current matrix. This modifies the matrix and causes learning.

```
this.layer.LayerMatrix = (MatrixMath.Add(this.layer.LayerMatrix,
```

```
                              this.matrixDelta));
```

Clear the errors for the next learning iteration.

```
  this.accMatrixDelta.Clear();
}
```

The **Learn** method on the **BackpropagationLayer** class is called once per layer.

Chapter Summary

In this chapter, you learned how a feedforward backpropagation neural network functions. The feedforward backpropagation neural network is actually composed of two neural network algorithms. It is not necessary to always use feedforward and backpropagation together, but this is often the case. Other training methods will be introduced in coming chapters. The term "feedforward" refers to a method by which a neural network recognizes a pattern. The term "backpropagation" describes a process by which the neural network will be trained.

A feedforward neural network is a network in which neurons are only connected to the next layer. There are no connections between neurons in previous layers or between neurons and themselves. Additionally, neurons are not connected to neurons beyond the next layer. As a pattern is processed by a feedforward design, the thresholds and connection weights will be applied.

Neural networks can be trained using backpropagation. Backpropagation is a form of supervised training. The neural network is presented with the training data, and the results from the neural network are compared with the expected results. The difference between the actual results and the expected results is the error. Backpropagation is a method whereby the weights and input threshold of the neural network are altered in a way that causes this error to be reduced.

Backpropagation is not the only way to train a feedforward neural network. Simulated annealing and genetic algorithms are two other common methods. The next chapter will demonstrate how a genetic algorithm can be used to train a neural network.

Vocabulary

Activation Function

Backpropagation

Derivative

Feedforward

Hyperbolic Tangent Activation Function

Learning Rate

Linear Activation Function

Momentum

Overfitting

Sigmoid Activation Function

Underfitting

Questions for Review

1.   What is an activation function? Explain when you might use the hyperbolic tangent activation function over the sigmoid activation function.

2.   How can you determine if an activation function is compatible with the backpropagation training method?

3.   Consider a neural network with one output neuron and three input neurons. The weights between the three input neurons and the one output neuron are 0.1, 0.2, and 0.3. The threshold is 0.5. What would be the output value for an input of 0.4, 0.5, and 0.6?

4.   Explain the role of the learning rate in backpropagation.

5.   Explain the role of the momentum in backpropagation.

CHAPTER 6: UNDERSTANDING GENETIC ALGORITHMS

- Introducing the Genetic Algorithm
- Understanding the Structure of a Genetic Algorithm
- Understanding How a Genetic Algorithm Works
- Implementing the Traveling Salesman Problem
- Neural Network Plays Tic-Tac-Toe

Backpropagation is not the only way to train a neural network. This chapter will introduce genetic algorithms (GAs), which can be used to solve many different types of problems. We will begin by exploring how to use a genetic algorithm to solve a problem independent of a neural network. The genetic algorithm will then be applied to a feedforward neural network.

Genetic Algorithms

Both genetic algorithms and simulated annealing are evolutionary processes that may be utilized to solve search space and optimization problems. However, genetic algorithms differ substantially from simulated annealing.

Simulated annealing is based on a thermodynamic evolutionary process, whereas genetic algorithms are based on the principles of Darwin's theory of evolution and the field of biology. Two features introduced by GAs, which distinguish them from simulated annealing, are the inclusion of a population and the use of a genetic operator called "crossover" or recombination. These features will be discussed in more detail later in this chapter.

A key component of evolution is natural selection. Organisms poorly suited to their environment tend to die off, while organisms better suited to their current environment are more likely to survive. The surviving organisms produce offspring that have many of the better qualities possessed by their parents. As a result, these children tend to be "better suited" to their environment, and are more likely to survive, mate, and produce future generations. This process is analogous to Darwin's "survival of the fittest" theory, an ongoing process of evolution in which life continues to improve over time. The same concepts that apply to natural selection apply to genetic algorithms as well.

When discussing evolution, it is important to note that sometimes a distinction is made between microevolution and macroevolution. Microevolution refers to small changes that occur in the overall genetic makeup of a population over a relatively short period of time. These changes are generally small adaptations to an existing species, and not the introduction of a whole new species. Microevolution is caused by factors such as natural selection and mutation. Macroevolution refers to significant changes in a population over a long period of time. These changes may result in a new species. The concepts of genetic algorithms are consistent with microevolution.

Background of Genetic Algorithms

John Holland, a professor at the University of Michigan, developed the concepts associated with genetic algorithms through research with his colleagues and students. In 1975, he published a book, Adaptation in Natural and Artificial Systems, in which he presents the theory behind genetic algorithms and explores their practical application. Holland is considered the father of genetic algorithms.

Another significant contributor to the area of genetic algorithms is David Goldberg. Goldberg studied under Holland at the University of Michigan and has written a collection of books, including Genetic Algorithms in Search, Optimization, and Machine Learning (1989), and more recently, The Design of Innovation (2002).

Uses for Genetic Algorithms

Genetic algorithms are adaptive search algorithms, which can be used for many purposes in many fields, such as science, business, engineering, and medicine. GAs are adept at searching large, nonlinear search spaces. A nonlinear search space problem has a large number of potential solutions and the optimal solution cannot be solved by conventional iterative means. GAs are most efficient and appropriate for situations in which:

- the search space is large, complex, or not easily understood;
- there is no programmatic method that can be used to narrow the search space;
- traditional optimization methods are inadequate.

Table 6.1 lists some examples.

Table 6.1: Common Uses for Genetic Algorithms

Purpose	Common Uses
Optimization	Production scheduling, call routing for call centers, routing for transportation, determining electrical circuit layouts
Design	Machine learning: designing neural networks, designing and controlling robots
Business applications	Utilized in financial trading, credit evaluation, budget allocation, fraud detection

Many optimization problems are nonlinear in behavior and are too complex for traditional methods. The set of possible solutions for such a problem can be enormous (e.g., determining the optimum route for a traveling salesperson or determining the optimum design for an electrical circuit layout). A genetic algorithm possesses the ability to search large and complex search spaces to efficiently determine near optimal solutions in a reasonable time frame by simulating biological evolution. Now that you have been introduced to some of the uses for genetic algorithms, we must examine how to actually construct one.

Understanding Genetic Algorithms

Genetic algorithms closely resemble the biological model of chromosomes and genes. Individual organisms in a genetic algorithm generally consist of a single chromosome. These chromosomes are composed of genes. By manipulating the genes, new chromosomes are created, which possess different traits. These manipulations occur through crossover and mutation, just as they occur in nature. Crossover is analogous to the biological process of mating, and mutation is one way in which new information can be introduced into an existing population.

Understanding Genes

In a genetic algorithm, genes represent individual components of a solution. This is a very important concept in the analysis of a problem for which a genetic algorithm is to be used. To effectively solve a problem, you must determine a way to break it into its related components, or genes. The genes will then be linked together to form a chromosome. Life forms in this simulation consist of a single chromosome; therefore, each chromosome will represent one possible solution to a problem.

Later in this chapter, we will examine the traveling salesman problem. You will be shown how to decompose the solution for this problem into individual genes. Additionally, in this chapter you will be shown how to make the individual weights in a neural network represent the genes in the chromosome.

It is important to note that there is a finite number of genes that are used. Individual genes are not modified as the organisms evolve. It is the chromosomes that evolve when the order and makeup of their genes are changed.

Understanding Chromosomes

As explained above, each organism in our genetic algorithm contains one chromosome. As a result, each chromosome can be thought of as an "individual" or a solution composed of a collection of parameters to be optimized. These parameters are genes, which you learned about in the previous section. Each chromosome is initially assigned a random solution or collection of genes. This solution is used to calculate a "fitness" level, which determines the chromosome's suitability or "fitness" to survive—as in Darwin's theory of natural selection. If a chromosome has a high level of "fitness," it has a higher probability of mating and staying alive.

How Genetic Algorithms Work

A genetic algorithm begins by creating an initial population of chromosomes that are given a random collection of genes. It then continues as follows:

1. Create an initial population of chromosomes.

2. Evaluate the fitness or "suitability" of each chromosome that makes up the population.

3. Based on the fitness level of each chromosome, select the chromosomes that will mate, or those that have the "privilege" to mate.

4. Crossover (or mate) the selected chromosomes and produce offspring.

5. Randomly mutate some of the genes of the chromosomes.

6. Repeat steps three through five until a new population is created.

7. The algorithm ends when the best solution has not changed for a preset number of generations.

Genetic algorithms strive to determine the optimal solution to a problem by utilizing three genetic operators. These operators are selection, crossover, and mutation. GAs search for the optimal solution until specific criteria are met and the process terminates. The results of the process include good solutions, as compared to one "optimal" solution, for complex problems (such as "NP-hard" problems). NP-hard refers to problems which cannot be solved in polynomial time. Most problems solved with computers today are not NP-hard and can be solved in polynomial time. A polynomial is a mathematical expression involving exponents and variables. A P-Problem, or polynomial problem, is a problem for which the number of steps to find the answer is bounded by a polynomial. An NP-hard problem does not increase exponentially, but often increases at a much greater rate, described by the factorial operator (n!). One example of an NP-hard problem is the traveling salesman problem, which will be discussed later in this chapter.

Initial Population

To recap, the population of a genetic algorithm is comprised of organisms, each of which usually contains a single chromosome. Chromosomes are comprised of genes, and these genes are usually initialized to random values based on defined boundaries. Each chromosome represents one complete solution to the defined problem. The genetic algorithm must create the initial population, which is comprised of multiple chromosomes or solutions.

Each chromosome in the initial population must be evaluated. This is done by evaluating its "fitness" or the quality of its solution. The fitness is determined through the use of a function specified for the problem the genetic algorithm is designed to solve.

Suitability and the Privilege to Mate

In a genetic algorithm, mating is used to create a new and improved population. The "suitability" to mate refers to whether or not chromosomes are qualified to mate, or whether they have the "privilege" to mate.

Determining the specific chromosomes that will mate is based upon each individual chromosome's fitness. The chromosomes are selected from the old population, mated, and children are produced, which are new chromosomes. These new children are added to the existing population. The updated population is used for selection of chromosomes for the subsequent mating.

Mating

We will now examine the crossover process used in genetic algorithms to accomplish mating. Mating is achieved by selecting two parents and taking a "splice" from each of their gene sequences. These splices effectively divide the chromosomes' gene sequences into three parts. The children are then created based on genes from each of these three sections.

The process of mating combines genes from two parents into new offspring chromosomes. This is useful in that it allows new chromosomes to inherit traits from each parent. However, this method can also lead to a problem in which no new genetic material is introduced into the population. To introduce new genetic material, the process of mutation is used.

Mutation

Mutation is used to introduce new genetic material into a population. Mutation can be thought of as natural experiments. These experiments introduce a new, somewhat random, sequence of genes into a chromosome. It is completely unknown whether or not this mutation will produce a desirable attribute, and it does not really matter, since natural selection will determine the fate of the mutated chromosome.

If the fitness of the mutated chromosome is higher than the general population, it will survive and likely be allowed to mate with other chromosomes. If the genetic mutation produces an undesirable feature, then natural selection will ensure that the chromosome does not live to mate.

An important consideration for any genetic algorithm is the mutation level that will be used. The mutation level is generally expressed as a percentage. The example program that will be examined later in this chapter will use a mutation level of 10%. Selection of a mutation level has many ramifications. For example, if you choose a mutation level that is too high, you will be performing nothing more than a random search. There will be no adaptation; instead, a completely new solution will be tested until no better solution can be found.

Implementation of a Generic Genetic Algorithm

Now that you understand the general structure of a genetic algorithm, we will examine a common problem to which they are often applied. To implement a generic genetic algorithm, several classes have been created:

- Chromosome
- GeneticAlgorithm
- MateWorker

The **Chromosome** class implements a single chromosome. The **GeneticAlgorithm** class is used to control the training process. It implements the **Train** interface and can be used to train feedforward neural networks.

Mating

Mating is performed either in the base **Chromosome** class or in a subclass. Subclasses can implement their own **Mate** methods if specialization is needed. However, the examples in this book do not require anything beyond the base **Chromosome** class's **Mate** method. We will now examine how the **Mate** method works. The signature for the **Mate** method of the **Chromosome** class is shown here:

```
public void Mate(Chromosome<GENE_TYPE> father,
                 Chromosome<GENE_TYPE> offspring1,
                 Chromosome<GENE_TYPE> offspring2)
```

The mating process treats the genes of a chromosome as a long array of elements. For this neural network, these elements will be **double** variables taken from the weight matrix. For the traveling salesman problem, these elements will represent cities at which the salesman will stop; however, these elements can represent anything. Some genes will be taken from the mother and some will be taken from the father. Two offspring will be created. Figure 6.1 shows how the genetic material is spliced by the **Mate** method.

Figure 6.1: Mating two chromosomes.

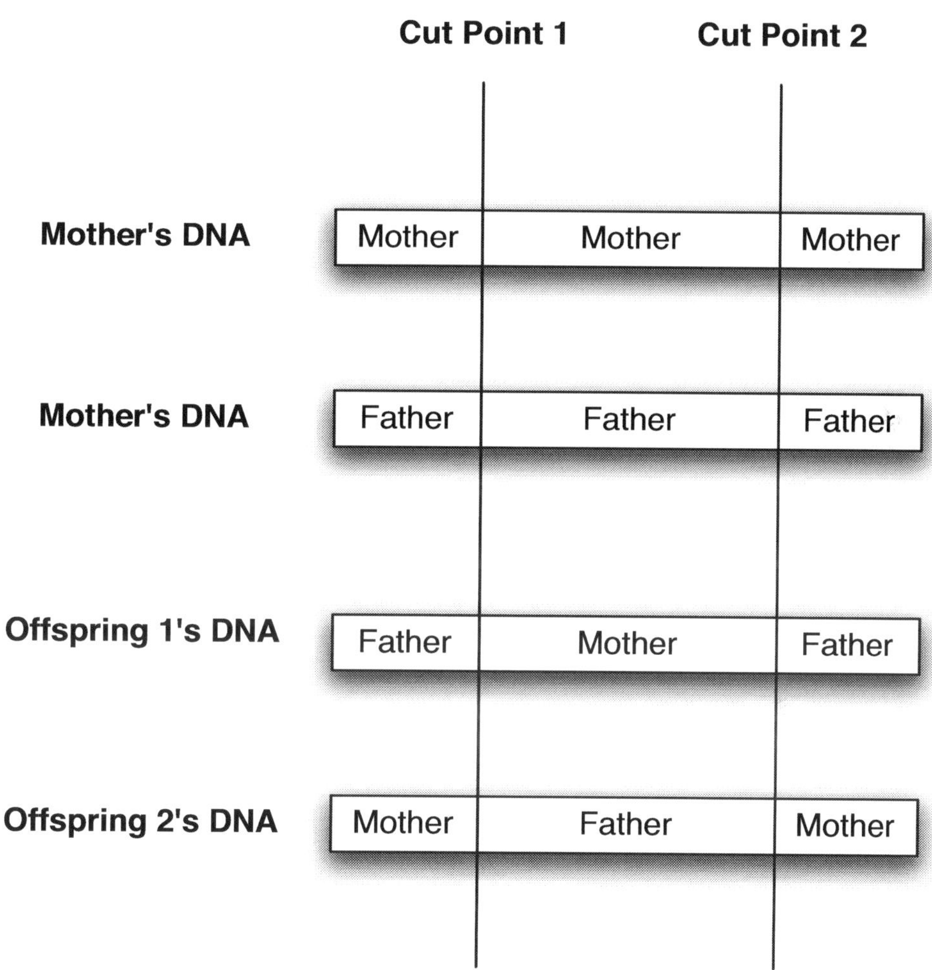

As you can see, two cut-points are created between the father and the mother. Some genetic material is taken from each region, defined by the cut-points, to create the genetic material for each offspring.

First, the length of the gene array is determined.

```
int geneLength = this.Genes.Length;
```

Two cut-points must then be established. The first cut-point is randomly chosen. Because all "cuts" will be of a constant length, the first cut-point cannot be chosen so far in the array that there is not a sufficiently long section left to allow the full cut length to be taken. The second cut-point is simply the cut length added to the first cut-point.

```
Random rand = new Random();

int cutpoint1 = (int)(rand.NextDouble() * (geneLength - this.
GA.CutLength));
int cutpoint2 = cutpoint1 + this.GA.CutLength;
```

Two arrays are then allocated that are big enough to hold the two offspring.

```
IList<GENE_TYPE> taken1 = new List<GENE_TYPE>();
IList<GENE_TYPE> taken2 = new List<GENE_TYPE>();
```

There are three regions of genetic material that must now be considered. The first is the area between the two cut-points. The other two are the areas before and after the cut-points.

```
for (int i = 0; i < geneLength; i++)
{
  if ((i < cutpoint1) || (i > cutpoint2))
  {
  }
  else
  {
    offspring1.SetGene(i, father.GetGene(i));
    offspring2.SetGene(i, this.GetGene(i));
    taken1.Add(offspring1.GetGene(i));
    taken2.Add(offspring2.GetGene(i));
  }
}
```

Now that the middle section has been handled, the two outer sections must be addressed.

```
for (int i = 0; i < geneLength; i++)
{
  if ((i < cutpoint1) || (i > cutpoint2))
  {
    if (this.GA.PreventRepeat)
    {
      offspring1.SetGene(i, GetNotTaken(this, taken1));
      offspring2.SetGene(i, GetNotTaken(father, taken2));
    }
    else
    {
```

```
    offspring1.SetGene(i, this.GetGene(i));
    offspring2.SetGene(i, father.GetGene(i));
  }
 }
}
```

Calculate the cost for the two offspring.

```
offspring1.CalculateCost();
offspring2.CalculateCost();
```

A random number is used to see if the first offspring should be mutated.

```
if (rand.NextDouble() < this.geneticAlgorithm.MutationPercent)
{
  offspring1.Mutate();
}
```

Likewise, mutating the second offspring is considered.

```
if (rand.NextDouble() < this.geneticAlgorithm.MutationPercent)
{
  offspring2.Mutate();
}
```

The exact process for mutation varies depending on the problem being solved. For a neural network application, some weight matrix value is scaled by a random percentage. For the traveling salesman problem, two random stops on the trip are swapped.

Multithreading Issues

Most new computers being purchased today are multicore. Multicore processors can execute programs considerably faster if they are written to be multithreaded. Neural network training, in particular, can benefit from multithreading. While backpropagation can be somewhat tricky to multithread, genetic algorithms are fairly easy. The **GeneticAlgorithm** class provided in this book is designed to use a thread pool, if one is provided. A complete discussion of C#'s built-in thread-pooling capabilities is beyond the scope of this book; however, the basics will be covered.

To use C#'s built-in thread pool, a class must be created that processes one unit of work. The real challenge in writing code that executes well on a multicore processor is breaking the work down into small packets that can be divided among the threads.

For the generic genetic algorithm, the work packets are performed by the **MateWorker** class. **MateWorker** objects are created during each iteration of the training. These objects are created for each mating that must occur. Once all of the **MateWorker** objects are created, they are handed off to a thread pool. The **MateWorker** class is shown in Listing 6.1.

Listing 6.1: The MateWorker Class (MateWorker.cs)

```csharp
using System;
using System.Collections.Generic;
using System.Linq;
using System.Text;

using System.Threading;

namespace HeatonResearchNeural.Genetic
{
    class MateWorker<GENE_TYPE>
    {
        private Chromosome<GENE_TYPE> mother;
        private Chromosome<GENE_TYPE> father;
        private Chromosome<GENE_TYPE> child1;
        private Chromosome<GENE_TYPE> child2;
        private ManualResetEvent eventHandler;

        /// <summary>
        /// Construct a MateWorker class to handle one mating.
        /// </summary>
        /// <param name="mother">The mother to mate.</param>
        /// <param name="father">The father to mate.</param>
        /// <param name="child1">The first offspring.</param>
        /// <param name="child2">The second offspring.</param>
        public MateWorker(Chromosome<GENE_TYPE> mother,
            Chromosome<GENE_TYPE> father,
            Chromosome<GENE_TYPE> child1,
            Chromosome<GENE_TYPE> child2)
        {
            this.mother = mother;
            this.father = father;
            this.child1 = child1;
            this.child2 = child2;
        }

        /// <summary>
        /// Set the event that will be used to signal when
        /// the mating is complete.
        /// </summary>
        /// <param name="eventHandler">The event object
        /// to use.</param>
        public void SetEvent(ManualResetEvent eventHandler)
        {
            this.eventHandler = eventHandler;
        }
```

```
/// <summary>
/// Perform the mating.
/// </summary>
public void Call()
{
    this.mother.Mate(this.father,
            this.child1,
            this.child2);
    if (this.eventHandler != null)
    {
        this.eventHandler.Set();
    }
}
}
```

As you can see from the above listing, the class is provided with everything that it needs to mate two chromosomes and produce two offspring. The actual work is done inside the **Call** method. The work consists of nothing more than calling the **Mate** method of one of the parents.

The Traveling Salesman Problem

In this section you will be introduced to the traveling salesman problem (TSP). Genetic algorithms are commonly used to solve the traveling salesman problem, because the TSP is an NP-hard problem that generally cannot be solved by traditional iterative algorithms.

Understanding the Traveling Salesman Problem

The traveling salesman problem involves a "traveling salesman" who must visit a certain number of cities. The task is to identify the shortest route for the salesman to travel between the cities. The salesman is allowed to begin and end at any city, but must visit each city once. The salesman may not visit a city more than once.

This may seem like an easy task for a normal iterative program, however, consider the speed with which the number of possible combinations grows as the number of cities increases. If there are one or two cities, only one step is required. Three increases the possible routes to six. Table 6.2 shows how quickly these combinations grow.

Table 6.2: Number of Steps to Solve TSP with a Conventional Program

Number of Cities	Number of Steps
1	1
2	1
3	6
4	24
5	120
6	720
7	5,040
8	40,320
9	362,880
10	3,628,800
11	39,916,800
12	479,001,600
13	6,227,020,800
...	...
50	$3.041 * 10^{64}$

The formula behind the above table is the factorial. The number of cities, n, is calculated using the factorial operator (!). The factorial of some arbitrary value n is given by n * (n − 1) * (n − 2) * ... * 3 * 2 * 1. As you can see from the above table, these values become incredibly large when a program must do a "brute force" search. The sample program that we will examine in the next section finds a solution to a 50-city problem in a matter of minutes. This is done by using a genetic algorithm, rather than a normal brute-force approach.

Implementing the Traveling Salesman Problem

So far, we have discussed the basic principles of genetic algorithms and how they are used. Now it is time to examine a C# example. In this section, you will be shown a complete application that is capable of finding solutions to the TSP. As this program is examined, you will be shown how the user interface is constructed, and also how the genetic algorithm itself is implemented.

Using the Traveling Salesman Program

The traveling salesman program itself is very easy to use. This program displays the cities, shown as dots, and the current best solution. The number of generations and the mutation percentage are also shown. As the program runs, these values are updated. The final output from the program is shown in Figure 6.2.

Figure 6.2: The traveling salesman program.

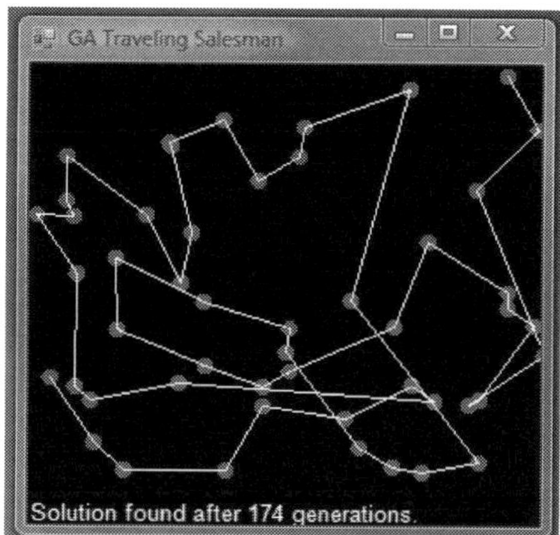

As the program is running, you will see white lines change between the green cities. Eventually, a path will begin to emerge. The path currently being displayed is close to the shortest path in the entire population.

When the program is nearly finished, you will notice that new patterns are not introduced; the program seems to stabilize. Yet, you will also notice that additional generations are still being calculated. This is an important part of the genetic algorithm—knowing when it is done! It is not as straightforward as it might seem. You do not know how many steps are required, nor do you know the shortest distance.

Termination criteria must be specified, so the program will know when to stop. This particular program stops when the optimal solution does not change for 100 generations. Once this has happened, the program indicates that it has found a solution after the number of generations indicated, which includes the 99 generations that did not change the solution. Now that you have seen how this GA program works, we will examine how it was constructed. We will begin by examining the user interface.

Overall Structure

The traveling salesman program uses five C# classes. It is important to understand the relationship between the individual classes that make up the traveling salesman program. These classes, and their functions, are summarized in Table 6.3.

Table 6.3: Classes Used for the GA Version of the Traveling Salesman

Class	Purpose
City	This class stores individual city coordinates. It also contains methods that are used to calculate the distance between cities.
GeneticTravelingSalesman	This class implements the user interface and performs general initialization.
TSPChromosome	This class implements the chromosome. It is the most complex class of the program, as it implements most of the functionality of the genetic algorithm.
TSPGeneticAlgorithm	This class implements the genetic algorithm. It is used to perform the training and process the chromosomes.
WorldMap	This class assists the GeneticTravelingSalesman class by drawing the map of cities.

Most of the work is done by the **TSPChromosome** class. This class is covered in the next section.

Traveling Salesman Chromosomes

When implementing a genetic algorithm using the classes provided in this book, you must generally create your own cost calculation method, named **CalculateCost**, as well as your own mutation function, named **Mutate**. The signature for the traveling salesman problem's **CalculateCost** method is shown here:

```
override public void CalculateCost()
```

Calculating the cost for the traveling salesman problem is relatively easy; the distance between each of the cities is summed. The program begins by initializing a running cost variable to zero and looping through the entire list of cities.

```
double cost = 0.0;
for (int i = 0; i < this.cities.Length - 1; i++)
{
```

For each city, the distance between this city and the next is calculated.

```
double dist = this.cities[GetGene(i)]
  .proximity(this.cities[GetGene(i + 1)]);
```

The distance is added to the total cost.

```
cost += dist;
}
```

Finally, the cost is saved to an instance variable.

```
this.Cost = cost;
```

A **Mutate** method is also provided. The signature for the **Mutate** method is shown here:

```
override public void Mutate()
```

First, the length is obtained and two random cities are chosen to be swapped.

```
Random rand = new Random();
int length = this.Genes.Length;
int iswap1 = (int) (rand.NextDouble() * length);
int iswap2 = (int)(rand.NextDouble() * length);
```

The two cities are then swapped.

```
int temp = GetGene(iswap1);
SetGene(iswap1, GetGene(iswap2));
SetGene(iswap2, temp);
```

The preceding code shows you how the generic genetic algorithm provided in this book was extended to solve a general problem like the traveling salesman. In the next section, classes will be provided that will allow you to use the generic algorithm to train a neural network using training sets in place of backpropagation.

XOR Operator

In the last chapter, backpropagation was used to solve the XOR operator problem. In this section, you will see how a genetic algorithm, the **TrainingSetNeuralG eneticAlgorithm** class, can be used to train for the XOR operator. This version of the XOR solver can be seen in Listing 6.2.

Listing 6.2: XOR with a Genetic Algorithm (GeneticXOR.cs)

```
using System;
using System.Collections.Generic;
using System.Linq;
using System.Text;

using HeatonResearchNeural.Feedforward;
using HeatonResearchNeural.Feedforward.Train.Genetic;

namespace Chapter6GeneticXOR
{
    class Program
    {

        public static double[][] XOR_INPUT ={
```

```csharp
    new double[2] { 0.0, 0.0 },
    new double[2] { 1.0, 0.0 },
        new double[2] { 0.0, 1.0 },
    new double[2] { 1.0, 1.0 } };

public static double[][] XOR_IDEAL = {
    new double[1] { 0.0 },
    new double[1] { 1.0 },
    new double[1] { 1.0 },
    new double[1] { 0.0 } };

static void Main(string[] args) {
    FeedforwardNetwork network = new FeedforwardNetwork();
    network.AddLayer(new FeedforwardLayer(2));
    network.AddLayer(new FeedforwardLayer(3));
    network.AddLayer(new FeedforwardLayer(1));
    network.Reset();

    // train the neural network
    TrainingSetNeuralGeneticAlgorithm train =
            new TrainingSetNeuralGeneticAlgorithm(
            network,
            true,
            XOR_INPUT,
            XOR_IDEAL,
            5000,
            0.1,
            0.25);

    int epoch = 1;

    do {
            train.Iteration();
            Console.WriteLine("Epoch #" + epoch
                    + " Error:" + train.Error);
            epoch++;
    } while ((epoch < 5000) && (train.Error > 0.001));

    network = train.Network;

    // test the neural network
    Console.WriteLine("Neural Network Results:");
    for (int i = 0; i < XOR_IDEAL.Length; i++) {
            double []actual =
                    network.ComputeOutputs(XOR_INPUT[i]);
            Console.WriteLine(XOR_INPUT[i][0] + ","
                    + XOR_INPUT[i][1]
```

```
                              + ", actual=" + actual[0]
                              + ",ideal=" + XOR_IDEAL[i][0]);
        }
```

The above listing is very similar to the XOR solver from the last chapter. The main difference is in the following lines:

```
TrainingSetNeuralGeneticAlgorithm train =
new TrainingSetNeuralGeneticAlgorithm(
network, true, XOR_INPUT, XOR_IDEAL, 5000, 0.1, 0.25);
```

As you can see, several parameters are passed to the constructor of the training class. First, the network to be trained is passed. The value of **true** specifies that all of the initial life forms should have their weight matrixes randomly initialized. The input and ideal arrays are also provided, just as they are with the backpropagation algorithm. The value of 5000 specifies the size of the population. The value 0.1 indicates that 10% of the population will be chosen to mate. The 10% will be able to mate with any life form in the top 25%.

Calculate Cost

A specialized method is then used to calculate the cost for the XOR pattern recognition. The signature for the cost calculation method is shown here:

```
override public void CalculateCost()
```

First, the contents of the chromosome are copied back into the neural network.

```
this.UpdateNetwork();
```

The root mean square error of the neural network can be used as a cost. The RMS error will be calculated just as it was in previous chapters. The **input** and **ideal** arrays are copied to local variables.

```
double[][] input =
    this.getTrainingSetNeuralGeneticAlgorithm().Input;
double[][] ideal =
    this.getTrainingSetNeuralGeneticAlgorithm().Ideal;
```

The neural network's **CalculateError** function is used to calculate the error of the neural network given the **input** and **ideal** arrays.

```
this.Cost  = this.Network.CalculateError(input, ideal);
```

Although the XOR program uses a specialized cost calculation method, the program uses the same mating method as previously discussed.

Mutate

Mutation is handled by a specialized **Mutate** function. The signature for this mutate function is shown here:

```
override public void Mutate()
```

The mutation method begins by obtaining the number of genes in a chromosome. Each gene will be scaled using a random percentage.

```
Random rand = new Random();

int length = this.Genes.Length;
```

The function loops through all of the genes.

```
for (int i = 0; i < length; i++)
{
```

It obtains a gene's value and multiplies it by a random ratio within a specified range.

```
    double d = GetGene(i);
    double ratio = (int)((RANGE * rand.NextDouble()) - RANGE);
    d *= ratio;
    SetGene(i, d);
}
```

The result is that each weight matrix element is randomly changed.

Tic-Tac-Toe

The game of tic-tac-toe, also called naughts and crosses in many parts of the world, can be an interesting application of neural networks trained by genetic algorithms. Tic-tac-toe has very simple rules. Most human players quickly grow bored with the game, since it is so easy to learn. Once two people have mastered tic-tac-toe, games almost always result in a tie.

The simple rules for tic-tac-toe are as follows: One player plays X and another plays O. They take turns placing these characters on a 3x3 grid until one player gets three in a row. If the grid is filled before one of them gets three in a row, then the game is a draw. Figure 6.3 shows a game of tic-tac-toe in progress.

Figure 6.3: The game of tic-tac-toe.

There are many implementations of tic-tac-toe in C#. This book makes use of one by Thomas David Baker, which was released as open source software. It provides several players that can be matched for games:

- Boring – Just picks the next open spot.
- Human – Allows a human to play.
- Logical – Uses logic to play a near perfect game.
- MinMax – Uses the min-max algorithm to play a perfect game.
- Random – Moves to random locations.

Each player can play any other player. A class simply has to implement the **Player** interface and it can play against the others. Some of the players are more advanced. This gives the neural network several levels of players to play against.

The most advanced player is the min-max player. This player uses a min-max algorithm. A min-max algorithm uses a tree to plot out every possible move. This technique can be used in a game as simple as tic-tac-toe; however, it would not be effective for a game with an extremely large number of combinations, such as chess or go.

The example for this chapter creates a class named **PlayerNeural**. This class uses a neural network to play against the other players. The neural player will not play a perfect game. Yet, it will play reasonably well against some of the provided players.

The goal is not to produce a perfect player using only a neural network, but to demonstrate the use of neural networks. Many games use a hybrid approach for optimal results. The min-max algorithm, together with a neural network to prune entire branches of the search tree can be a very effective combination. We will, however, implement a pure neural-network approach.

The tic-tac-toe example illustrates a very important concept. Thus far, we have only trained neural networks using training sets. The tic-tac-toe example will not use training sets. Rather, the neural network will be matched against any of the other players and a genetic algorithm will be used to train it. Since a genetic algorithm uses "natural selection" it is particularly well suited to learning to play a game.

Using the Sample Tic-Tac-Toe Implementation

There are many options available with this version of tic-tac-toe. There are several command line options that allow you to specify which two players will play against each other. The general format of a command is as follows:

```
NeuralTicTacToe [Command] [Player 1] [Player 2]
```

The command also specifies the mode in which the program should run. The following modes are available:

- game – Play a single game.
- match – Play 100 games.
- train – Train (and save) a neural network.

You must choose the two players. The following options are available:

- Boring
- Human
- Logic
- MinMax
- NeuralBlank
- NeuralLoad
- Random

For example, to play a match between the MinMax algorithm and the Random player, use the following command:

```
NeuralTicTacToe Match MinMax Random
```

If you would like to train a new blank neural network against the random player, you would use the following command:

```
NeuralTicTacToe Train NeuralBlank Random
```

This will train a blank neural network; but be aware it can take a considerable amount of time. The genetic algorithm will use a thread pool, so a multicore computer will help. Once the training is complete, the neural network will be saved to disk. It will be saved with the name "tictactoe.net". The download for this book contains an example "tictactoe.net" file that is already trained for tic-tac-toe. This neural network took nearly 20 hours to train on my computer. Appendix A explains how to download the examples for this book.

To play a trained neural network, use the following command:

```
NeuralTicTacToe Play NeuralLoad Human
```

The sample neural network will always load and save a neural network named "tictactoe.net".

Saving and Loading Neural Networks

You may be wondering how to load and save the neural networks in this book. These networks can be loaded and saved using regular C# serialization techniques. For example, the following command saves a neural network:

```
SerializeObject.Save("filename.net", neuralNetwork);
```

Loading a neural network is almost as easy. The following command loads a neural network from disk.

```
FeedforwardNetwork result =
(FeedforwardNetwork)SerializeObject.Load("neuralnet.net");
```

Some of the neural networks in this book take a considerable amount of time to train. Thus, it is valuable to save the neural network so it can be quickly reloaded later.

Structure of the Tic-Tac-Toe Neural Network

One of the most important questions that a neural network programmer must always consider is how to structure the neural network. Perhaps the most obvious way to structure a neural network for tic-tac-toe is with nine inputs and nine outputs. The nine inputs will specify the current board configuration. The nine outputs will allow the neural network to specify where it wants to move.

The first version of the example used this configuration. It did not work particularly well. One problem is that the neural network had to spend considerable time just learning the valid and invalid moves. Furthermore, this configuration did not play very well against the other players.

The final version of the neural network has a configuration with nine inputs and a single output. Rather than asking the neural network where to move, this structure asks the neural network if a proposed board position is favorable. Whenever it is the neural player's turn, every possible move is determined. There can be at most nine possible moves. A temporary board is constructed that indicates what the game board would look like after each of these possible moves. Each board is then presented to the neural network. The board position that receives the highest value from the output neuron will be the next move.

Neural Player

The **Player** interface requires that the **PlayerNeural** class include a **GetMove** method. This method determines the next move the neural player will make. The signature for the **GetMove** method is shown here:

```
public Move GetMove(int[,] board, Move prev, int color)
```

First, two local variables are established. The **bestMove** variable will hold the best move found so far. The **bestScore** variable will hold the score of the **bestMove** variable.

```
Move bestMove = null;
double bestScore = double.MinValue;
```

Next, all of the potential moves on the board's grid are examined.

```
for (int x = 0; x < 3; x++)
{
  for (int y = 0; y < 3; y++)
  {
```

A sample board is constructed to represent this potential move.

```
    Move move = new Move((int)x, (int)y, color);
```

The potential move is examined to determine if it is valid.

```
    if (Board.IsEmpty(board, move))
    {
```

If the potential move is valid, then the **TryMove** method is called to see what score its board position would provide.

```
      double d = TryMove(board, move);
```

If the score for that board position beats the current best score, then this move is saved as the best move encountered thus far.

```
if ((d > bestScore) || (bestMove == null))
{
  bestScore = d;
  bestMove = move;
}
}
```

Finally, the best move is returned.

```
return bestMove;
```

The **GetMove** method makes use of the **TryMove** method to build a temporary board for each possible move. The signature for the **TryMove** method is shown here:

```
private double TryMove(int[,] board, Move move)
{
```

First, an **input** array is constructed for the neural network. A local variable **index** is kept that will remember the current position within the **input** array.

```
double[] input = new double[9];
int index = 0;
```

Next, every position of the board grid is considered.

```
for (int x = 0; x < 3; x++)
{
  for (int y = 0; y < 3; y++)
  {
```

Each square on the grid is checked and the input array is set to reflect the status of that square.

```
if (board[x, y] == TicTacToe.NOUGHTS)
{
  input[index] = -1;
}
else if (board[x, y] == TicTacToe.CROSSES)
{
  input[index] = 1;
}
else if (board[x, y] == TicTacToe.EMPTY)
{
  input[index] = 0;
}
```

If the square contains an "X" (cross), then a value of −1 is inserted into the input array. If the square contains an "O" (nought), then a value of 1 is placed in the array.

If the square contains the current move, then the input is set to –1, or a value of "X," which is what the neural player is playing.

```
if ((x == move.x) && (y == move.y))
{
   input[index] = -1;
}
```

The next element of the input array is then examined.

```
index++;
   }
}
```

Finally, the output for this input array is computed.

```
double[] output = this.network.ComputeOutputs(input);
return output[0];
```

The output is returned to the caller. The higher this value, the more favorable the board position.

Chromosomes

The tic-tac-toe neural network is trained using a genetic training algorithm. Each chromosome is tested by playing 100 games against its opponent. This causes a score to be generated that allows each chromosome's effectiveness to be evaluated. Each chromosome has a **CalculateCost** method that performs this operation. The signature for **CalculateCost** is shown here:

```
override public void CalculateCost()
{
```

First, the neural network is updated using the gene array.

```
this.UpdateNetwork();
```

Next, a **PlayerNeural** player is constructed to play against the chosen component. To keep this example simple, the neural network player is always player one, and thus always moves first.

```
PlayerNeural player1 = new PlayerNeural(this.Network);
```

The second player is created, and a match is played.

```
Player player2;

player2 = (Player)Assembly.GetExecutingAssembly().
CreateInstance(this.GetTicTacToeGenetic().getOpponent().FullName);

ScorePlayer score = new ScorePlayer(player1, player2, false);
```

The match is managed by the **ScorePlayer** class. This class allows two players to play 100 games and a score is generated. The score then becomes the cost for this chromosome.

Chapter Summary

In this chapter, you were introduced to genetic algorithms. Genetic algorithms provide one approach for finding potential solutions to complex NP-hard problems. An NP-hard problem is a problem for which the number of steps required to solve the problem increases at a very high rate as the number of units in the program increases.

An example of an NP-hard problem, which was examined in this chapter, is the traveling salesman problem. The traveling salesman problem attempts to identify the shortest path for a salesman traveling to a certain number of cities. The number of possible paths that a program has to search increases factorially as the number of cities increases.

To solve such a problem, a genetic algorithm is used. The genetic algorithm creates a population of chromosomes. Each of the chromosomes is one path through the cities. Each leg in that journey is a gene. The best chromosomes are determined and they are allowed to "mate." The mating process combines the genes of two parents. The chromosomes that have longer, less desirable, paths are not allowed to mate. Because the population has a fixed size, the less desirable chromosomes are purged from memory. As the program continues, natural selection causes the better-suited chromosomes to mate and produce better and better solutions.

The actual process of mating occurs by splitting the parent chromosomes into three splices. These splices are then used to build new chromosomes. The result of all of this will be two offspring chromosomes. Unfortunately, the mating process does not introduce new genetic material. New genetic material is introduced through mutation.

Mutation randomly changes the genes of some of the newly created offspring. This introduces new traits. Many of these mutations will not be well suited for the particular problem and will be purged from memory. However, others can be used to advance an otherwise stagnated population. Mutation is also introduced to help find an optimal solution.

Thus far in this book you have been shown how to train neural networks with backpropagation and genetic algorithms. Neural networks can also be trained by a technique that simulates the way a molten metal cools. This process is called simulated annealing. Simulated annealing will be covered in the next chapter.

Vocabulary

Chromosome

Evolution

Gene

Mate

Min-Max Algorithm

Multicore

Mutate

Population

Thread Pool

Questions for Review

1. What is the role of a chromosome in a genetic algorithm? What is the role of a gene?

2. How can a neural network be expressed as a chromosome and genes?

3. What is the role of mutation in a genetic algorithm?

4. How can the cost be calculated for a potential traveling salesman solution? For a neural network?

5. For what types of problems are genetic algorithms best suited? For what types of problems are they not well suited?

CHAPTER 7: UNDERSTANDING SIMULATED ANNEALING

- What is Simulated Annealing?
- For What is Simulated Annealing Used?
- Implementing Simulated Annealing in C#
- Applying Simulated Annealing to the Traveling Salesman Problem

In chapter 6, "Understanding Genetic Algorithms," you were introduced to genetic algorithms and how they can be used to train a neural network. In this chapter you will learn about another popular algorithm you can use, simulated annealing. As you will see, it can also be applied to other situations.

The sample program that will be presented in this chapter solves the traveling salesman problem, as did the genetic algorithm in chapter 6. However, in this program, simulated annealing will be used in place of the genetic algorithm. This will allow you to see some of the advantages that simulated annealing offers over a genetic algorithm.

We will begin with a general background of the simulated annealing process. We will then construct a class that is capable of using simulated annealing to solve the traveling salesman problem. Finally, we will explore how simulated annealing can be used to train a neural network.

Simulated Annealing Background

Simulated annealing was developed in the mid 1970s by Scott Kirkpatrick and several other researchers. It was originally developed to better optimize the design of integrated circuit (IC) chips by simulating the actual process of annealing.

Annealing is the metallurgical process of heating up a solid and then cooling it slowly until it crystallizes. The atoms of such materials have high-energy values at very high temperatures. This gives the atoms a great deal of freedom in their ability to restructure themselves. As the temperature is reduced, the energy levels of the atoms decrease. If the cooling process is carried out too quickly, many irregularities and defects will be seen in the crystal structure. The process of cooling too rapidly is known as rapid quenching. Ideally, the temperature should be reduced slowly to allow a more consistent and stable crystal structure to form, which will increase the metal's durability.

Simulated annealing seeks to emulate this process. It begins at a very high temperature, at which the input values are allowed to assume a wide range of random values. As the training progresses, the temperature is allowed to fall, thus restricting the degree to which the inputs are allowed to vary. This often leads the simulated annealing algorithm to a better solution, just as a metal achieves a better crystal structure through the actual annealing process.

Simulated Annealing Applications

Given a specified number of inputs for an arbitrary equation, simulated annealing can be used to determine those inputs that will produce the minimum result for the equation. In the case of the traveling salesman, this equation is the calculation of the total distance the salesman must travel. As we will learn later in this chapter, this equation is the error function of a neural network.

When simulated annealing was first introduced, the algorithm was very popular for integrated circuit (IC) chip design. Most IC chips are composed of many internal logic gates. These gates allow the chip to accomplish the tasks that it was designed to perform. Just as algebraic equations can often be simplified, so too can IC chip layouts. Simulated annealing is often used to find an IC chip design that has fewer logic gates than the original. The result is a chip that generates less heat and runs faster.

The weight matrix of a neural network provides an excellent set of inputs for the simulated annealing algorithm to minimize. Different sets of weights are used for the neural network until one is found that produces a sufficiently low return from the error function.

Understanding Simulated Annealing

The previous sections discussed the background of the simulated annealing algorithm and presented various applications for which it is used. In this section, you will be shown how to implement the simulated annealing algorithm. We will first examine the algorithm and then we will develop a simulated annealing algorithm class that can be used to solve the traveling salesman problem, which was introduced in chapter 6.

The Structure of a Simulated Annealing Algorithm

There are several distinct steps that the simulated annealing process must go through as the temperature is reduced and randomness is applied to the input values. Figure 7.1 presents a flowchart of this process.

Figure 7.1: Overview of the simulated annealing process.

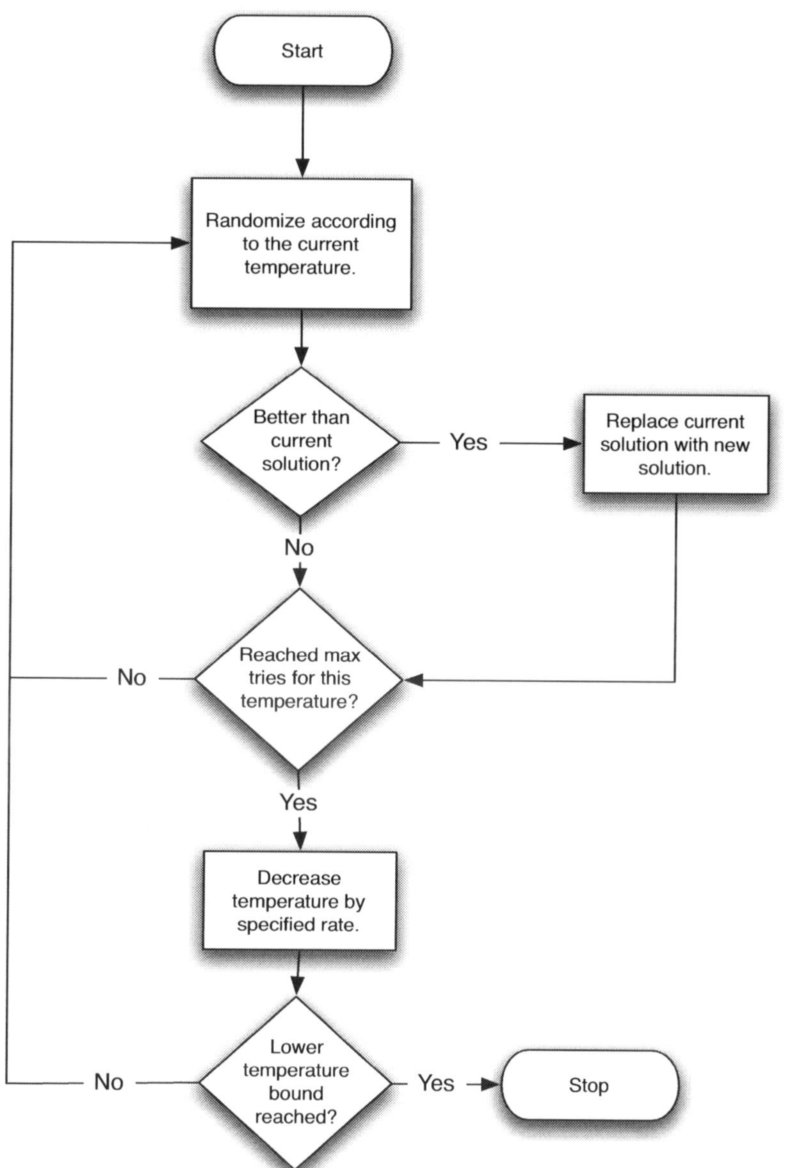

As you can see in Figure 7.1, there are two major processes that take place in the simulated annealing algorithm. First, for each temperature, the simulated annealing algorithm runs through a number of cycles. The number of cycles is predetermined by the programmer. As a cycle runs, the inputs are randomized. In the case of the traveling salesman problem, these inputs are the order of the cities that the traveling salesman will visit. Only randomizations which produce a better-suited set of inputs will be retained.

Once the specified number of training cycles have been completed, the temperature can be lowered. Once the temperature is lowered, it is determined whether or not the temperature has reached the lowest temperature allowed. If the temperature is not lower than the lowest temperature allowed, then the temperature is lowered and another cycle of randomizations will take place. If the temperature is lower than the lowest temperature allowed, the simulated annealing algorithm terminates.

At the core of the simulated annealing algorithm is the randomization of the input values. This randomization is ultimately what causes simulated annealing to alter the input values that the algorithm is seeking to minimize. The randomization process must often be customized for different problems. In this chapter we will discuss randomization methods that can be used for both the traveling salesman problem and neural network training. In the next section, we will examine how this randomization occurs.

How Are the Inputs Randomized?

An important part of the simulated annealing process is how the inputs are randomized. The randomization process takes the previous input values and the current temperature as inputs. The input values are then randomized according to the temperature. A higher temperature will result in more randomization; a lower temperature will result in less randomization.

There is no specific method defined by the simulated annealing algorithm for how to randomize the inputs. The exact nature by which this is done often depends upon the nature of the problem being solved. When comparing the methods used in the simulated annealing examples for the neural network weight optimization and the traveling salesman problem, we can see some of the differences.

Simulated Annealing and Neural Networks

The method used to randomize the weights of a neural network is somewhat simpler than the traveling salesman's simulated annealing algorithm, which we will discuss next. A neural network's weight matrix can be thought of as a linear array of floating point numbers. Each weight is independent of the others. It does not matter if two weights contain the same value. The only major constraint is that there are ranges that all weights must fall within.

Thus, the process generally used to randomize the weight matrix of a neural network is relatively simple. Using the temperature, a random ratio is applied to all of the weights in the matrix. This ratio is calculated using the temperature and a random number. The higher the temperature, the more likely it is that the ratio will cause a larger change in the weight matrix. A lower temperature will most likely produce a smaller change. This is the method that is used for the simulated annealing algorithm that will be presented later in this chapter.

Simulated Annealing and the Traveling Salesman Problem

The method used to randomize the path of the traveling salesman is somewhat more complex than the method used to randomize the weights of a neural network. This is because there are constraints that exist on the path of the traveling salesman problem that do not exist when optimizing the weight matrix of the neural network. The most significant constraint is that the randomization of the path must be controlled enough to prevent the traveling salesman from visiting the same city more than once, and at the same time ensure that he does visit each city once; no cities may be skipped.

You can think of the traveling salesman randomization as the reordering of elements in a fixed-size list. This fixed-size list is the path that the traveling salesman must follow. Since the traveling salesman can neither skip nor revisit cities, his path will always have the same number of "stops" as there are cities.

As a result of the constraints imposed by the traveling salesman problem, most randomization methods used for this problem change the order of the previous path through the cities. By simply rearranging the data, and not modifying original values, we can be assured that the final result of this reorganization will neither skip, nor revisit cities.

This is the method that is used to randomize the traveling salesman's path in the example in this chapter. Using a combination of the temperature and distance between two cities, the simulated annealing algorithm determines if the positions of the two cities should be changed. You will see the actual C# implementation of this method later in this chapter.

Temperature Reduction

There are several different methods that can be used for temperature reduction; we will examine two. The most common is to simply reduce the temperature by a fixed amount through each cycle. This is the method that is used in this chapter for the traveling salesman problem.

Another method is to specify a beginning and ending temperature. To use this method, we must calculate a ratio at each step in the simulated annealing process. This is done by using an equation that guarantees that the step amount will cause the temperature to fall to the ending temperature in the number of cycles specified. Equation 7.1 describes how to logarithmically decrease the temperature between a beginning and ending temperature. It calculates the ratio and ensures that the temperature naturally decreases for each cycle.

Equation 7.1: Scaling the Temperature

$$step = e^{\frac{\ln\left(\frac{s}{e}\right)}{c-1}}$$

The variables are **s** for starting temperature, **e** for ending temperature, and **c** for cycle count. The equation can be implemented in C# as follows:

```
double ratio = Math.Exp(Math.Log(this.StopTemperature
                        / this.StartTemperature)
                        / (this.Cycles - 1));
```

The above line calculates a ratio that should be multiplied against the current temperature. This will produce a change that will cause the temperature to reach the ending temperature in the specified number of cycles. This method is used later in this chapter when simulated annealing is applied to neural network training.

Implementing Simulated Annealing

The source code accompanying this book provides a generic simulated annealing class. This abstract class is named **SimulatedAnnealing** and can be used to implement a simulated annealing solution for a variety of problems. We will use this simulated annealing class for both the neural network example and the traveling salesman problem.

This section will describe how the generic **SimulatedAnnealing** class works. The application of simulated annealing to neural networks and the traveling salesman problem will be covered later in this chapter.

Inputs to the Simulated Annealing Algorithm

There are several variables that must be set on the **SimulatedAnnealing** class for it to function properly. These variables are usually set by the constructor of one of the classes that subclass the **SimulatedAnnealing** class. Table 7.1 summarizes these inputs.

Table 7.1: Simulated Annealing Inputs

Variable	Purpose
StartTemperature	The temperature at which to start.
StopTemperature	The temperature at which to stop.
Cycles	The number of cycles to be used.

The simulated annealing training algorithm works very much like every other training algorithm in this book. Once it is set up, it progresses through a series of iterations.

Processing Iterations

The SimulatedAnnealing class contains a method named **Iteration** that is called to process each iteration of the training process.

```
public void Iteration()
{
```

First, an array is created to hold the best solution.

```
UNIT_TYPE[] bestArray;
```

Next, the starting error is determined.

```
this.Error = DetermineError();
bestArray = this.GetArrayCopy();
```

The training process is then cycled through a specified number of times. For each training pass, the **Randomize** method is called. This method is abstract and must be implemented for any problem that is to be solved by simulated annealing.

```
this.temperature = this.StartTemperature;

for (int i = 0; i < this.cycles; i++)
{
  double curError;
  Randomize();
```

The error is determined after **Randomize** has been called.

```
  curError = DetermineError();
```

If this was an improvement, then the newly created array is saved.

```
if (curError < this.Error)
{
  bestArray = this.GetArrayCopy();
  this.Error = curError;
```

```
}
```

Once the cycle is complete, the best array is stored.

```
this.PutArray(bestArray);
```

A ratio is calculated that will decrease the temperature to the desired level. This is the C# implementation of Equation 7.1, which was shown earlier.

```
double ratio = Math.Exp(Math.Log(this.StopTemperature
  / this.StartTemperature)
  / (this.Cycles - 1));
```

The temperature is scaled by this amount.

```
this.temperature *= ratio;
```

This simulated annealing class is, of course, abstract; thus it only implements the simulated annealing algorithm at a primitive level. The examples in this chapter that actually put the **SimulatedAnnealing** class to use must implement the **Randomize** function for their unique situations.

Simulated Annealing for the Traveling Salesman Problem

Simulated annealing can provide potential solutions to the traveling salesman problem. The traveling salesman problem was introduced in chapter 6, "Understanding Genetic Algorithms." Aside from the fact that the traveling salesman problem from this chapter uses simulated annealing, it is the same as the program presented in chapter 6.

The simulated annealing traveling salesman problem implements a special version of the **SimulatedAnnealing** class. The class is named **TSPSimulatedAnnealing**. The most important method is the **Randomize** method. The signature for the **Randomize** method is shown here:

```
override public void Randomize()
{
```

First, the **length** of the path is determined.

```
int length = this.path.Length;
```

Next, we iterate through the loop a number of times equal to the temperature. The higher the temperature, the more iterations. The more iterations, the more "excited" the underlying path becomes and the more changes made.

```
Random rand = new Random();

for (int i = 0; i < this.temperature; i++)
{
```

Two random index locations are chosen inside the path.

```
int index1 = (int)Math.Floor(length * rand.NextDouble());
int index2 = (int)Math.Floor(length * rand.NextDouble());
```

A basic distance number is calculated based on the two random points.

```
double d = Distance(index1, index1 + 1) + Distance(index2,
index2 + 1) - Distance(index1, index2) - Distance(index1 + 1,
index2 + 1);
```

If the distance calculation is greater than zero, then the array elements in the path are excited.

```
if (d > 0) {
```

The index locations, **index1** and **index2**, are sorted if necessary.

```
if (index2 < index1)
{
  int temp = index1;
  index1 = index2;
  index2 = temp;
}
```

All cities between the two random index points are sorted.

```
for (; index2 > index1; index2--)
{
  int temp = this.path[index1 + 1];
  this.path[index1 + 1] = this.path[index2];
  this.path[index2] = temp;
  index1++;
}
```

When the new path is returned to the **Iteration** function, it will be evaluated. If it is an improvement over the last path, it will be retained.

Simulated Annealing for Neural Networks

Simulated annealing can also be applied to neural networks. This book provides a class named **NeuralSimulatedAnnealing**. By making use of the generic **SimulatedAnnealing** class introduced earlier in this chapter, this class implements a training solution for neural networks. Listing 7.1 shows a simple program that uses simulated annealing to train a neural network for the XOR operator.

Listing 7.1: Simulated Annealing and the XOR Operator (AnnealXOR.cs)

```
using System;
using System.Collections.Generic;
using System.Linq;
```

```csharp
using System.Text;

using HeatonResearchNeural.Feedforward;
using HeatonResearchNeural.Feedforward.Train.Anneal;

namespace Chapter6XOR
{
    class AnnealXOR
    {

        public static double[][] XOR_INPUT ={
            new double[2] { 0.0, 0.0 },
            new double[2] { 1.0, 0.0 },
                new double[2] { 0.0, 1.0 },
            new double[2] { 1.0, 1.0 } };

        public static double[][] XOR_IDEAL = {
            new double[1] { 0.0 },
            new double[1] { 1.0 },
            new double[1] { 1.0 },
            new double[1] { 0.0 } };

        static void Main(string[] args)
        {
            FeedforwardNetwork network = new FeedforwardNetwork();
            network.AddLayer(new FeedforwardLayer(2));
            network.AddLayer(new FeedforwardLayer(3));
            network.AddLayer(new FeedforwardLayer(1));
            network.Reset();

            // train the neural network
            NeuralSimulatedAnnealing train =
                    new NeuralSimulatedAnnealing(
                network, XOR_INPUT, XOR_IDEAL, 10, 2, 100);

            int epoch = 1;

            do
            {
                train.Iteration();
                Console.WriteLine("Epoch #" + epoch
                        + " Error:" + train.Error);
                epoch++;
            } while ((epoch < 5000) && (train.Error > 0.001));

            network = train.Network;
```

```
        // test the neural network
        Console.WriteLine("Neural Network Results:");
        for (int i = 0; i < XOR_IDEAL.Length; i++)
        {
            double[] actual =
                    network.ComputeOutputs(XOR_INPUT[i]);
            Console.WriteLine(XOR_INPUT[i][0] + ","
                    + XOR_INPUT[i][1]
                    + ", actual=" + actual[0]
                    + ",ideal=" + XOR_IDEAL[i][0]);
        }
    }
  }
}
```

The **NeuralSimulatedAnnealing** class implements the **Train** interface, and thus can be used just like backpropagation and genetic algorithms discussed in earlier chapters. The **NeuralSimulatedAnnealing** is instantiated as follows:

```
NeuralSimulatedAnnealing train =
    new NeuralSimulatedAnnealing(
    network, XOR_INPUT, XOR_IDEAL, 10, 2, 100);
```

The **NeuralSimulatedAnnealing** class implements a special **Randomize** method. This method excites the state of the neural network in a way that is very similar to how the traveling salesman implementation works. The signature for the **Randomize** method is shown here:

```
override public void Randomize()
```

First, **MatrixCODEC** is used to serialize the neural network into an array of **double** variables.

```
Random rand = new Random();
double[] array = MatrixCODEC.NetworkToArray(this.network);
```

We then loop through the array.

```
for (int i = 0; i < array.Length; i++)
{
```

Each array element is randomly excited based on the temperature.

```
  double add = 0.5 - (rand.NextDouble());
  add /= this.StartTemperature;
  add *= this.temperature;
  array[i] = array[i] + add;
}
```

Finally, **MatrixCODEC** is used to turn the array back into a neural network.

```
MatrixCODEC.ArrayToNetwork(array, this.network);
```

When this new neural network is returned to the **Iteration** function, it will be evaluated. If it is an improvement, it will be retained.

Chapter Summary

In this chapter, you learned about the simulated annealing algorithm. The simulated annealing algorithm is based on the actual process of annealing. The key point behind the annealing process is that a metal that is allowed to cool slowly will form more consistent, and therefore stronger, crystal structures. The reason being that the higher temperatures result in higher energy levels for the atoms that make up the metal. At the higher energy levels, the atoms have greater freedom of movement. As the metal cools, this freedom of movement is curtailed. This allows the atoms to settle into consistent crystal patterns.

The process of simulated annealing is very similar to the actual annealing process. A series of input values are presented to the simulated annealing algorithm. The simulated annealing algorithm wants to optimize these input values so that an arbitrary equation can be minimized. Examples of equations to be minimized include the error function for a neural network, or the distance that a traveling salesman travels. The input values, which drive the simulated annealing algorithm, can be the weight matrix of a neural network or the current route between cities that a traveling salesman is traveling.

To present a relatively simple example of how to use simulated annealing, this chapter once again turned to the traveling salesman problem. The traveling salesman problem was also used in chapter 6 in conjunction with genetic algorithms. Reusing the traveling salesman problem allows us to easily compare the performance of genetic algorithms with simulated annealing.

Vocabulary

Annealing

Annealing Cycles

Excite

Simulated Annealing

Temperature

Questions for Review

1.   Describe the metallurgical annealing process.

2.   How are the array elements randomized when finding solutions for the traveling salesman problem?

3.   How are the array elements randomized when training a neural network?

4.   What is the difference between a cycle and an iteration in the simulated annealing algorithm presented in this chapter?

5.   How do we ensure that the temperature changes naturally between cycles?

CHAPTER 8: PRUNING NEURAL NETWORKS

- What is Pruning?
- Incremental Pruning
- Selective Pruning
- Pruning Examples

In chapters 6 and 7, we saw that you can use simulated annealing and genetic algorithms to train neural networks. These two techniques employ various algorithms to better fit the weights of a neural network to the problem to which it is being applied. However, these techniques do nothing to adjust the structure of the neural network.

In this chapter, we will examine two algorithms that can be used to actually modify the structure of a neural network. This structural modification will not generally improve the error rate of the neural network, but it can make the neural network more efficient. The modification is accomplished by analyzing how much each neuron contributes to the output of the neural network. If a particular neuron's connection to another neuron does not significantly affect the output of the neural network, the connection will be pruned. Through this process, connections and neurons that have only a marginal impact on the output are removed.

This process is called pruning. In this chapter, we will examine how pruning is accomplished. We will begin by examining the pruning process in greater detail and will discuss some of the popular methods. Finally, this chapter will conclude by providing two examples that demonstrate pruning.

Understanding Pruning

Pruning is a process used to make neural networks more efficient. Unlike genetic algorithms or simulated annealing, pruning does not increase the effectiveness of a neural network. The primary goal of pruning is to decrease the amount of processing required to use the neural network.

Pruning can be especially effective when performed on a large neural network that is taking too long to execute. Pruning works by analyzing the connections of the neural network. The pruning algorithm looks for individual connections and neurons that can be removed from the neural network to make it operate more efficiently. By pruning unneeded connections, the neural network can be made to execute faster. This allows the neural network to perform more work in a given amount of time. In the next two sections we will examine how to prune both connections and neurons.

Pruning Connections

Connection pruning is central to most pruning algorithms. The individual connections between the neurons are analyzed to determine which connections have the least impact on the effectiveness of the neural network. One of the methods that we will examine will remove all connections that have a weight below a certain threshold value. The second method evaluates the effectiveness of the neural network as certain weights are considered for removal. Connections are not the only thing that can be pruned. By analyzing which connections were pruned, we can also prune individual neurons.

Pruning Neurons

Pruning focuses primarily on the connections between the individual neurons of the neural network. However, individual neurons can be pruned as well. One of the pruning algorithms that we will examine later in this chapter is designed to prune neurons as well as connections.

To prune individual neurons, the connections between each neuron and the other neurons must be examined. If one particular neuron is surrounded entirely by weak connections, there is no reason to keep that neuron. If we apply the criteria discussed in the previous section, we can end up with neurons that have no connections. This is because all of the neuron's connections were pruned. Such a neuron can then be pruned itself.

Improving or Degrading Performance

It is possible that pruning a neural network may improve its performance. Any modifications to the weight matrix of a neural network will always have some impact on the accuracy of the recognitions made by the neural network. A connection that has little or no impact on the neural network may actually be degrading the accuracy with which the neural network recognizes patterns. Removing such a weak connection may improve the overall output of the neural network.

Unfortunately, it is also possible to decrease the effectiveness of the neural network through pruning. Thus, it is always important to analyze the effectiveness of the neural network before and after pruning. Since efficiency is the primary benefit of pruning, you must be careful to evaluate whether an improvement in the processing time is worth a decrease in the neural network's effectiveness. The program in the example that we will examine later in this chapter will evaluate the overall effectiveness of the neural network both before and after pruning. This will give us an idea of what effect the pruning process had on the effectiveness of the neural network.

Pruning Algorithms

We will now review exactly how pruning takes place. In this section we will examine two different methods for pruning. These two methods work in somewhat opposite ways. The first method, incremental pruning, works by gradually increasing the number of hidden neurons until an acceptable error rate has been obtained. The second method, selective pruning, works by taking an existing neural network and decreasing the number of hidden neurons as long as the error rate remains acceptable.

Incremental Pruning

Incremental pruning is a trial and error approach to finding an appropriate number of hidden neurons. This method is summarized in Figure 8.1.

Figure 8.1: Flowchart of the incremental pruning algorithm.

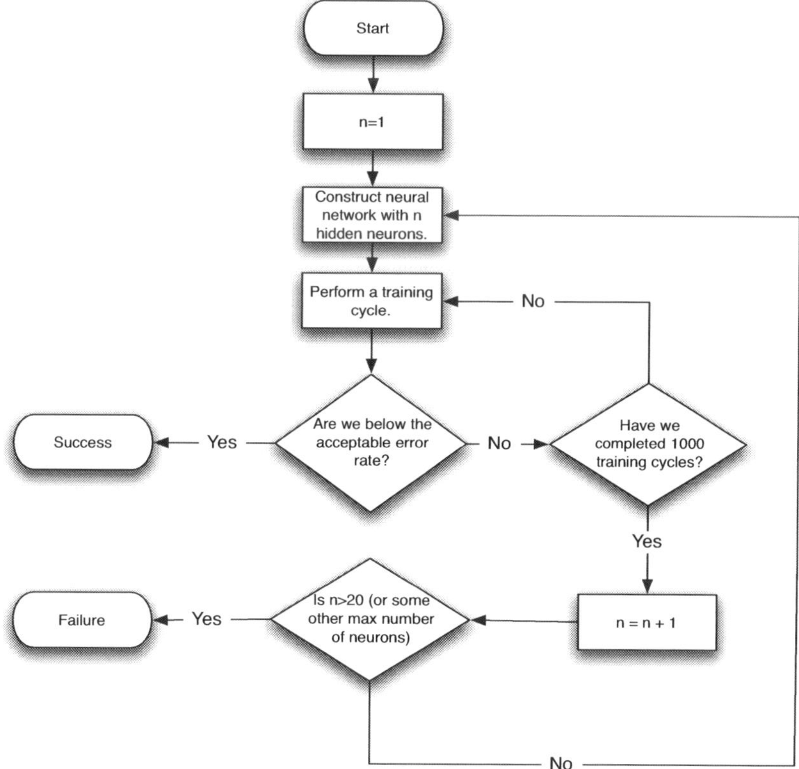

The incremental pruning algorithm begins with an untrained neural network. It then attempts to train the neural network many times. Each time, it uses a different set of hidden neurons.

The incremental training algorithm must be supplied with an acceptable error rate. It is looking for the neural network with the fewest number of hidden neurons that will cause the error rate to fall below the desired level. Once a neural network that can be trained to fall below this rate is found, the algorithm is complete.

As you saw in chapter 5, "Feedforward Backpropagation Neural Networks," it is often necessary to train for many cycles before a solution is found. The incremental pruning algorithm requires the entire training session to be completed many times. Each time a new neuron is added to the hidden layer, the neural network must be retrained. As a result, it can take a long time for the incremental pruning algorithm to run.

The neural network will train for different numbers of hidden neurons, beginning initially with a single neuron. Because the error rate does not drop sufficiently fast, the single hidden neuron neural network will quickly be abandoned. Any number of methods can be used to determine when to abandon a neural network. The method that will be used in this chapter is to check the current error rate after intervals of 1,000 cycles. If the error does not decrease by a single percentage point, then the search will be abandoned. This allows us to quickly abandon hidden layer sizes that are too small for the intended task.

One advantage of the incremental pruning algorithm is that it will usually create neural networks with fewer hidden neurons than the other methods. The biggest disadvantage is the amount of processor time that it takes to run this algorithm. Now that you have been introduced to the incremental pruning algorithm, we will examine the selective pruning algorithm.

Selective Pruning

The selective pruning algorithm differs from the incremental pruning algorithm in several important ways. One of the most notable differences is the beginning state of the neural network. No training was required before beginning the incremental pruning algorithm. This is not the case with the selective pruning algorithm. The selective pruning algorithm works by examining the weight matrixes of a previously trained neural network. The selective training algorithm will then attempt to remove neurons without disrupting the output of the neural network. The algorithm used for selective pruning is shown in Figure 8.2.

Figure 8.2: Flowchart of the selective pruning algorithm.

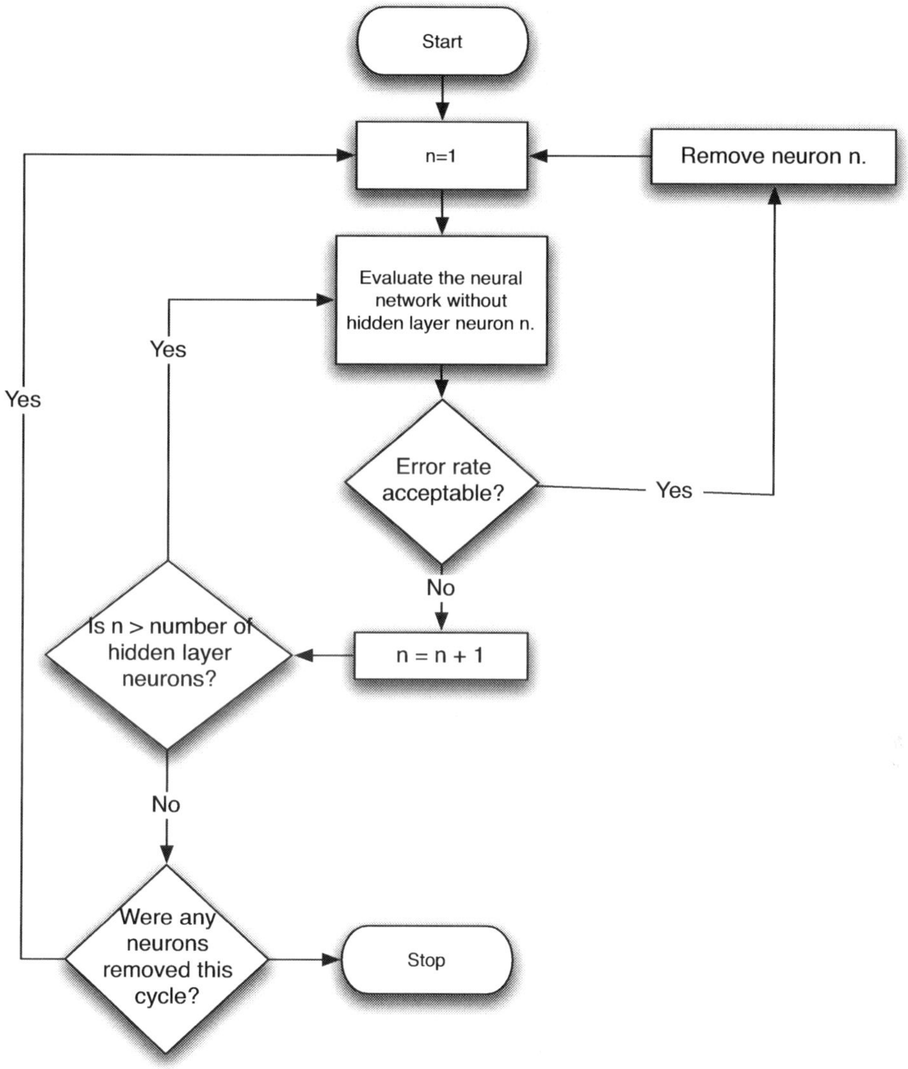

As you can see, the selective pruning algorithm is something of a trial and error approach. The selective pruning algorithm attempts to remove neurons from the neural network until no more neurons can be removed without degrading the performance of the neural network.

To begin this process, the selective pruning algorithm loops through each of the hidden neurons. For each hidden neuron encountered, the error level of the neural network is evaluated both with and without the specified neuron. If the error rate jumps beyond a predefined level, the neuron will be retained and the next neuron will be evaluated. If the error rate does not jump by much, the neuron will be removed.

Once the program has evaluated all neurons, the program repeats the process. This cycle continues until the program has made one pass through the hidden neurons without removing a single neuron. Once this process is complete, a new neural network is achieved that performs acceptably close to the original, yet has fewer hidden neurons.

The major advantage of the selective pruning algorithm is that it takes very little processing time to complete. The program in the example presented later in this chapter requires under one second to prune a neural network with 10 hidden layer neurons. This is considerably less time than the incremental pruning algorithm described in the previous section.

Implementing Pruning

Now that it has been explained how the pruning algorithms work, you will be shown how to implement them in C#. In this section, we will examine a general class that is designed to prune feedforward backpropagation neural networks. The name of this class is simply "Prune." This class accepts a "Network" class and performs either incremental or selective pruning. We will begin by examining the prune class. We will then examine the incremental and selective algorithms within the class.

The Prune Class

The Prune class contains all of the methods and properties that are required to prune a feedforward backpropagation neural network. There are several properties that are used internally by many of the methods that make up the **Prune** class. These properties are summarized in Table 8.1.

Table 8.1: Variables Used for the Prune Process

Variable	Purpose
backprop	The backpropagation object to be pruned.
cycles	The number of cycles.
done	Flag to indicate if the incremental pruning process is done or not.
error	The current error.
ideal	The ideal results from the training set.
hiddenNeuronCount	The number of hidden neurons.
markErrorRate	Used to determine if training is still effective. Holds the error level determined in the previous 1000 cycles. If no significant drop in error occurs for 1000 cycles, training ends.
maxError	The maximum acceptable error.
momentum	The desired momentum.
rate	The desired learning rate (for backpropagation).
sinceMark	Used with markErrorRate. This is the number of cycles since the error was last marked.
train	The training set.

You will now be shown how the selective and incremental pruning algorithms are implemented. We will begin with incremental pruning.

Incremental Pruning

As you will recall from earlier in this chapter, the process of incremental pruning involves increasing the number of neurons in the hidden layer until the neural network is able to be trained sufficiently well. This should automatically lead us to a good number of hidden neurons. The constructor used to implement incremental pruning is very simple. It collects the required parameters and stores them in the class's properties.

The parameters required by the incremental pruning constructor are the usual parameters needed to perform backpropagation training of a feedforward neural network. The learning rate and momentum are both required. These backpropagation constants are discussed in greater detail in chapter 5. Additionally, a training set, along with the ideal outputs for the training set, are also required.

The final parameter that is required by the incremental pruning constructor is the minimum acceptable error. This is the error rate that is sufficient for a neural network to be trained. As the incremental pruning algorithm progresses, it will try to train neural networks with various numbers of hidden neurons. The final number of hidden neurons will be determined by the neural network with the fewest number of hidden neurons that is able to be trained to reach this error level.

The **Prune** class contains two constructors; one is for incremental pruning and the other is for selective pruning. The constructor for the **Prune** class to be used with incremental pruning is shown here:

```
public Prune(double rate, double momentum,
                double[][] train, double[][] ideal,
                double maxError)
```

This provides the class with the training and ideal sets to be used with backpropagation, as well as a maximum acceptable error.

Starting the Incremental Pruning Process

To begin the process of incremental pruning, you must call the **StartIncremental** method. This sets up the **Prune** class for a new pruning run. The signature for the **StartIncremental** method is shown here.

```
public void StartIncremental()
```

First, some of the properties are set to their initial values. One such property is the number of neurons that will exist in the hidden layer. Initially, we begin with one single neuron in the hidden layer.

```
this.hiddenNeuronCount = 1;
this.cycles = 0;
this.done = false;
```

A new **FeedforwardNetwork** object is created to hold the neural network that will be prepared as the training progresses.

```
this.currentNetwork = new FeedforwardNetwork();
```

Next, the layers are added to the network.

```
this.currentNetwork.AddLayer(new FeedforwardLayer(this.train[0].
Length));
this.currentNetwork.AddLayer(new FeedforwardLayer(
                this.hiddenNeuronCount));
this.currentNetwork
                .AddLayer(new FeedforwardLayer(this.ideal[0].
Length));
this.currentNetwork.Reset();
```

A backpropagation object is created to train the network.

```
this.backprop = new Backpropagation(this.currentNetwork, this.
train, this.ideal, this.rate, this.momentum);
```

Now, the incremental prune algorithm is ready to begin. In the next section, you will see how the main loop of the incremental algorithm is constructed.

Main Loop of the Incremental Algorithm

The incremental pruning algorithm is processor intensive and may take some time to run. This is because the incremental algorithm is literally trying different numbers of hidden neurons, in a trial and error fashion, until a network is identified that has the fewest number of neurons while producing an acceptable error level.

The incremental pruning algorithm is designed so that a background thread can rapidly call the **PruneIncremental** method until the **Done** property indicates that the algorithm is done. Of course, the **PruneIncremental** method can be called from the main thread, as well. The signature for the **PruneIncremental** method is shown here:

```
public void PruneIncramental()
```

If the work has already been done, then exit.

```
if (this.done)
{
   return;
}
```

The **PruneIncremental** method begins by first checking to see if it is already done. If the algorithm is already done, the **PruneIncremental** method simply returns.

The next step is to attempt a single training cycle for the neural network. The program calls **Increment**, which loops through all of the training sets and calculates the error based on the ideal outputs.

```
this.backprop.Iteration();
```

Once the training set has been presented, the root mean square (RMS) error is calculated. The RMS error was discussed in chapter 4, "How a Machine Learns." Calculating the RMS error allows the pruning algorithm to determine if the error has reached the desired level.

```
this.error = this.backprop.Error;
this.cycles++;
Increment();
```

Each time a training cycle is executed, the neural network must check to see if the number of hidden neurons should be increased or if training should continue with the current neural network.

Incrementing the Number of Neurons

To determine if the number of hidden neurons should be increased or not, the helper method named **Increment** is used. The **Increment** method keeps track of training progress for the neural network. If the training improvement for each cycle falls below a constant value, further training is deemed futile. In this case, we increment the number of hidden neurons and continue training.

The **Increment** method begins by setting a flag that indicates whether or not it should increment the number of hidden neurons. The default is **false**, which means do not increment the number of neurons. The signature for the increment method is shown here:

```
protected void Increment()
```

Start by setting the **doit** variable to false. This variable is set to **true** if a better neural network configuration is found.

```
bool doit = false;
```

The algorithm that this class uses to determine if further training is futile, works by examining the amount of improvement every 10,000 cycles. If the error rate does not change by more than one percent within 10,000 cycles, further training is deemed futile and the number of neurons in the hidden layer is incremented.

The following lines of code accomplish this evaluation. First, when the **markErrorRate** is zero, it means that we are just beginning and have not yet sampled the error rate. In this case, we initialize the **markErrorRate** and **sinceMark** variables.

```
if (this.markErrorRate == 0)
{
   this.markErrorRate = this.error;
   this.sinceMark = 0;
}
else
{
```

If the **markErrorRate** is not zero, then we are tracking errors. We should increase the **sinceMark** cycle counter and determine if more than 10,000 cycles have been completed since we last sampled the error rate.

```
this.sinceMark++;
if (this.sinceMark > 10000)
{
```

If more than 10,000 cycles have passed, we check to see if the improvement between the **markErrorRate** and current error rate is less than one percent. If this is the case, then we set the flag to indicate that the number of hidden neurons should be incremented.

```
if ((this.markErrorRate - this.error) < 0.01)
{
  doit = true;
}
```

The error rate is then sampled again.

```
    this.markErrorRate = this.error;
    this.sinceMark = 0;
  }
}
```

If the error rate is below the acceptable error, then we have found the number of neurons we will recommend for the neural network. We can now set the **done** flag to **true**.

```
if (this.error < this.maxError)
{
  this.done = true;
}
```

If the flag is set, we increment the number of neurons as follows:

```
if (doit)
{
  this.cycles = 0;
  this.hiddenNeuronCount++;

  this.currentNetwork = new FeedforwardNetwork();
  this.currentNetwork.AddLayer(new FeedforwardLayer(
    this.train[0].Length));
  this.currentNetwork.AddLayer(new FeedforwardLayer(
    this.hiddenNeuronCount));
  this.currentNetwork.AddLayer(new FeedforwardLayer(
                    this.ideal[0].Length));
  this.currentNetwork.Reset();

  this.backprop = new Backpropagation(this.currentNetwork,
    this.train, this.ideal, this.rate, this.momentum);
  }
}
```

As you can see, a new neural network is constructed after the number of hidden neurons is increased. Also, the cycle count is reset to zero, because we will begin training a new neural network.

You should now be familiar with how the incremental pruning algorithm is implemented. Later in this chapter, we will construct a sample program that makes use of this algorithm. For now, we will cover the implementation of the second pruning algorithm, the selective pruning algorithm.

Selective Pruning

Now that you have seen how the incremental pruning algorithm was implemented, we will examine the implementation of the selective pruning algorithm. In some ways, the selective pruning algorithm works in reverse of the incremental pruning algorithm. Where the incremental pruning algorithm starts small and grows, the selective pruning algorithm starts with a large, pretrained neural network, and selects neurons for removal.

To use selective pruning, you can make use of a simplified version of the Prune constructor. Selective pruning does not need to know anything about the learning rate or momentum of the backpropagation process, because it does not involve the backpropagation algorithm. The simplified version of the constructor is shown below.

```
public Prune(double rate, double momentum,
   double[][] train, double[][] ideal,
   double maxError)
```

As you can see, you are only required to pass a neural network training set and the ideal results to the selective pruning algorithm. The constructor is very simple and merely stores the values that it was passed. We will now examine the implementation of the selective pruning methods. We will begin by examining the main loop of the algorithm.

Main Loop of the Selective Pruning Algorithm

The main loop of the selective pruning algorithm is much less processor intensive than the incremental pruning algorithm. The incremental pruning algorithm that we examined in the previous section was designed to run as a background thread due to the large number of cycles that might be required to find a solution. This is not the case with the selective pruning algorithm.

The selective pruning algorithm is designed to evaluate the performance of the neural network when each hidden neuron is removed. If the performance of the neural network does not degrade substantially with the removal of a neuron, that neuron will be removed permanently. This process will continue until no additional neurons can be removed without substantially degrading the performance of the neural network. Thus, the selective pruning algorithm is designed to perform the entire algorithm with one method call. There is no reason for a background thread, as this method should be able to perform its task almost instantaneously.

The method that should be called to prune a neural network selectively is the **PruneSelective** method. We will now examine how this method performs. The signature for this method is shown here:

```
public int PruneSelective()
```

Following is the body of the **PruneSelective** method.

```
int i = this.HiddenCount;
while (FindNeuron())
{
  ;
}
return (i - this.HiddenCount);
```

As you can see from the above code, the current number of hidden neurons is stored in the variable i for future use. We then enter a loop and iterate until no additional neurons can be removed. Finally, the **PruneSelective** method returns the number of neurons that were removed from the neural network. The new optimized neural network is stored in the **currentNetwork** property of the **Prune** class and can be accessed using the **CurrentNetwork** property.

The real work performed by the selective pruning algorithm is done by the **FindNeuron** method. It is the **FindNeuron** method that actually identifies and removes neurons that do not have an adverse effect on the error rate. The **FindNeuron** method will remove a neuron, if possible, and return **true**. If no neuron can be removed, the **FindNeuron** method returns a value of **false**. As you can see from the above code in the **PruneSelective** method, the **FindNeuron** method is called as long as the return value is **true**. The signature for the **FindNeuron** method is shown here:

```
protected bool FindNeuron()
```

We will now examine the contents of the **FindNeuron** method. This method begins by calculating the current error rate.

```
for (int i = 0; i < this.HiddenCount; i++)
{
```

The error rate is then recalculated, and we evaluate the effect this has on the quality of the neural network. As long as the quality is still below **maxError**, we continue pruning.

```
FeedforwardNetwork trial = this.ClipHiddenNeuron(i);
double e2 = DetermineError(trial);
if (e2 < this.maxError)
{
```

If we have an acceptable network when the neuron is removed, we exit the method and **true** is returned. The value of **true** indicates that the neuron was removed, and we should attempt to remove additional neurons.

```
this.currentNetwork = trial;
return true;
}
```

If no neurons were removed, **false** is returned. This indicates that further processing with be of no additional value.

```
return false;
```

You will now be shown the process by which neurons are removed from the neural network.

Removing Neurons

Removing a neuron from a **FeedforwardLayer** object is a relatively straightforward process. The task of removing an individual hidden neuron is encapsulated inside the **Prune** method of the **FeedforwardLayer** class in the ClipHidden-Neuron method. The first thing that the **ClipHiddenNeuron** method does is create a new neural network with one less neuron.

```
public void Prune(int neuron)
```

First, it deletes the row of this layer's matrix that corresponds to the targeted neuron.

```
if (this.matrix != null)
{
    this.LayerMatrix = (MatrixMath.DeleteRow(this.matrix, neuron));
}
```

Next, it deletes the column on the previous layer's matrix that corresponds to the targeted neuron.

```
FeedforwardLayer previous = this.Previous;
if (previous != null)
{
    if (previous.LayerMatrix != null)
    {
        previous.LayerMatrix =  (MatrixMath.DeleteCol(
                previous.LayerMatrix, neuron));
    }
}
}
```

This completes the process for removing the targeted neuron and concludes how the **Prune** class is constructed. We covered both incremental and selective pruning. We will now see how to make use of this class in a C# program.

Using the Prune Class

In this section, we will examine two programs that are provided as examples to demonstrate the use of the Prune class. These examples demonstrate the two pruning methods that we have discussed in this chapter. We will begin with the incremental pruning example.

The Incremental Pruning Example

This example is based on the XOR problem that was presented in chapter 5. Thus, the complete code for this program will not be shown here. Rather, the additional code that was added to the XOR example in chapter 5 to support pruning is shown. You can see the output from the incremental pruning example in Figure 8.3.

Figure 8.3: The incremental pruning example.

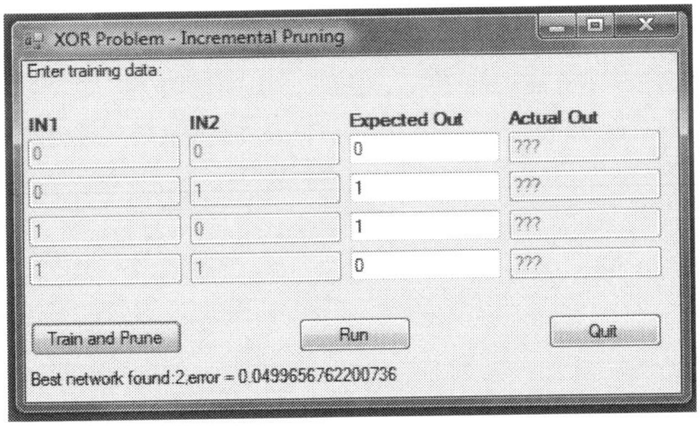

When the "Prune/Train" button is pressed, a background thread is created. This background thread executes the prune example's **ThreadProc** method. We will now examine the contents of the **ThreadProc** method.

The signature for the **ThreadProc** method is shown here:

```
public void ThreadProc()
```

The **ThreadProc** method begins by reading any data entered by the user. Both the training sets and the ideal results are read from the window. Next, a **Prune** object is created named **prune**. This object will use a learning rate of 0.7 and a momentum of 0.5. The **StartIncremental** method is called to prepare for incremental pruning.

```
int update = 0;

Prune prune = new Prune(0.7, 0.5, PruneIncrementalForm.XOR_INPUT,
this.ObtainIdeal(), 0.05);
prune.StartIncremental();
Prune prune = new Prune(0.7, 0.5, xorData, xorIdeal, 0.05);
prune.StartIncremental();
```

As long as the pruning algorithm is not done, the loop will continue.

```
while (!prune.Done) {
```

One iteration of incremental training will be performed.

```
prune.PruneIncramental();
update++;
```

The screen is updated every ten iterations.

```
if (update == 10) {
  this.SetText( "Cycles:" + prune.Cycles
    + ",Hidden Neurons:" + prune.HiddenNeuronCount
    + ", Current Error=" + prune.Error);
  update = 0;
}
}
```

Finally, the system reports the best network found.

```
this.SetText( "Best network found:" + prune.HiddenNeuronCount
+ ",error = " + prune.Error);
```

This network is then copied to the current network.

```
this.network = prune.CurrentNetwork;
```

In this section, you have seen how the Prune class was used to implement an incremental pruning of a neural network. In the next section, you will see how to use the Prune class for a selective pruning of a neural network.

The Selective Pruning Example

This selective pruning example is also based on the XOR problem that was shown in chapter 5; thus, the complete code is not shown here. Rather, only the additional code that was added to the XOR example in chapter 5 to support selective pruning is presented. You can see the output from the incremental pruning example in Figure 8.4.

Figure 8.4: The selective pruning example.

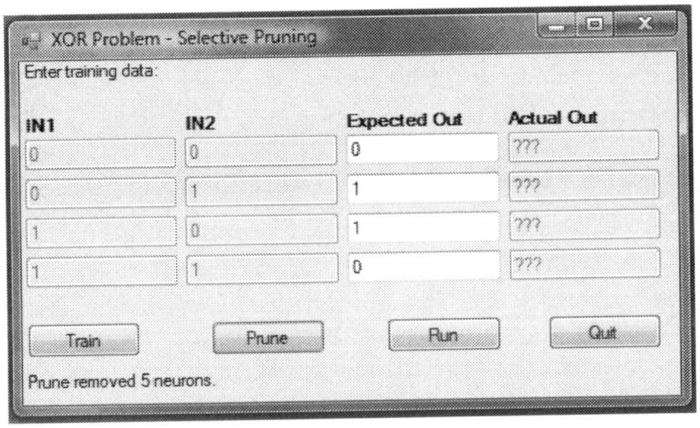

Because the selective pruning example requires that a neural network already be present to prune, you should begin by clicking the "Train" button. This will train the neural network using the backpropagation method. The neural network shown in this example initially contains ten neurons in the hidden layer. Clicking the "Prune" button will begin a selective pruning and attempt to remove some of the neurons from the hidden layer.

The code necessary to implement a selective pruning algorithm is very simple. Because this algorithm executes very quickly, there is no need for a background thread. This greatly simplifies the use of the selective pruning algorithm. When the "Prune" button is clicked, the **Click** event is executed. The signature for the **Click** event is shown here:

```
private void btnPrune_Click(object sender, EventArgs e)
```

The **Prune** method begins by obtaining the data from the grid.

```
Prune prune = new Prune(this.network,
        PruneSelectiveForm.XOR_INPUT, this.ObtainIdeal(), 0.05);
int count = prune.PruneSelective();
this.network = prune.CurrentNetwork;
this.SetText("Prune removed " + count + " neurons.");
```

Next, a **Prune** object is instantiated. The **PruneSelective** method is called which returns a count of the neurons that were removed during the prune. This value is displayed to the user and the new network is copied to the current network. The user may now run the network to see, first hand, the performance of the neural network. You will find that the selective pruning algorithm is usually able to eliminate two or three neurons. While this leaves more neurons than the incremental algorithm, significantly less processor time is required, and there is no need to retrain the neural network.

Chapter Summary

As you learned in this chapter, it is possible to prune neural networks. Pruning a neural network removes connections and neurons in order to make the neural network more efficient. The goal of pruning is not to make the neural network more effective at recognizing patterns, but to make it more efficient. There are several different algorithms for pruning a neural network. In this chapter, we examined two of these algorithms.

The first algorithm we examined was called the incremental pruning algorithm. This algorithm trains new neural networks as the number of hidden neurons is increased. The incremental pruning algorithm eventually settles on the neural network that has the fewest neurons in the hidden layer, yet still maintains an acceptable error level. While the incremental algorithm will often find the ideal number of hidden neurons, in general, it takes a considerable amount of time to execute.

The second algorithm we examined was called the selective pruning algorithm. The selective pruning algorithm begins with a neural network that has already been trained. The algorithm then removes hidden neurons as long as the error stays below a specified level. Although the selective pruning algorithm will often not find the optimal number of neurons it will execute considerably faster than the incremental algorithm.

The primary goal of neural network pruning is to improve efficiency. By pruning a neural network, you are able to create a neural network that will execute faster and require fewer processor cycles. If your neural network is already operating sufficiently fast, you must evaluate whether the pruning is justified. Even when efficiency is of great importance, you must weigh the trade-offs between efficiency and a reduction in the effectiveness of your neural network.

Thus far, this book has focused primarily on using neural networks to recognize patterns. Neural networks can also be taught to predict future trends. By providing a neural network with a series of time-based values, it can predict subsequent values. The next two chapters will focus on predictive neural networks. This type of neural network is sometimes called a temporal neural network.

Vocabulary

Connection Significance

Incremental Pruning

Pruning

Selective Pruning

Questions for Review

1. Describe the steps in the incremental pruning method.

2. Describe the steps in the selective pruning method.

3. You have a neural network that has already been trained and produces good results. However, you wonder if you might be able to remove several hidden neurons. Which pruning method would you use to accomplish this? Why?

4. You would like to remove a neuron from the hidden layer. What, if anything, must be done to the weight matrix between the input layer and the hidden layer? What, if anything, must be done to the weight matrix between the hidden layer and the output layer?

5. Which pruning method must use one of the learning algorithms as part of its process.

CHAPTER 9: PREDICTIVE NEURAL NETWORKS

- Creating Input and Output Neurons for Prediction
- How to Create Training Sets for a Predictive Neural Network
- Predicting the Sine Wave

Neural networks are particularly good at recognizing patterns. Pattern recognition can be used to predict future patterns in data. A neural network used to predict future patterns is call a predictive, or temporal neural network. A predictive neural network can be used to predict future events, such as stock market trends and sun spot cycles.

This chapter will introduce predictive neural networks through an example network coded to predict the sine wave. The next chapter will present a neural network that attempts to predict the S&P 500.

How to Predict with a Neural Network

Many different kinds of neural networks can be used for prediction. This book will use the feedforward neural network to attempt to learn patterns in data and predict future values. Like all problems applied to neural networks, prediction is a matter of intelligently determining how to configure input and interpret output neurons for a problem.

There are many ways to model prediction problems. This book will focus on one specific technique, which involves taking known data, partitioning it into training sets, and applying it to input neurons. A smaller number of output neurons then represent the future data. Following is a discussion of how to set up input and output neurons for a simple prediction.

Setting Up Input and Output Neurons for Prediction

Consider a simple series of numbers, such as the sequence shown here:

1, 2, 3, 4, 3, 2, 1, 2, 3, 4, 3, 2, 1

A neural network that predicts numbers from this sequence might use three input neurons and a single output neuron. For example, a training set might look like Table 9.1.

Table 9.1: Sample Training Sets for a Predictive Neural Network

Set	Input	Ideal Output
1	1,2,3	4
2	2,3,4	3
3	3,4,3	2
4	4,3,2	1

As you can see, the neural network is prepared to receive several data samples in a sequence. The output neuron then predicts how the sequence will be continued. The idea is that you can now feed any sequence of three numbers, and the neural network will predict the fourth number. Each data point is called a time slice. Therefore, each input neuron represents a known time slice. The output neurons represent future time slices.

Of course this is a very simple example. It is possible to include additional data that might influence the next value. In chapter 10, we will attempt to predict the S&P 500 and will include the current interest rate.

Selecting Data for Prediction

There are several methods for selecting input data for prediction. In the above example, each training set value occurred directly adjacent to the next. This is not always possible. The amount of input data may produce too many training sets. This will be the case for the neural network presented in the next chapter, since we will have easy access to the S&P 500 financial information going all the way back to 1950, as well as prime interest rates. This will be more data than will be practical to work with to train the neural network.

In the example presented in the table above, the actual values are simply input into the neural network. For a simple example, such as the sine wave, this works just fine. However, you may want to feed the neural network percentage increases and cause the output neurons to predict future percentage increases or decreases. This technique will be expanded upon in chapter 10 when a predictive neural network is applied to the S&P 500.

Another consideration for the training set data is to leave enough data to be able to evaluate the performance of the predictive neural network. For example, if the goal is to train a neural network for stock market prediction, perhaps only data prior to 2005 should be used to train the neural network. Everything past 2005 can then be used to evaluate how well the trained neural network is performing.

Predicting the Sine Wave

The example in this chapter is relatively simple. A neural network is presented that predicts the sine wave. The sine wave is mathematically predictable, so in many ways it is not a good example for illustrating a predictive neural network; however, the sine wave is easily understood and varies over time. This makes it a good introduction to predictive neural networks. Chapter 10 will expand upon this and use a neural network to attempt to provide some insight into stock market prediction.

The sine wave can be seen by plotting the trigonometric sine function. Figure 9.1 shows the sine wave.

Figure 9.1: The sine wave.

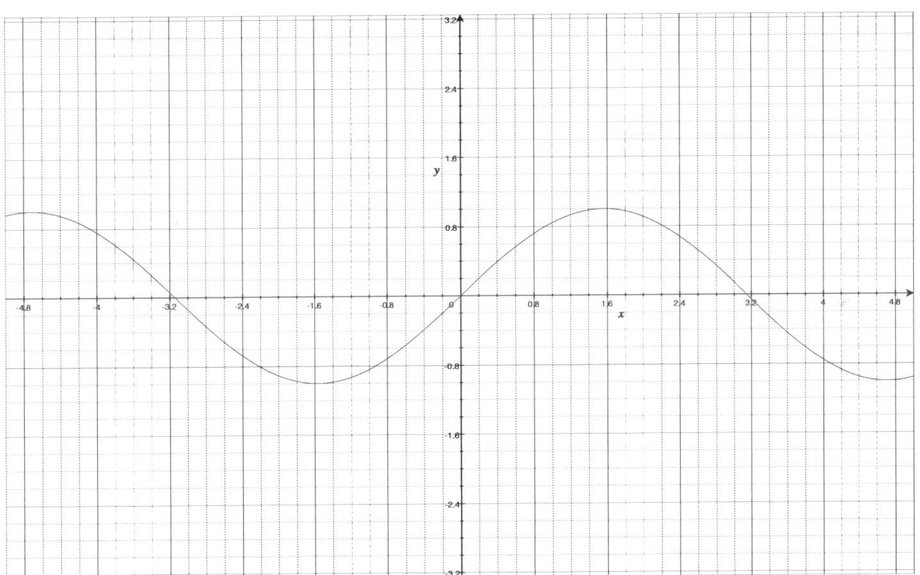

The sine wave function is used to begin training the neural network. Backpropagation is used to train for the sine wave predictor. When the sine wave example is first executed, you will see the results of the training process. Listing 9.1 shows typical output from the sine wave predictor's training process.

Listing 9.1: Training the Sine Wave Predictor

```
Iteration #1 Error:0.48120350975475823 Iteration #2 Er-
ror:0.36753445768855236 Iteration #3 Error:0.3212066601426759
Iteration #4 Error:0.2952410514715732 Iteration #5 Er-
ror:0.2780102928778258 Iteration #6 Error:0.26556861969786527
Iteration #7 Error:0.25605359706505776 Iteration #8 Er-
ror:0.24842242500053566 Iteration #9 Error:0.24204767544134156 It-
```

```
eration #10 Error:0.23653845782593882
...
Iteration #4990 Error:0.02319397662897425 Iteration #4991 Er-
ror:0.02319310934886356 Iteration #4992 Error:0.023192242246688515
Iteration #4993 Error:0.02319137532183077 Iteration #4994 Er-
ror:0.02319050857367858 Iteration #4995 Error:0.02318964200159761
Iteration #4996 Error:0.02318877560498862 Iteration #4997 Er-
ror:0.02318790938322986 Iteration #4998 Error:0.02318704333705867
Iteration #4999 Error:0.02318617746180174502
```

In the beginning, the error rate is fairly high at 48%. This quickly begins to fall off to 36.7% by the second iteration. By the time the 4,999th iteration has occurred, the error rate has fallen to 2.3%. The program is designed to stop before hitting the 5,000th iteration. This succeeds in reducing the error rate to less than 3%.

Additional training would produce a better error rate; however, by limiting the iterations, the program is able to finish in only a few minutes on a regular computer. This program took about two minutes to execute on an Intel Core2 Dual 2mghtz computer.

Once the training is complete, the sine wave is presented to the neural network for prediction. The output from this prediction is shown in Listing 9.2.

Listing 9.2: Predicting the Sine Wave

```
5:Actual=0.76604:Predicted=0.7892166200864351:Difference=2.32% 6:A
ctual=0.86602:Predicted=0.8839210963512845:Difference=1.79% 7:Ac
tual=0.93969:Predicted=0.934526031234053:Difference=0.52% 8:Act
ual=0.9848:Predicted=0.9559577688326862:Difference=2.88% 9:Actu
al=1.0:Predicted=0.9615566601973113:Difference=3.84% 10:Actual=
0.9848:Predicted=0.9558060932656686:Difference=2.90% 11:Actual=
0.93969:Predicted=0.9354447787244102:Difference=0.42% 12:Actual
=0.86602:Predicted=0.8894014978439005:Difference=2.34% 13:Actua
l=0.76604:Predicted=0.801342405700056:Difference=3.53% 14:Actua
l=0.64278:Predicted=0.6633506809125252:Difference=2.06% 15:Actu
al=0.49999:Predicted=0.4910483600917853:Difference=0.89% 16:Act
ual=0.34202:Predicted=0.31286152780645105:Difference=2.92% 17:A
ctual=0.17364:Predicted=0.14608325263568134:Difference=2.76%
18:Actual=0.0:Predicted=-0.008360016796238434:Difference=0.84%
19:Actual=-0.17364:Predicted=-0.15575381460132823:Difference=1.79%
20:Actual=-0.34202:Predicted=-0.3021775158559559:Difference=3.98%
...
490:Actual=-0.64278:Predicted=-0.6515076637590029:Difference=0.87%
491:Actual=-0.76604:Predicted=-0.8133333939237001:Difference=4.73%
492:Actual=-0.86602:Predicted=-0.9076496572125671:Difference=4.16%
493:Actual=-0.93969:Predicted=-0.9492579517460149:Difference=0.96%
494:Actual=-0.9848:Predicted=-0.9644567437192423:Difference=2.03%
```

```
495:Actual=-1.0:Predicted=-0.9664801515670861:Difference=3.35%
496:Actual=-0.9848:Predicted=-0.9579489752650393:Difference=2.69%
497:Actual=-0.93969:Predicted=-0.9340105440194074:Difference=0.57%
498:Actual=-0.86602:Predicted=-0.8829925066754494:Difference=1.70%
499:Actual=-0.76604:Predicted=-0.7913823031308845:Difference=2.53%
```

As you can see, both the actual and predicted values are shown for each element. The neural network was only trained for the first 250 elements; yet, the neural network is able to predict well beyond these first 250. You will also notice that the difference between the actual values and the predicted values rarely exceeds 3%.

Obtaining Sine Wave Data

A class named **ActualData** is provided that will hold the actual "calculated" data for the sine wave. The **ActualData** class also provides convenience methods that can be used to construct the training sets. The **ActualData** class is shown in Listing 9.3.

Listing 9.3: Actual Sine Wave Data (ActualData.cs)

```csharp
using System;
using System.Collections.Generic;
using System.Linq;
using System.Text;

namespace Chapter09Predict
{
    class ActualData
    {
        public static double SinDEG(double deg)
        {
            double rad = deg * (Math.PI / 180);
            double result = Math.Sin(rad);
            return ((int)(result * 100000.0)) / 100000.0;
        }

        private double[] actual;
        private int inputSize;

        private int outputSize;

        public ActualData(int size, int inputSize, int outputSize)
        {
            this.actual = new double[size];
            this.inputSize = inputSize;
            this.outputSize = outputSize;

            int angle = 0;
```

```
        for (int i = 0; i < this.actual.Length; i++)
        {
            this.actual[i] = SinDEG(angle);
            angle += 10;
        }
    }

    public void GetInputData(int offset, double[] target)
    {
        for (int i = 0; i < this.inputSize; i++)
        {
            target[i] = this.actual[offset + i];
        }
    }

    public void GetOutputData(int offset, double[] target)
    {
        for (int i = 0; i < this.outputSize; i++)
        {
            target[i] = this.actual[offset
                + this.inputSize + i];
        }
    }

    }
}
```

The constructor for the **ActualData** class initializes the internal variables to the values of the sine wave. The signature for the constructor for the **ActualData** class is shown here:

```
public ActualData(int size, int inputSize, int outputSize)
```

Three arguments are passed into the **ActualData** constructor. The **size** argument defines how many values of the sine wave will be considered. The **inputSize** argument specifies the number of input neurons. The **outputSize** argument specifies the number of output neurons.

First, a **double** array is allocated that is large enough to hold all of the requested sine wave values. Then, the arguments are copied to instance variables.

```
this.actual = new double[size];
this.inputSize = inputSize;
this.outputSize = outputSize;
```

The sine wave data starts at angle zero.

```
int angle = 0;
```

We then loop through the number of requested values.

```
for (int i = 0; i < this.actual.Length; i++)
```

For each requested value, the sine is calculated using an angle expressed in degrees.

```
  this.actual[i] = SinDEG(angle);
  angle += 10;
}
```

The looping continues with an angle increment of 10 degrees.

Constructing Training Sets for the Sine Wave

As you will recall from previous chapters, you can provide training sets to train the feedforward neural network. These training sets consist of two arrays. The first array specifies input values for the neural network. The second array specifies the ideal outputs for each of the input values. The **ActualData** class provides two methods to retrieve each of these arrays. The first method, named **GetInputData**, is shown here:

```
public void GetInputData(int offset, double[] target)
```

The **offset** variable specifies the offset in the actual data at which copying begins. The **target** array will receive the actual values. The **GetInputData** method simply continues by copying the appropriate values into the **target** array.

```
for (int i = 0; i < this.inputSize; i++)
{
  target[i] = this.actual[offset + i];
}
```

The **GetOutputData** method retrieves the ideal values with which the neural network will be trained. The signature for the **GetOutputData** method is shown here:

```
public void GetOutputData(int offset, double[] target)
```

As above, the **offset** variable specifies the offset in the actual data at which to begin copying ideal values. The **target** array will receive the ideal values. The **GetInputData** method simply continues by copying the appropriate values into the **target** array.

```
for (int i = 0; i < this.outputSize; i++)
{
  target[i] = this.actual[offset + this.inputSize + i];
}
```

The above loop will populate the target array with the actual values. Table 9.2 shows these values.

Table 9.2: Sine Wave Training Data

Input 1	Input 2	Input 3	Input 4	Input 5	Output 1
0.0	0.17364	0.34202	0.49999	0.64278	0.76604
0.17364	0.34202	0.49999	0.64278	0.76604	0.86602
0.34202	0.49999	0.64278	0.76604	0.86602	0.93969
0.49999	0.64278	0.76604	0.86602	0.93969	0.9848
0.64278	0.76604	0.86602	0.93969	0.9848	1.0
0.76604	0.86602	0.93969	0.9848	1.0	0.9848
0.86602	0.93969	0.9848	1.0	0.9848	0.93969
0.93969	0.9848	1.0	0.9848	0.93969	0.86602
0.9848	1.0	0.9848	0.93969	0.86602	0.76604
1.0	0.9848	0.93969	0.86602	0.76604	0.64278
0.9848	0.93969	0.86602	0.76604	0.64278	0.49999
0.93969	0.86602	0.76604	0.64278	0.49999	0.34202
0.86602	0.76604	0.64278	0.49999	0.34202	0.17364
0.76604	0.64278	0.49999	0.34202	0.17364	0.0
0.64278	0.49999	0.34202	0.17364	0.0	-0.17364
0.49999	0.34202	0.17364	0.0	-0.17364	-0.34202
0.34202	0.17364	0.0	-0.17364	-0.34202	-0.5
0.17364	0.0	-0.17364	-0.34202	-0.5	-0.64278
0.0	-0.17364	-0.34202	-0.5	-0.64278	-0.76604
-0.17364	-0.34202	-0.5	-0.64278	-0.76604	-0.86602
-0.34202	-0.5	-0.64278	-0.76604	-0.86602	-0.93969
-0.5	-0.64278	-0.76604	-0.86602	-0.93969	-0.9848
-0.64278	-0.76604	-0.86602	-0.93969	-0.9848	-1.0
-0.76604	-0.86602	-0.93969	-0.9848	-1.0	-0.9848
-0.86602	-0.93969	-0.9848	-1.0	-0.9848	-0.93969
-0.93969	-0.9848	-1.0	-0.9848	-0.93969	-0.86602
-0.9848	-1.0	-0.9848	-0.93969	-0.86602	-0.76604

These training values will be used in the next section to train the neural network.

Training the Sine Wave Predictor

The sine wave predictor uses a hyperbolic tangent activation function, rather than the sigmoid activation function that many of the neural networks in this book have used. This is because the sine function returns numbers between -1 and 1. This can be seen in Table 9.2. The sigmoid function can only handle numbers between 0 and 1, and thus would fail when presented with the values of the sine function.

As mentioned earlier, the neural network is trained with a backpropagation algorithm. Backpropagation was covered in chapter 5, "Feedforward Backpropagation Neural Networks." When using the hyperbolic tangent as an activation function, it is important to use a low learning rate and momentum. Otherwise, the adjustments will be too large and the network may fail to converge on an acceptable error rate.

The training occurs in the **TrainNetworkBackprop** method. The signature for the **TrainNetworkBackprop** is shown here:

```
private void TrainNetworkBackprop()
```

This method begins by creating a **Backpropagation** object to train the network. A learning rate of 0.001 and a momentum of 0.1 are used. These are sufficiently small to properly train this neural network.

```
Train train = new Backpropagation(this.network, this.input,
   this.ideal, 0.001, 0.1);
```

A local variable named **epoch** is created to count the number of training epochs.

```
int epoch = 1;
```

The loop is entered, and then for each training epoch the **Iteration** method is called on the **train** object.

```
do
{
  train.Iteration();
  Console.WriteLine("Iteration #" + epoch + " Error:"
    + train.Error);
  epoch++;
} while ((epoch < 5000) && (train.Error > 0.01));
```

This continues until either 5,000 epochs have passed, or the error rate is less than 1%.

Predicting the Future of the Sine Wave

To see how effective the neural network is at predicting the future of the sine wave, the **Display** method should be called. The signature for the **Display** method is shown here:

```
private void Display()
```

Input and output arrays need to be created to hold the input to the neural network, as well as its output.

```
double[] input = new double[SineWave.INPUT_SIZE];
double[] output = new double[SineWave.OUTPUT_SIZE];
```

Next, we loop through all of the actual data. The neural network was not trained on all of the actual data, so some of this will be prediction.

```
for (int i = SineWave.INPUT_SIZE; i < SineWave.ACTUAL_SIZE; i++)
{
```

We obtain the input and output data from the actual data array. The output data are the ideal values. We compare the actual output of the neural network to this data.

```
this.actual.GetInputData(i - SineWave.INPUT_SIZE, input);
this.actual.GetOutputData(i - SineWave.INPUT_SIZE, output);
```

A **StringBuilder** is created to hold the formatted data.

```
StringBuilder str = new StringBuilder();
str.Append(i);
str.Append(":Actual=");
for (int j = 0; j < output.Length; j++)
{
  if (j > 0)
  {
    str.Append(',');
  }
  str.Append(output[j]);
}
```

The neural network is called to compute its prediction.

```
double[] predict = this.network.ComputeOutputs(input);
```

The predicted value is displayed with the actual value.

```
str.Append(":Predicted=");
for (int j = 0; j < output.Length; j++)
{
  if (j > 0)
  {
    str.Append(',');
  }
  str.Append(predict[j]);
}
```

The difference is also displayed as a percentage.

```
str.Append(":Difference=");

ErrorCalculation error = new ErrorCalculation();
error.UpdateError(predict, output);

str.Append(error.CalculateRMS().ToString("N2"));

Console.WriteLine(str.ToString());
}
```

Finally, the line for this actual value is output. This neural network does a reasonably good job of predicting future values. There are many different ways that the input data can be presented for prediction. In the next chapter we will explore how to create neural networks that attempt to predict financial markets.

Chapter Summary

The feedforward neural network is very adept at recognizing patterns. Used properly, a feedforward neural network can be used to predict future patterns. Such neural networks are called predictive, or temporal neural networks. A predictive neural network is not one specific type of neural network; rather, it is any type of neural network used for prediction. This book uses feedforward neural networks for all prediction examples.

Implementing a feedforward neural network that predicts is simply a matter of properly constructing the input and output neurons. Time is divided into several blocks, called time slices. For example, a neural network may have five known time slices followed by an unknown time slice. This would produce a neural network with five input neurons and one output neuron. Such a neural network would be trained using known actual data in groups of six time slices. The first five time slices in each group would be the input neurons. The sixth would be the ideal output. To have the neural network predict, you would simply provide five known time slices to the input neurons. The output from the output neuron would be the neural network's prediction for the sixth time slice.

An entire book could easily be written on predictive neural networks. This chapter introduced predictive neural networks at a basic level by predicting the sine wave. Perhaps one of the most common applications of predictive neural networks is predicting movement in financial markets. The next chapter will provide an introduction to programming neural networks for financial market predictions.

Vocabulary

Actual Data

Predictive Neural Network

Sine Wave

Temporal Neural Network

Time Slice

Questions for Review

1.   Can a self-organizing map be used for prediction? If so, how would you set up the input and output neurons?

2.   When a feedforward neural network is used for prediction, what do the input neurons represent? What do the output neurons represent?

3.   You have 500 time slices of information. How could you use this data to both train and test a predictive neural network.

4.   How would you choose between using a hyperbolic tangent and a sigmoid function as the activation function for a predictive neural network?

5.   Why might you use more than one output neuron in a predictive neural network?

CHAPTER 10: APPLICATION TO THE FINANCIAL MARKETS

- Creating Input and Output Neurons for Prediction
- How to Create Training Sets for a Predictive Neural Network
- Predicting the Sine Wave

In the last chapter, you saw that neural networks can be used to predict trends in numeric data, as in the sine wave example. Predicting the sine wave was useful in demonstrating how to create neural networks that can predict, but it has little real world application. The purpose of chapter 9 was to introduce the fundamentals of how to predict with a neural network. This chapter builds upon the material presented in chapter 9 by providing you with a foundation for applying neural networks to financial market problems.

In this chapter, a relatively simple program is presented that attempts to predict the S&P 500 index. The keyword in the last sentence is "attempts." This chapter is for educational purposes only and is by no means an investment strategy, since past performance is no indication of future returns. The material presented here can be used as a starting point from which to adapt neural networks to augment your own investment strategy.

Collecting Data for the S&P 500 Neural Network

Before we discuss how to predict direction in the S&P 500, we should first clarify what the S&P 500 is and how it functions.

"The S&P 500 is a stock market index containing the stocks of 500 Large-Cap corporations, most of which are American. The index is the most notable of the many indices owned and maintained by Standard & Poor's, a division of McGraw-Hill. S&P 500 is used in reference not only to the index but also to the 500 companies that have their common stock included in the index."

Figure 10.1 shows movement in the S&P 500 since 1950.

Figure 10.1: The S&P 500 stock index.

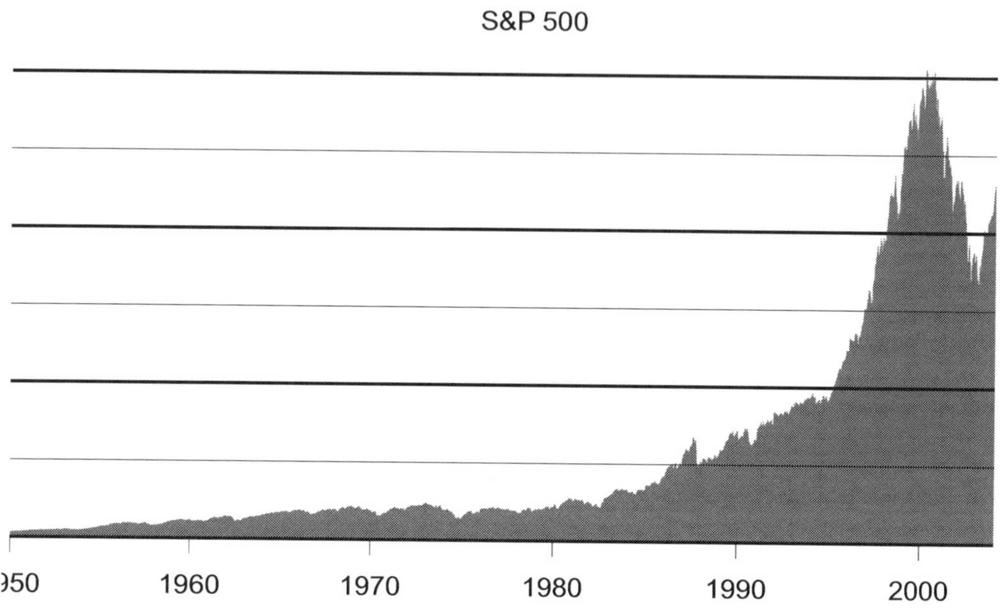

Historical S&P 500 values will be used to predict future S&P 500 values; however, the S&P 500 data will not be considered in a vacuum. The current prime interest rate will also be adjusted to aid in the detection of patterns. The prime interest rate is defined as follows:

"Prime rate is a term applied in many countries to a reference interest rate used by banks. The term originally indicated the rate of interest at which banks lent to favored customers, [...] though this is no longer always the case. Some variable interest rates may be expressed as a percentage above or below prime rate."

Figure 10.2 shows the US prime interest rate over time.

Figure 10.2: US prime interest rate.

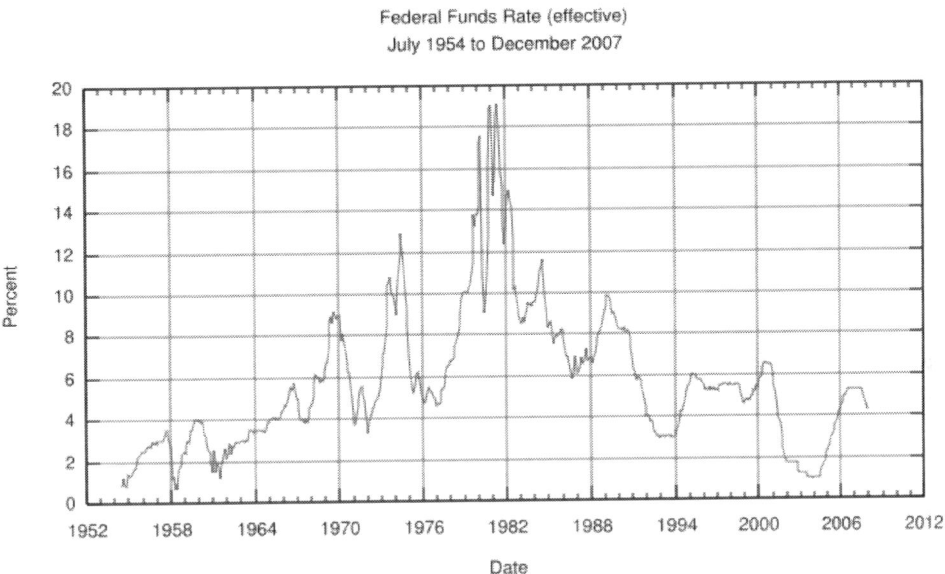

The neural network presented in this chapter must be provided with both the S&P 500 historical data and the prime interest rate historical data. The program is designed to receive both data inputs in comma separated value (CSV) files.

Obtaining S&P 500 Historical Data

When you download the examples for this book, you will also be downloading a set of S&P 500 historical data. The data provided was current as of May 2008. If you would like more current financial data, you can obtain it from many sites on the Internet, free of charge. One such site is Yahoo! Finance. Historical S&P 500 data from the 1950s to present can be accessed at the URL:

```
http://finance.yahoo.com/q/hp?s=%5EGSPC
```

The file **sp500.csv**, which is included with the companion download for this book, contains historical S&P 500 data from the 1950s to May 14, 2008. Data from this file is shown in Listing 10.1.

Listing 10.1: S&P 500 Historical Data (sp500.csv)

```
Date,Open,High,Low,Close,Volume,Adj Close 2008-04-
18,1369.00,1395.90,1369.00,1390.33,4222380000,1390.33 2008-
04-17,1363.37,1368.60,1357.25,1365.56,3713880000,1365.56
2008-04-16,1337.02,1365.49,1337.02,1364.71,4260370000,1364.71
```

```
2008-04-15,1331.72,1337.72,1324.35,1334.43,3581230000,1334.43
2008-04-14,1332.20,1335.64,1326.16,1328.32,3565020000,1328.32
2008-04-11,1357.98,1357.98,1331.21,1332.83,3723790000,1332.83
2008-04-10,1355.37,1367.24,1350.11,1360.55,3686150000,1360.55
2008-04-09,1365.50,1368.39,1349.97,1354.49,3556670000,1354.49
2008-04-08,1370.16,1370.16,1360.62,1365.54,3602500000,1365.54
2008-04-07,1373.69,1386.74,1369.02,1372.54,3747780000,1372.54
2008-04-04,1369.85,1380.91,1362.83,1370.40,3703100000,1370.40
...
1950-01-23,16.92,16.92,16.92,16.92,1340000,16.92 1950-
01-20,16.90,16.90,16.90,16.90,1440000,16.90 1950-
01-19,16.87,16.87,16.87,16.87,1170000,16.87 1950-
01-18,16.85,16.85,16.85,16.85,1570000,16.85
1950-01-17,16.86,16.86,16.86,16.86,1790000,16.86
1950-01-16,16.72,16.72,16.72,16.72,1460000,16.72
1950-01-13,16.67,16.67,16.67,16.67,3330000,16.67 1950-
01-12,16.76,16.76,16.76,16.76,2970000,16.76 1950-
01-11,17.09,17.09,17.09,17.09,2630000,17.09 1950-
01-10,17.03,17.03,17.03,17.03,2160000,17.03
1950-01-09,17.08,17.08,17.08,17.08,2520000,17.08
1950-01-06,16.98,16.98,16.98,16.98,2010000,16.98
1950-01-05,16.93,16.93,16.93,16.93,2550000,16.93 1950-
01-04,16.85,16.85,16.85,16.85,1890000,16.85 1950-01-
03,16.66,16.66,16.66,16.66,1260000,16.66
```

A CSV file contains data such that each line is a record and commas separate individual fields within each line. As mentioned earlier, the example presented in this chapter also uses prime interest rate data.

Obtaining Prime Interest Rate Data

There are many Internet sites that provide historical prime interest rate data. The companion download for this book contains a file named **prime.csv**. This file contains prime interest rates from approximately the same time period as the S&P 500 data provided. The contents of **prime.csv** are shown in Listing 10.2.

Listing 10.2: Prime Interest Rate Historical Data

```
date,prime
1955-08-04,3.25
1955-10-14,3.50
1956-04-13,3.75
1956-08-21,4.00
1957-08-06,4.50
1958-01-22,4.00
1958-04-21,3.50
1958-09-11,4.00
1959-05-18,4.50
```

```
...
2005-12-13,7.25
2006-01-31,7.50
2006-03-28,7.75
2006-05-10,8.00
2006-06-29,8.25
2007-09-18,7.75
2007-10-31,7.50
2007-12-11,7.25
2008-01-22,6.50
2008-01-30,6.00
2008-03-18,5.25
```

The data in this file will be combined with the S&P 500 data to form the actual data to be used to train the S&P 500 neural network.

Running the S&P 500 Prediction Program

There are two modes of operation for the S&P 500 prediction application. The mode of operation depends upon the command line arguments provided to the program. If no command line arguments are specified, then the neural network is loaded from the file **sp500.net**. If the command argument FULL is specified, then the neural network will train a new neural network and save it to disk under the name **sp500.net**.

It can take many hours to completely train the neural network. Therefore, you will not want to run it in full mode every time. However, if you choose to change some of the training parameters, you should retrain the neural network and generate a new **sp500.net** file. The companion download contains an **sp500.net** file that has been trained within 2% accuracy of the training sets.

If you run the program in full training mode, the following output will be produced:

Listing 10.3: Training the SP500 Neural Network

```
Samples read: 14667 Iteration(Backprop) #1
Error:0.6999154401150052 Iteration(Backprop) #2
Error:0.6464464887928701 Iteration(Backprop) #3 Er-
ror:0.584286620498403 Iteration(Backprop) #4
Error:0.5161413540009822 Iteration(Backprop) #5
Error:0.44688028770366317 Iteration(Backprop) #6 Er-
ror:0.3832980672593392 Iteration(Backprop) #7
  Error:0.33189098575632436 Iteration(Backprop) #8
Error:0.2958585679317178 Iteration(Backprop) #9
Error:0.2738894563079073 Iteration(Backprop) #10
Error:0.2619015539956993

...
```

```
Iteration(Backprop)  #2038  Error:0.020032706833329087
Iteration(Backprop)  #2039  Error:0.02002936831637675
Iteration(Backprop)  #2040  Error:0.020026031153749693
Iteration(Backprop)  #2041  Error:0.020022695344982695
Iteration(Backprop)  #2042  Error:0.02001936088961063
Iteration(Backprop)  #2043  Error:0.02001602778716852
Iteration(Backprop)  #2044  Error:0.0200126960371914
Iteration(Backprop)  #2045  Error:0.020009365639214557
Iteration(Backprop)  #2046  Error:0.020006036592773283
Iteration(Backprop)  #2047  Error:0.020002708897403004
Iteration(Backprop)  #2048  Error:0.019999382552639385
```

As you can see, it took a considerable number of training iterations to train the neural network to the desired level. Immediately after the training for this network was complete, the neural network was run in prediction mode and the following output was produced:

Listing 10.4: Predicting the SP500 Neural Network

```
2007-01-03:Start=1416.6,Actual % Change=-0.12%,Predicted % Change=
1.78%:Difference=1.90%
2007-01-04:Start=1418.34,Actual % Change=0.12%,Predicted % Change=
1.39%:Difference=1.27%
2007-01-05:Start=1409.71,Actual % Change=-0.61%,Predicted %
Change= 1.06%:Difference=1.67%
2007-01-08:Start=1412.84,Actual % Change=0.22%,Predicted % Change=
1.28%:Difference=1.06%
2007-01-09:Start=1412.11,Actual % Change=-0.05%,Predicted %
Change= 1.35%:Difference=1.41%
2007-01-10:Start=1414.85,Actual % Change=0.19%,Predicted % Change=
0.87%:Difference=0.67%
2007-01-11:Start=1423.82,Actual % Change=0.63%,Predicted % Change=
0.53%:Difference=0.11%
2007-01-12:Start=1430.73,Actual % Change=0.49%,Predicted % Change=
1.42%:Difference=0.94%
2007-01-16:Start=1431.9,Actual % Change=0.08%,Predicted % Change=
1.71%:Difference=1.63%
...
2008-03-27:Start=1325.76,Actual % Change=-1.15%,Predicted %
Change= 2.85%:Difference=3.99%
2008-03-28:Start=1315.22,Actual % Change=-0.80%,Predicted %
Change= 3.20%:Difference=4.00%
2008-03-31:Start=1322.7,Actual % Change=0.57%,Predicted % Change=
-0.78%:Difference=1.34%
2008-04-01:Start=1370.18,Actual % Change=3.59%,Predicted % Change=
-0.43%:Difference=4.02%
2008-04-02:Start=1367.53,Actual % Change=-0.19%,Predicted %
Change= 1.30%:Difference=1.49%
```

```
2008-04-03:Start=1369.31,Actual % Change=0.13%,Predicted % Change=
-0.56%:Difference=0.69%
2008-04-04:Start=1370.4,Actual % Change=0.08%,Predicted % Change=
1.30%:Difference=1.22%
2008-04-07:Start=1372.54,Actual % Change=0.16%,Predicted % Change=
2.25%:Difference=2.09%
2008-04-08:Start=1365.54,Actual % Change=-0.51%,Predicted %
Change= 2.09%:Difference=2.60%
2008-04-09:Start=1354.49,Actual % Change=-0.81%,Predicted %
Change= 2.23%:Difference=3.04%
2008-04-10:Start=1360.55,Actual % Change=0.45%,Predicted % Change=
1.50%:Difference=1.05%
2008-04-11:Start=1332.83,Actual % Change=-2.04%,Predicted %
Change= -0.94%:Difference=1.10%
2008-04-14:Start=1328.32,Actual % Change=-0.34%,Predicted %
Change= -1.25%:Difference=0.91%
2008-04-15:Start=1334.43,Actual % Change=0.46%,Predicted % Change=
0.43%:Difference=0.03%
2008-04-16:Start=1364.71,Actual % Change=2.27%,Predicted % Change=
-0.03%:Difference=2.30%
2008-04-17:Start=1365.56,Actual % Change=0.06%,Predicted % Change=
-0.02%:Difference=0.08%
2008-04-18:Start=1390.33,Actual % Change=1.81%,Predicted % Change=
1.04%:Difference=0.77%
```

As you can see from the above data, the prediction is far from perfect, although it does generally stay within an accuracy range of 10%. It could easily fare much better, or far worse, as additional data becomes available.

Creating the Actual S&P 500 Data

As mentioned earlier, the actual neural network input data is composed of both the prime interest rate and S&P 500 historical data. This data is stored in a class named **SP500Actual**. This class is shown in Listing 10.5.

Listing 10.5: Storing Actual S&P 500 Data (SP500Actual.cs)

```
using System;
using System.Collections.Generic;
using System.Linq;
using System.Text;

using HeatonResearchNeural.Util;

namespace Chapter10SP500
{
    class SP500Actual
```

```csharp
{
    private List<InterestRate> rates =
        new List<InterestRate>();
    private List<FinancialSample> samples =
        new List<FinancialSample>();
    private int inputSize;
    private int outputSize;

    public SP500Actual(int inputSize, int outputSize)
    {
        this.inputSize = inputSize;
        this.outputSize = outputSize;
    }

    public void CalculatePercents()
    {
        double prev = -1;
        foreach (FinancialSample sample in this.samples)
        {
            if (prev != -1)
            {
                double movement = sample.GetAmount() - prev;
                double percent = movement / prev;
                sample.SetPercent(percent);
            }
            prev = sample.GetAmount();
        }
    }

    public void GetInputData(int offset, double[] input)
    {
        Object[] samplesArray = this.samples.ToArray();
        // get SP500 & prime data
        for (int i = 0; i < this.inputSize; i++)
        {
            FinancialSample sample =
                (FinancialSample)samplesArray[offset
                    + i];
            input[i] = sample.GetPercent();
            input[i + this.outputSize] = sample.GetRate();
        }
    }

    public void GetOutputData(int offset, double[] output)
    {
        Object[] samplesArray = this.samples.ToArray();
```

```csharp
    for (int i = 0; i < this.outputSize; i++)
    {
        FinancialSample sample =
           (FinancialSample)samplesArray[offset
                + this.inputSize + i];
        output[i] = sample.GetPercent();
    }


}

public double GetPrimeRate(DateTime date)
{
    double currentRate = 0;

    foreach (InterestRate rate in this.rates)
    {
        if (rate.GetEffectiveDate().CompareTo(date) > 0)
        {
            return currentRate;
        }
        else
        {
            currentRate = rate.GetRate();
        }
    }
    return currentRate;
}

public IList<FinancialSample> GetSamples()
{
    return this.samples;
}

public void Load(String sp500Filename,
    String primeFilename)
{
    LoadSP500(sp500Filename);
    LoadPrime(primeFilename);
    StitchInterestRates();
    CalculatePercents();
}

public void LoadPrime(String primeFilename)
{
    ReadCSV csv = new ReadCSV(primeFilename);
```

```csharp
        while (csv.Next())
        {
            DateTime date = csv.GetDate("date");
            double rate = csv.GetDouble("prime");
            InterestRate ir = new InterestRate(date, rate);
            this.rates.Add(ir);
        }

        csv.Close();
        this.rates.Sort();
    }

    public void LoadSP500(String sp500Filename)
    {
        ReadCSV csv = new ReadCSV(sp500Filename);
        while (csv.Next())
        {
            DateTime date = csv.GetDate("date");
            double amount = csv.GetDouble("adj close");
            FinancialSample sample = new FinancialSample();
            sample.SetAmount(amount);
            sample.SetDate(date);
            this.samples.Add(sample);
        }
        csv.Close();
        this.samples.Sort();
    }

    public int Size()
    {
        return this.samples.Count;
    }

    public void StitchInterestRates()
    {
        foreach (FinancialSample sample in this.samples)
        {
            double rate = GetPrimeRate(sample.GetDate());
            sample.SetRate(rate);
        }
    }
}
```

There are several functions that this class provides. These functions will be explored in the next sections.

Financial Samples

The primary purpose for the SP500Actual class is to provide an SP500 quote and the prime interest rate for any given day that the US stock market was open. Additionally, the percent change between the current quote and the previous quote is stored. Together, these values are called a sample. Samples are stored in the **FinancialSample** class. The **FinancialSample** class is shown in Listing 10.6.

Listing 10.6: Financial Samples (FinancialSample.cs)

```
using System;
using System.Collections.Generic;
using System.Linq;
using System.Text;

using HeatonResearchNeural.Util;

namespace Chapter10SP500
{
    class FinancialSample : IComparable<FinancialSample>
    {
        private double amount;
        private double rate;
        private DateTime date;
        private double percent;

        public int CompareTo(FinancialSample other)
        {
            return GetDate().CompareTo(other.GetDate());
        }

        public double GetAmount()
        {
            return this.amount;
        }

        public DateTime GetDate()
        {
            return this.date;
        }

        public double GetPercent()
        {
            return this.percent;
        }

        public double GetRate()
```

```csharp
        {
            return this.rate;
        }
        public void SetAmount(double amount)
        {
            this.amount = amount;
        }


        public void SetDate(DateTime date)
        {
            this.date = date;
        }


        public void SetPercent(double percent)
        {
            this.percent = percent;
        }


        public void SetRate(double rate)
        {
            this.rate = rate;
        }


        override public String ToString()
        {
            StringBuilder result = new StringBuilder();
            result.Append(ReadCSV.DisplayDate(this.date));
            result.Append(", Amount: ");
            result.Append(this.amount);
            result.Append(", Prime Rate: ");
            result.Append(this.rate);
            result.Append(", Percent from Previous: ");
            result.Append(this.percent.ToString("N2"));
            return result.ToString();
        }

    }
}
```

Another important feature of the **FinancialSample** class is that it implements the **IComparable** interface. This allows the **FinancialSample** objects to be added to a sorted C# collection and be ordered by their dates.

Get Prime Rate for a Day

The prime interest rate data file, named **prime.csv**, only contains the prime interest rate for days on which the interest rate changed. Therefore, a special method is required to determine what the interest rate was on a specific date. This method is called **GetPrimeRate**. The signature for **GetPrimeRate** is shown here:

```
public double GetPrimeRate(DateTime date)
```

First, a variable is defined to hold the last rate found, which is the current rate. This variable is named **currentRate**.

```
double currentRate = 0;
```

Next, the method loops through all of the interest rates. These interest rates are stored in a sorted list, so the interest rates for the earliest dates occur first.

```
foreach (InterestRate rate in this.rates)
```

As soon as the first interest rate is found with a date beyond the date of interest, then the rate stored in **currentRate** is the interest rate for the specified date. If the variable **currentRate** has not yet been set, then the specified date is earlier than the dates for our data. If this is the case, then we have no interest rate data for the specified date and a value of **null** is returned.

```
if (rate.GetEffectiveDate().CompareTo(date) > 0)
{
  return currentRate;
}
else
{
```

Otherwise, the specified date has not yet been reached, so the **currentRate** variable is updated.

```
    currentRate = rate.GetRate();
    }
  }
```

If we reach the end of the list, then the final interest rate is simply returned. We assume that the rate has not changed since our last data value and specified date. As long as our interest rate file is up to date, and the specified date is not in the future, this is a valid assumption.

```
return currentRate;
}
```

Since the **GetPrimeRate** method must iterate to find the interest rate, calling it is somewhat expensive; therefore, each S&P 500 sample must be "stitched" to the correct interest rate.

Stitching the Rates to Ranges

The **StitchInterestRates** function is called to find the appropriate interest rate for each of the **FinancialSample** objects. The signature for the **StitchInterestRates** method is shown here:

```
public void StitchInterestRates()
```

We begin by looping through all the **FinancialSample** objects.

```
foreach (FinancialSample sample in this.samples)
```

For each **FinancialSample** object, we obtain the prime interest rate.

```
    double rate = GetPrimeRate(sample.GetDate());
    sample.SetRate(rate);
    }
}
```

This process is continued until all the **FinancialSample** objects have been processed.

To train the neural network, input and ideal data must be created. The next two sections discuss how this is done.

Creating the Input Data

To create input data for the neural network, the **GetInputDate** method of the **SP500Actual** class is used. The signature for the **GetInputData** method is shown here:

```
public void GetInputData(int offset, double[] input)
```

Two arguments are passed to the **GetInputData** method. The **offset** argument specifies the zero-based index at which the input data is to be extracted. The **input** argument provides a **double** array into which the financial samples will be copied. This array also specifies the number of **FinancialSample** objects to process. Sufficient **FinancialSample** objects will be processed to fill the array.

First, an array of references to the samples is obtained.

```
Object[] samplesArray = this.samples.ToArray();
```

Next, we loop forward, according to the size of the **input** array.

```
for (int i = 0; i < this.inputSize; i++)
{
```

Each **FinancialSample** object is then obtained.

```
FinancialSample sample = (FinancialSample)samplesArray[offset +
i];
```

Both the percent change and rate for each sample are copied. The neural network then uses these two values to make a prediction.

```
input[i] = sample.GetPercent();
input[i + this.outputSize] = sample.GetRate();
}
```

As you can see, the input to the neural network consists of percentage changes and the current level of the prime interest rate. Using the percentage changes is different than how input was handled for the neural network presented in chapter 9. In chapter 9, the actual numbers were added to the neural network. The program in this chapter will instead track percentage moves. In general, the S&P 500 has increased over its history, and has not often revisited ranges. Therefore, more patterns can be found by tracking the percent changes, rather than actual point values.

Creating the Ideal Output Data

For supervised training, the ideal outputs must also be calculated from known data. While the inputs include both interest rate and quote data, the outputs only contain quote percentage data. We are attempting to predict percentage movement in the S&P 500; we are not attempting to predict fluctuations in the prime interest rate.

The ideal output data is created by calling the **GetOutputData** method. The signature for the **GetOutputData** method is shown here:

```
public void GetOutputData(int offset, double[] output)
{
```

Two arguments are passed to the **GetInputData**. The **offset** argument specifies the zero-based index at which the output data is to be extracted. The **output** argument provides a **double** array into which the financial samples will be copied. This array also specifies the number of **FinancialSample** objects to be processed. Sufficient **FinancialSample** objects will be processed to fill the array.

First, an array of references to the samples is obtained.

```
Object[] samplesArray = this.samples.ToArray();
```

Next, we loop through the samples.

```
for (int i = 0; i < this.outputSize; i++)
{
```

For each sample, we copy only the percentage change to the output array.

```
FinancialSample sample = (FinancialSample)samplesArray[offset
                    + this.inputSize + i];
output[i] = sample.GetPercent();
}
```

The prime interest rate is not copied, because the neural network is not trying to predict fluctuations in the prime interest rate. The neural network is only predicting fluctuations in the S&P 500 index.

Training the S&P 500 Network

A combination of backpropagation and simulated annealing is used to train this neural network. A complex network such as this often benefits from a hybrid training approach.

Local Minima

The error for a backpropagation training algorithm has a tendency to encounter the local minima problem. Ideally, you should train until the global minimum is reached. However, the backpropagation algorithm can sometimes mistake a local minimum for the global minimum. Consider Figure 10.3.

Figure 10.3: Global and Local Minima

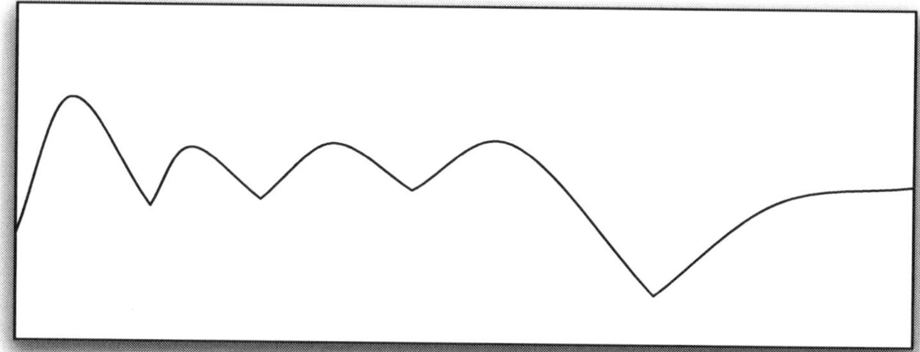

As you can see in Figure 10.3, there are four local minima. Only one of these local minima is the global minimum. To avoid the local minima problem, a hybrid training algorithm is used.

Hybrid Training

The main class for the S&P 500 prediction example is **PredictSP500**. This class should be executed to run this example. The **PredictSP500** class is shown in Listing 10.7:

Listing 10.7: Try to Predict the S&P 500 (PredictSP500.cs)

```
using System;
using System.Collections.Generic;
using System.Linq;
using System.Text;

using HeatonResearchNeural.Activation;
using HeatonResearchNeural.Feedforward;
using HeatonResearchNeural.Feedforward.Train;
using HeatonResearchNeural.Feedforward.Train.Backpropagation;
using HeatonResearchNeural.Feedforward.Train.Anneal;
using HeatonResearchNeural.Util;

namespace Chapter10SP500
{
    class PredictSP500
    {

        public const int TRAINING_SIZE = 500;
        public const int INPUT_SIZE = 10;
        public const int OUTPUT_SIZE = 1;
        public const int NEURONS_HIDDEN_1 = 20;
        public const int NEURONS_HIDDEN_2 = 0;
        public const double MAX_ERROR = 0.02;
        public DateTime PREDICT_FROM =
            ReadCSV.ParseDate("2007-01-01");
        public DateTime LEARN_FROM =
            ReadCSV.ParseDate("1980-01-01");

        static void Main(string[] args)
        {
            PredictSP500 predict = new PredictSP500();
            if (args.Length > 0 && args[0].Equals(
            "full", StringComparison.CurrentCultureIgnoreCase))
                predict.Run(true);
            else
                predict.Run(false);
        }

        private double[][] input;
```

```csharp
private double[][] ideal;
private FeedforwardNetwork network;

private SP500Actual actual;

public void CreateNetwork()
{
    ActivationFunction threshold = new ActivationTANH();
    this.network = new FeedforwardNetwork();
    this.network.AddLayer(new FeedforwardLayer(threshold,
            PredictSP500.INPUT_SIZE * 2));
    this.network.AddLayer(new FeedforwardLayer(threshold,
            PredictSP500.NEURONS_HIDDEN_1));
    if (PredictSP500.NEURONS_HIDDEN_2 > 0)
    {
        this.network.AddLayer(
          new FeedforwardLayer(threshold,
               PredictSP500.NEURONS_HIDDEN_2));
    }
    this.network.AddLayer(new FeedforwardLayer(threshold,
            PredictSP500.OUTPUT_SIZE));
    this.network.Reset();
}

public void Display()
{
    double[] present = new double[INPUT_SIZE * 2];
    double[] predict = new double[OUTPUT_SIZE];
    double[] actualOutput = new double[OUTPUT_SIZE];

    int index = 0;
    foreach (FinancialSample sample in
         this.actual.GetSamples())
    {
        if (sample.GetDate().CompareTo(
          this.PREDICT_FROM) > 0)
        {
            StringBuilder str = new StringBuilder();
            str.Append(ReadCSV.DisplayDate(
                sample.GetDate()));
            str.Append(":Start=");
            str.Append(sample.GetAmount());

            this.actual.GetInputData(index -
                INPUT_SIZE, present);
```

```csharp
            this.actual.GetOutputData(index -
                INPUT_SIZE, actualOutput);

            predict = this.network.
                ComputeOutputs(present);
            str.Append(",Actual % Change=");
            str.Append(actualOutput[0].ToString("N2"));
            str.Append(",Predicted % Change= ");
            str.Append(predict[0].ToString("N2"));

            str.Append(":Difference=");

            ErrorCalculation error =
                new ErrorCalculation();
            error.UpdateError(predict, actualOutput);
            str.Append(error.CalculateRMS().
                ToString("N2"));

            //

            Console.WriteLine(str.ToString());
        }

        index++;
    }
}

private void GenerateTrainingSets()
{
    this.input = new double[TRAINING_SIZE][];
    this.ideal = new double[TRAINING_SIZE][];

    // find where we are starting from
    int startIndex = 0;
    foreach (FinancialSample sample in
        this.actual.GetSamples())
    {
        if (sample.GetDate().CompareTo(
          this.LEARN_FROM) > 0)
        {
            break;
        }
        startIndex++;
    }

    // create a sample factor across the training area
```

```
            int eligibleSamples = TRAINING_SIZE - startIndex;
            if (eligibleSamples == 0)
            {
                Console.WriteLine(
        "Need an earlier date for LEARN_FROM or a smaller number for
TRAINING_SIZE.");
                return;
            }
            int factor = eligibleSamples / TRAINING_SIZE;

            // grab the actual training data from that point
            for (int i = 0; i < TRAINING_SIZE; i++)
            {
                this.actual.GetInputData(startIndex + (i
                    * factor), this.input[i]);
                this.actual.GetOutputData(startIndex + (i
                    * factor), this.ideal[i]);
            }
        }


        public void LoadNeuralNetwork()
        {
            this.network = (FeedforwardNetwork)
                SerializeObject.Load("sp500.net");
        }


        public void Run(bool full)
        {
            try
            {
                this.actual = new SP500Actual(
                    INPUT_SIZE, OUTPUT_SIZE);
                this.actual.Load("sp500.csv", "prime.csv");

                Console.WriteLine("Samples read: "
                    + this.actual.Size());

                if (full)
                {
                    CreateNetwork();
                    GenerateTrainingSets();

                    TrainNetworkHybrid();

                    SaveNeuralNetwork();
                }
```

```
            else
            {
                LoadNeuralNetwork();
            }

            Display();

        }
        catch (Exception e)
        {
            Console.WriteLine(e);
            Console.WriteLine(e.StackTrace);
        }
    }


public void SaveNeuralNetwork()
{
    SerializeObject.Save("sp500.net", this.network);
}


private void TrainNetworkHybrid()
{
    Train train = new Backpropagation(this.network,
            this.input,
            this.ideal, 0.00001, 0.1);
    double lastError = Double.MaxValue;
    int epoch = 1;
    int lastAnneal = 0;

    do
    {
        train.Iteration();
        double error = train.Error;

        Console.WriteLine("Iteration(Backprop) #"
          + epoch + " Error:"
                + error);

        if (error > 0.05)
        {
            if ((lastAnneal > 100)
 && (error > lastError || Math.Abs(error - lastError) < 0.0001))
            {
                TrainNetworkAnneal();
                lastAnneal = 0;
            }
```

```
                }

                lastError = train.Error;
                epoch++;
                lastAnneal++;
            } while (train.Error > MAX_ERROR);
        }


        private void TrainNetworkAnneal()
        {
            Console.WriteLine(
 "Training with simulated annealing for 5 iterations");
            // train the neural network
            NeuralSimulatedAnnealing train =
                    new NeuralSimulatedAnnealing(
                      this.network, this.input,
                      this.ideal, 10, 2, 100);

            int epoch = 1;

            for (int i = 1; i <= 5; i++)
            {
                train.Iteration();
                Console.WriteLine("Iteration(Anneal) #"
                  + epoch + " Error:"
                        + train.Error);
                epoch++;
            }
        }
    }
}
```

The **PredictSP500** class implements the hybrid training, as well as attempts
to predict future S&P 500 values with the newly trained neural network. The hybrid
training works by alternating between backpropagation training and simulated annealing. The training begins with backpropagation and switches to simulated annealing when backpropagation is no longer efficiently training the network. Once simulated annealing has been used for a number of cycles, the program switches back to
backpropagation.

Listing 10.8 shows the output from hybrid training.

Listing 10.8: Hybrid Training Output

```
Iteration(Backprop) #1511 Error:0.1023912889542664
Iteration(Backprop) #1512 Error:0.10237590385794164
Iteration(Backprop) #1513 Error:0.10236112842990429
```

```
Iteration(Backprop)  #1514  Error:0.10234696743296834
Iteration(Backprop)  #1515  Error:0.10233342565770161
Iteration(Backprop)  #1516  Error:0.10232050792236635
Iteration(Backprop)  #1517  Error:0.10230821907285384

...
Iteration(Backprop)  #1518  Error:0.10229656398261411
Iteration(Backprop)  #1519  Error:0.10228554755257999
Iteration(Backprop)  #1520  Error:0.10227517471108645
Iteration(Backprop)  #1521  Error:0.10226545041378378
Training with simulated annealing for 5 iterations
Iteration(Anneal) #1
Error:0.042124954651261835  Iteration(Anneal)  #2
Error:0.042124954651261835  Iteration(Anneal)  #3
Error:0.042124954651261835  Iteration(Anneal)  #4
Error:0.042124954651261835  Iteration(Anneal)  #5
Error:0.042124954651261835  Iteration(Backprop)  #1522
Error:0.04137291563937421  Iteration(Backprop)  #1523
Error:0.0407959588007687  Iteration(Backprop)  #1524
Error:0.04031691771522145  Iteration(Backprop)  #1525
Error:0.03987729279067175  Iteration(Backprop)  #1526
Error:0.03945727030649545  Iteration(Backprop)  #1527
Error:0.03905037926667383  Iteration(Backprop)  #1528
Error:0.038654238218587864  Iteration(Backprop)  #1529
Error:0.03826781584914556  Iteration(Backprop)  #1530
Error:0.03789057258057805  Iteration(Backprop)  #1531
Error:0.03752216093273823  Iteration(Backprop)  #1532
Error:0.03716231245175569  Iteration(Backprop)  #1533
Error:0.03681079335044474

...
```

As you can see from the above code, backpropagation is used through iteration 1,521. The improvement between iterations 1,520 and 1,521 was not sufficient, so simulated annealing was employed for five iterations. Before the simulated annealing was used, the error rate was around 10%. After the simulated annealing, the error rate dropped rapidly to around 4%. Simulated annealing was successful in avoiding the local minimum that the above training session was approaching.

The hybrid training algorithm is implemented in the **TrainNeuralNetworkHybrid** method. The signature for the **TrainNeuralNetworkHybrid** method is shown here:

```
private void TrainNetworkHybrid()
```

The hybrid training begins just like a regular backpropagation training session. A backpropagation trainer is implemented with a low training rate and a low momentum.

```
Train train = new Backpropagation(this.network, this.input,
```

```
                        this.ideal, 0.00001, 0.1);
```

We keep track of the last error, so we can gauge the performance of the training algorithm. Initially, this last error value is set very high so that it will be properly initialized during the first iteration.

```
double lastError = Double.MaxValue;
int epoch = 1;
```

We only use simulated annealing every 100 iterations; otherwise, as the improvements become very small towards the end of the training, simulated annealing would constantly be invoked. We use the **lastAnneal** variable to track how many epochs it has been since the last simulated annealing attempt.

```
int lastAnneal = 0;


do
{
  train.Iteration();
  double error = train.Error;
```

For every epoch, we update the progress.

```
Console.WriteLine("Iteration(Backprop) #" + epoch + " Error:"
+ error);
```

If the error is greater than 5%, then we will consider using simulated annealing. Once the error is less than 5%, it is usually best to just let backpropagation finish out the training.

```
  if (error > 0.05)
  {
```

We must now consider if we would like to use simulated annealing. If it has been 100 iterations since we last used simulated annealing and the error rate has not improved by one hundredth of a percent, then we will try to train the neural network using simulated annealing.

```
    if ((lastAnneal > 100) && (error > lastError || Math.Abs(error
- lastError) < 0.0001))
    {
```

To train using simulated annealing, we call the **TrainNetworkAnneal** method. This method works very much like our previous examples of simulated annealing, so it will not be repeated here. After the simulated annealing training has completed, the **lastAnneal** variable is set to zero so that we can once again keep track of how many epochs it has been since simulated annealing training was last used.

```
      TrainNetworkAnneal();
      lastAnneal = 0;
    }
```

```
}
```

We keep track of the last error and the epoch number.

```
lastError = train.Error;
epoch++;
lastAnneal++;
} while (train.Error > MAX_ERROR);
```

The **MAX_ERROR** constant for this example is set to 2%. It is possible to train this example to less than 1%, but it takes nearly one million epochs and several days of training.

Attempting to Predict the S&P 500

This example uses the **Display** method to attempt to predict the S&P 500. The signature for the **Display** method is shown here:

```
public void Display()
```

Three arrays are created. The **present** array holds the "present values" upon which the prediction will be based. The **predict** array will hold the predicted S&P 500 values. The **actualOutput** array will contain the actual values from the historical S&P 500 data. The **actualOutput** array will be compared against the **present** array to determine the effectiveness of the neural network.

```
double[] present = new double[INPUT_SIZE * 2];
double[] predict = new double[OUTPUT_SIZE];
double[] actualOutput = new double[OUTPUT_SIZE];
```

We loop through all of the **FinancialSample** objects that fall in the range for which this prediction is to be made.

```
int index = 0;
foreach (FinancialSample sample in this.actual.GetSamples())
{
```

If this **FinancialSample** object falls in the range after the **PREDICT_FROM** constant, then we should attempt to predict based on it.

```
if (sample.GetDate().CompareTo(this.PREDICT_FROM) > 0)
{
```

We create a **StringBuilder** that will build the line of text to be displayed and append the date on which the sample was taken.

```
StringBuilder str = new StringBuilder();
str.Append(ReadCSV.DisplayDate(sample.GetDate()));
```

The starting value of the S&P 500 for this time slice is then displayed.

```
str.Append(":Start=");
```

```
str.Append(sample.GetAmount());
```

The input values for the neural network are obtained, as well as the ideal output values.

```
this.actual.GetInputData(index - INPUT_SIZE, present);
this.actual.GetOutputData(index - INPUT_SIZE, actualOutput);
```

The outputs are then computed using the present values. This is the neural network's prediction.

```
predict = this.network.ComputeOutputs(present);
```

The actual change in percent for the S&P 500 is displayed.

```
str.Append(",Actual % Change=");
str.Append(actualOutput[0].ToString("N2"));
```

Next, the predicted change in percent is displayed.

```
str.Append(",Predicted % Change= ");
str.Append(predict[0].ToString("N2"));
```

The difference between the actual and predicted values is then displayed.

```
str.Append(":Difference=");
```

The error between the actual and the difference is then calculated using root mean square.

```
ErrorCalculation error = new ErrorCalculation();
error.UpdateError(predict, actualOutput);
str.Append(error.CalculateRMS().ToString("N2"));
```

Finally, the **StringBuilder** is displayed.

```
Console.WriteLine(str.ToString());
    }
  index++;
}
```

This same procedure is followed for every **FinancialSample** object provided.

This example serves as a basic introduction to financial prediction with neural networks. An entire book could easily be written about how to use neural networks with financial markets. There are many options available that will allow you to create more advanced financial neural networks. For example, additional inputs can be provided; individual stocks, and their relations to other stocks can be used; and hybrid approaches using neural networks and other forms of statistical analyses can be used. This example serves as a starting point.

Chapter Summary

Predicting the movement of financial markets is a very common area of interest for predictive neural networks. Application of neural networks to financial forecasting could easily fill a book. This book provides a brief introduction by presenting the basics of how to construct a neural network that attempts to predict price movement in the S&P 500 index.

To attempt to predict the S&P 500 index, both the prime interest rate and previous values of the S&P 500 are used. This attempts to find trends in the S&P 500 data that might be used to predict future price movement.

This chapter also introduced hybrid training. The hybrid training algorithm used in this chapter made use of both backpropgation and simulated annealing. Backpropagation is used until the backpropagation no longer produces a satisfactory reduction in the error rate. At this time, simulated annealing is used to help free the neural network from what might be a local minimum. A local minimum is a low point on the training chart, but not necessarily the lowest point. Backpropagation has a tendency to get stuck at a local minimum.

Though the feedforward neural network is one of the most common forms of neural networks, there are other neural network architectures that are also worth considering. In the next chapter, you will be introduced to a self-organizing map. A self-organizing map is often used to classify input into groups.

Vocabulary

Comma Separated Value (CSV) File

Global Minimum

Hybrid Training

Local Minima

Prime Interest Rate

S&P 500

Sample

Questions for Review

1.   This chapter explained how to use simulated annealing and backpropagation to form a hybrid training algorithm. How can a genetic algorithm be easily added to the mix? A genetic algorithm uses many randomly generated neural networks. How can this be used without discarding the previous work done by the backpropagation and simulated annealing algorithms?

2.   You would like to create a predictive neural network that predicts the price of an individual stock for the next five days. You will use the stock's prices from the previous ten days and the current prime interest rate. How many input neurons and how many output neurons will be used?

3.   Explain what a local minimum is and how it can be detrimental to neural network training. How can this be overcome?

4.   How can simulated annealing be used to augment backpropagation? How does the hybrid training algorithm presented in this chapter know when to engage simulated annealing?

5.   Why is it preferable to input percentage changes into financial neural network changes rather than actual stock prices? Which activation function would work well for percentage changes? Why?

CHAPTER 11: UNDERSTANDING THE SELF-ORGANIZING MAP

- What is a Self-Organizing Map?
- How is a Self-Organizing Map Used to Classify Patterns?
- Training a Self-Organizing Map
- Dealing with Neurons that do not Learn to Classify

In chapter 5, you learned about the feedforward backpropagation neural network. While the feedforward architecture is commonly used for neural networks, it is not the only option available. In this chapter, we will examine another architecture commonly used for neural networks, the self-organizing map (SOM).

The self-organizing map, sometimes called a Kohonen neural network, is named after its creator, Tuevo Kohonen. The self-organizing map differs from the feedforward backpropagation neural network in several important ways. In this chapter, we will examine the self-organizing map and see how it is implemented. Chapter 12 will continue by presenting a practical application of the self-organizing map, optical character recognition.

Introducing the Self-Organizing Map

The self-organizing map differs considerably from the feedforward backpropagation neural network in both how it is trained and how it recalls a pattern. The self-organizing map does not use an activation function or a threshold value.

In addition, output from the self-organizing map is not composed of output from several neurons; rather, when a pattern is presented to a self-organizing map, one of the output neurons is selected as the "winner." This "winning" neuron provides the output from the self-organizing map. Often, a "winning" neuron represents a group in the data that is presented to the self-organizing map. For example, in chapter 12 we will examine an OCR program that uses 26 output neurons that map input patterns to the 26 letters of the Latin alphabet.

The most significant difference between the self-organizing map and the feedforward backpropagation neural network is that the self-organizing map trains in an unsupervised mode. This means that the self-organizing map is presented with data, but the correct output that corresponds to the input data is not specified.

It is also important to understand the limitations of the self-organizing map. You will recall from earlier discussions that neural networks without hidden layers can only be applied to certain problems. This is the case with the self-organizing map. Self-organizing maps are used because they are relatively simple networks to construct and can be trained very rapidly.

How a Self-Organizing Map Recognizes a Pattern

We will now examine how the self-organizing map recognizes a pattern. We will begin by examining the structure of the self-organizing map. You will then be instructed on how to train the self-organizing map to properly recognize the patterns you desire.

The Structure of the Self-Organizing Map

The self-organizing map works differently than the feedforward neural network that we learned about in chapter 5, "Feedforward Backpropagation Neural Networks." The self-organizing map only contains an input neuron layer and an output neuron layer. There is no hidden layer in a self-organizing map.

The input to a self-organizing map is submitted to the neural network via the input neurons. The input neurons receive floating point numbers that make up the input pattern to the network. A self-organizing map requires that the inputs be normalized to fall between -1 and 1. Presenting an input pattern to the network will cause a reaction from the output neurons.

The output of a self-organizing map is very different from the output of a feedforward neural network. Recall from chapter 5 that if we have a neural network with five output neurons, we will receive an output that consists of five values. As noted earlier, this is not the case with the self-organizing map. In a self-organizing map, only one of the output neurons actually produces a value. Additionally, this single value is either **true** or **false**. Therefore, the output from the self-organizing map is usually the index of the neuron that fired (e.g. Neuron #5). The structure of a typical self-organizing map is shown in Figure 11.1.

Figure 11.1: A self-organizing map.

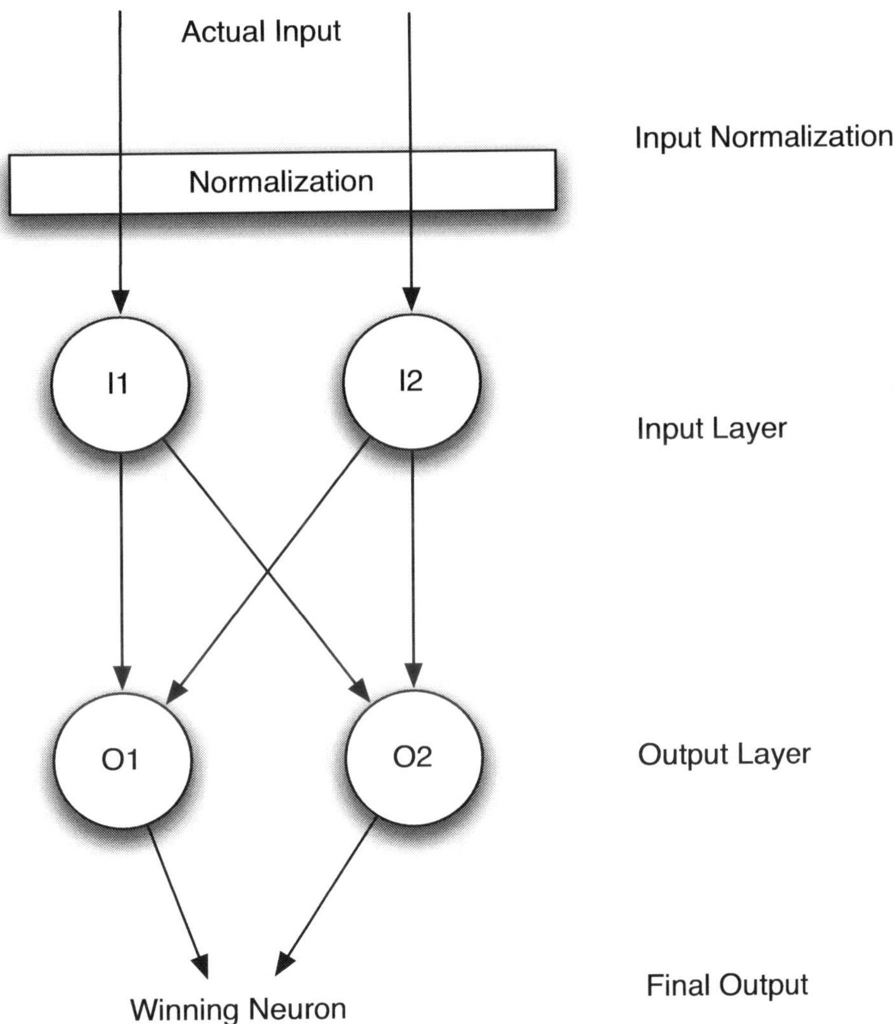

Now that you understand the structure of the self-organizing map, we will examine how the network processes information by considering a very simple self-organizing map. This network will have only two input neurons and two output neurons. The input to be given to the two input neurons is shown in Table 11.1.

Table 11.1: Sample Inputs to a Self-Organizing Map

Input Neuron 1 (I1)	0.5
Input Neuron 2 (I2)	0.75

We must also know the connection weights between the neurons. The connection weights are given in Table 11.2.

Table 11.2: Connection Weights in the Sample Self-Organizing Map

I1 -> O1	0.1
I2 -> O1	0.2
I1 -> O2	0.3
I2 -> O2	0.4

Using these values, we will now examine which neuron will win and produce output. We will begin by normalizing the input.

Normalizing the Input

The self-organizing map requires that its input be normalized. Thus, some texts refer to the normalization as a third layer. However, in this book, the self-organizing map is considered to be a two-layer network, because there are only two actual neuron layers at work.

The self-organizing map places strict limitations on the input it receives. Input to the self-organizing map must be between the values of −1 and 1. In addition, each of the input neurons must use the full range. If one or more of the input neurons were to only accept the numbers between 0 and 1, the performance of the neural network would suffer.

Input for a self-organizing map is generally normalized using one of two common methods, multiplicative normalization and z-axis normalization.

Multiplicative normalization is the simpler of the two methods, however z-axis normalization can sometimes provide a better scaling factor. The algorithms for these two methods will be discussed in the next two sections. We will begin with multiplicative normalization.

Multiplicative Normalization

To perform multiplicative normalization, we must first calculate the vector length of the input data, or vector. This is done by summing the squares of the input vector and then taking the square root of this number, as shown in Equation 11.1.

Equation 11.1: Multiplicative Normalization

$$f = \frac{1}{\sqrt{\sum_{i=0}^{n-1} x_i^2}}$$

The above equation produces the normalization factor that each input is multiplied by to properly scale them. Using the sample data provided in Tables 11.1 and 11.2, the normalization factor is calculated as follows:

```
1.0 / Math.Sqrt( (0.5 * 0.5) + (0.75 * 0.75) )
```

This produces a normalization factor of 1.1094.

Z-Axis Normalization

Unlike the multiplicative algorithm for normalization, the z-axis normalization algorithm does not depend upon the actual data itself; instead the raw data is multiplied by a constant. To calculate the normalization factor using z-axis normalization, we use Equation 11.2.

Equation 11.2: Z-Axis Normalization

$$f = \frac{1}{\sqrt{n}}$$

As can be seen in the above equation, the normalization factor is only dependent upon the size of the input, denoted by the variable n. This preserves absolute magnitude information. However, we do not want to disregard the actual inputs completely; thus, a synthetic input is created, based on the input values. The synthetic input is calculated using Equation 11.3.

Equation 11.3: Synthetic Input

$$s = f \sqrt{n - l^2}$$

The variable n represents the input size. The variable f is the normalization factor. The variable l is the vector length. The synthetic input will be added to the input vector that was presented to the neural network.

You might be wondering when you should use the multiplicative algorithm and when you should use the z-axis algorithm. In general, you will want to use the z-axis algorithm, since the z-axis algorithm preserves absolute magnitude. However, if most of the training values are near zero, the z-axis algorithm may not be the best choice. This is because the synthetic component of the input will dominate the other near-zero values.

Calculating Each Neuron's Output

To calculate the output, the input vector and neuron connection weights must both be considered. First, the dot product of the input neurons and their connection weights must be calculated. To calculate the dot product between two vectors, you must multiply each of the elements in the two vectors as shown in Equation 11.4.

Equation 11.4: Calculating the SOM Output

$$[0.5 \quad 0.75] * [0.1 \quad 0.2] = (0.5 * 0.75) + (0.1 * 0.2) = 0.395$$

As you can see from the above calculation, the dot product is 0.395. This calculation will have to be performed for each of the output neurons. In this example, we will only examine the calculations for the first output neuron. The calculations necessary for the second output neuron are carried out in the same way.

The output must now be normalized by multiplying it by the normalization factor that was determined in the previous step. You must multiply the dot product of 0.395 by the normalization factor of 1.1094. The result is an output of 0.438213. Now that the output has been calculated and normalized, it must be mapped to a bipolar number.

Mapping to a Bipolar Ranged Number

As you may recall from chapter 2, a bipolar number is an alternate way of representing binary numbers. In the bipolar system, the binary zero maps to −1 and the binary one remains a 1. Because the input to the neural network has been normalized to this range, we must perform a similar normalization on the output of the neurons. To make this mapping, we multiply by two and subtract one. For the output of 0.438213, the result is a final output of −0.123574.

The value −0.123574 is the output of the first neuron. This value will be compared with the outputs of the other neuron. By comparing these values we can determine a "winning" neuron.

Choosing the Winner

We have seen how to calculate the value for the first output neuron. If we are to determine a winning neuron, we must also calculate the value for the second output neuron. We will now quickly review the process to calculate the second neuron.

The same normalization factor is used to calculate the second output neuron as was used to calculate the first output neuron. As you recall from the previous section, the normalization factor is 1.1094. If we apply the dot product for the weights of the second output neuron and the input vector, we get a value of 0.45. This value is multiplied by the normalization factor of 1.1094, resulting in a value of 0.0465948. We can now calculate the final output for neuron 2 by converting the output of 0.0465948 to bipolar, which yields –0.9068104.

As you can see, we now have an output value for each of the neurons. The first neuron has an output value of –0.123574 and the second neuron has an output value of –0.9068104. To choose the winning neuron, we select the neuron that produces the largest output value. In this case, the winning neuron is the second output neuron with an output of –0.9068104, which beats the first neuron's output of –0.123574.

You have now seen how the output of the self-organizing map was derived. As you can see, the weights between the input and output neurons determine this output. In the next section we will see how these weights can be adjusted to produce output that is more suitable for the desired task. The training process modifies these weights and will be described in the next section.

How a Self-Organizing Map Learns

In this section, you will learn how to train a self-organizing map. There are several steps involved in the training process. Overall, the process for training a self-organizing map involves stepping through several epochs until the error of the self-organizing map is below an acceptable level. In this section, you will learn how to calculate the error rate for a self-organizing map and how to adjust the weights for each epoch. You will also learn how to determine when no additional epochs are necessary to further train the neural network.

The training process for the self-organizing map is competitive. For each training set, one neuron will "win." This winning neuron will have its weight adjusted so that it will react even more strongly to the input the next time it sees it. As different neurons win for different patterns, their ability to recognize that particular pattern will increase.

We will first examine the overall process of training the self-organizing map. The self-organizing map is trained by repeating epochs until one of two things happens: If the calculated error is below an acceptable level, the training process is complete. If, on the other hand, the error rate has changed by only a very small amount, this individual cycle will be aborted without any additional epochs taking place. If it is determined that the cycle is to be aborted, the weights will be initialized with random values and a new training cycle will begin.

Learning Rate

The learning rate is a variable that is used by the learning algorithm to adjust the weights of the neurons. The learning rate must be a positive number less than 1, and is typically 0.4 or 0.5. In the following sections, the learning rate will be specified by the symbol alpha.

Generally, setting the learning rate to a higher value will cause training to progress more quickly. However, the network may fail to converge if the learning rate is set to a number that is too high. This is because the oscillations of the weight vectors will be too great for the classification patterns to ever emerge.

Another technique is to start with a relatively high learning rate and decrease this rate as training progresses. This allows rapid initial training of the neural network that is then "fine tuned" as training progresses.

Adjusting Weights

The memory of the self-organizing map is stored inside the weighted connections between the input layer and the output layer. The weights are adjusted in each epoch. An epoch occurs when training data is presented to the self-organizing map and the weights are adjusted based on the results of this data. The adjustments to the weights should produce a network that will yield more favorable results the next time the same training data is presented. Epochs continue as more and more data is presented to the network and the weights are adjusted.

Eventually, the return on these weight adjustments will diminish to the point that it is no longer valuable to continue with this particular set of weights. When this happens, the entire weight matrix is reset to new random values; thus beginning a new cycle. The final weight matrix that will be used will be the best weight matrix from each of the cycles. We will now examine how weights are transformed.

The original method for calculating changes to weights, which was proposed by Kohonen, is often called the additive method. This method uses the following equation:

Equation 11.5: Adjusting the SOM Weights (Additive)

$$w^{t+1} = \frac{w^t + \alpha\, x}{length\left(w^t + \alpha\, x\right)}$$

The variable **x** is the training vector that was presented to the network. Variable **wt** is the weight of the winning neuron, and the result of the equation is the new weight. The double vertical bars represent the vector length. This equation will be implemented as a method in the self-organizing map example presented later in this chapter.

This additive method generally works well for most self-organizing maps; however, in cases for which the additive method shows excessive instability and fails to converge, an alternate method can be used. This method is called the subtractive method. The subtractive method uses the following equations:

Equation 11.6: Adjusting the SOM Weight (Subtractive)

$$e = x - w^t$$

$$w^{t+1} = w^t + \alpha e$$

These two equations describe the basic transformation that will occur on the weights of the network. In the next section, you will see how these equations are implemented as a C# program, and their use will be demonstrated.

Calculating the Error

Before we can understand how to calculate the error for the neural network, we must first define "error." A self-organizing map is trained in an unsupervised fashion, so the definition of error is somewhat different than the definition with which we are familiar.

In the previous chapter, supervised training involved calculating the error. The error was the difference between the anticipated output of the neural network and the actual output of the neural network. In this chapter, we are examining unsupervised training. In unsupervised training, there is no anticipated output; thus, you may be wondering exactly how we can calculate an error. The answer is that the error we are calculating is not a true error, or at least not an error in the normal sense of the word.

The purpose of the self-organizing map is to classify input into several sets. The error for the self-organizing map, therefore, provides a measure of how well the network is classifying input into output groups. The error itself is not used to modify the weights, as is the case in the backpropagation algorithm. There is no one official way to calculate the error for a self-organizing map, so we will examine two different methods in the following section as we explore how to implement a C# training method.

Implementing the Self-Organizing Map

Now that you have an understanding of how the self-organizing map functions, we will implement one using C#. In this section, we will see how several classes can be used together to create a self-organizing map. Following this section, you will be shown an example of how to use the self-organizing map classes to create a simple self-organizing map. Finally, in chapter 12, you will be shown how to construct a more complex application, based on the self-organizing map, that can recognize handwriting.

First, you must understand the structure of the self-organizing map classes that we are constructing. The classes used to implement the self-organizing map are summarized in Table 11.3.

Table 11.3: Classes Used to Implement the Self-organizing Map

Class	Purpose
NormalizeInput	Normalizes the input for the self-organizing map. This class implements the normalization method discussed earlier in this chapter.
SelfOrganizingMap	This is the main class that implements the self-organizing map.
TrainSelfOrganizingMap	Used to train the self-organizing map.

Now that you are familiar with the overall structure of the self-organizing map classes, we will examine each individual class. You will see how these classes work together to provide self-organizing map functionality. We will begin by examining how the training set is constructed using the **NormalizeInput** class.

The SOM Normalization Class

The **NormalizeInput** class receives all of the information that it will need from its constructor. The signature for the constructor is shown here:

```
public NormalizeInput(double[] input, NormalizationType type)
```

The constructor begins by storing the type of normalization requested. This can be either multiplicative or z-axis normalization.

```
this.type = type;
```

Next, the normalization factor and synthetic input values are calculated. The **CalculateFactors** method is explained in the next section.

```
CalculateFactors(input);
```

Finally, the input matrix is created. This includes the synthetic input. The **CreateInputMatrix** method is described in a section to follow.

```
this.inputMatrix = this.CreateInputMatrix(input, this.synth);
```

Calculating the Factors

The **CalculateFactors** method calculates both the normalization factor and the synthetic input value. The signature for the **CalculateFactors** method is shown here:

```
protected void CalculateFactors(double[] input)
```

First, the input array is converted to a column matrix.

```
Matrix.Matrix inputMatrix = Matrix.Matrix.
CreateColumnMatrix(input);
```

The vector length is then calculated for the **inputMatrix** variable.

```
double len = MatrixMath.VectorLength(inputMatrix);
```

The length of the vector is evaluated, to ensure it has not become too small.

```
len = Math.Max(len, VERYSMALL);
```

The number of inputs is determined and this value is stored in the **numInputs** variable.

```
int numInputs = input.Length;
```

Next, the type of normalization to be performed is determined.

```
if (this.type == NormalizationType.MULTIPLICATIVE)
{
```

If the type of normalization is multiplicative, then the reciprocal of the vector length is used as the normalization factor.

```
  this.normfac = 1.0 / len;
```

Because the normalization method is additive, no synthetic input is needed. We simply set the synthetic input variable to zero, so that it does not have any influence.

```
  this.synth = 0.0;
}
else
{
```

If z-axis normalization is being used, then the normalization factor is computed as the reciprocal of the square root of the number of inputs.

```
  this.normfac = 1.0 / Math.Sqrt(numInputs);
```

Now we must determine the synthetic input.

```
double d = numInputs - Math.Pow(len, 2);
```

If the synthetic input is calculated to be greater than zero, then we multiply it by the normalization factor.

```
if (d > 0.0)
{
  this.synth = Math.Sqrt(d) * this.normfac;
}
else
{
  this.synth = 0;
}
}
```

If the synthetic input is less than zero, then we set the synthetic input variable to zero.

Creating the Input Matrix

Now that the normalization factor and synthetic input have been determined, the input matrix can be created. The input matrix is created by the **CreateInputMatrix** method. The signature for the **CreateInputMatrix** method is shown here:

```
protected Matrix.Matrix CreateInputMatrix(double[] pattern,
                double extra)
```

First, a matrix is created that has one row and columns equal to one more than the length of the pattern. The extra column will hold the synthetic input.

```
Matrix.Matrix result = new Matrix.Matrix(1, pattern.Length + 1);
```

Next, all of the values from the pattern are inserted.

```
for (int i = 0; i < pattern.Length; i++)
{
  result[0, i] = pattern[i];
}
```

Finally, the synthetic input is added and the **result** variable is returned.

```
result[0, pattern.Length] = extra;

return result;
```

The input matrix is now ready for use.

The SOM Implementation Class

The self-organizing map is implemented in the class **TrainSelfOrganizingMap**. A pattern is presented to the SOM using a method named **Winner**. The signature for this method is shown here:

```
public int Winner(double[] input)
```

This method does little more than create a normalized matrix and send it on to a more advanced version of the **Winner** method that accepts a normalized matrix.

```
NormalizeInput normalizedInput = new NormalizeInput(input,
this.normalizationType);
```

The winning neuron is returned from this more advanced **Winner** method.

```
return Winner(normalizedInput);
```

This **Winner** method accepts a **NormizedInput** object. The signature for this method is shown here:

```
public int Winner(NormalizedInput input)
```

First, a local variable is created to hold the winning neuron. This variable is named **win**.

```
int win = 0;
```

As we progress, we keep track of the output neuron with the greatest output. One of the output neurons will win. We set the **biggest** variable to a very small number before we begin.

```
double biggest = Double.MinValue;
```

Then we loop over the output neurons.

```
for (int i = 0; i < this.outputNeuronCount; i++)
{
```

We obtain the row from the weight matrix that corresponds to this output neuron.

```
Matrix.Matrix optr = this.outputWeights.GetRow(i);
```

We then obtain the dot product between this row and the input pattern. This is the output for this neuron.

```
this.output[i] = MatrixMath.DotProduct(input.InputMatrix, optr)
* input.Normfac;
```

The output from the neuron is mapped to a number between −1 and 1.

```
this.output[i] = (this.output[i] + 1.0) / 2.0;
```

The number is evaluated to see if this is the biggest output so far.

```
if (this.output[i] > biggest)
{
  biggest = this.output[i];
  win = i;
}
```

If the output is above one or below zero, it is adjusted as necessary.

```
if (this.output[i] < 0)
{
  this.output[i] = 0;
}

if (this.output[i] > 1)
{
  this.output[i] = 1;
}
}
```

The winning neuron is then returned.

```
return win;
```

As you can see, the output is calculated very differently than the output of the feedforward networks seen earlier in this book. The self-organizing map is a competitive neural network; thus, the output from this neural network is the winning neuron.

The SOM Training Class

The self-organizing map is trained using different techniques than those used with the feedforward neural networks demonstrated thus far. The training is performed by a class named **TrainSelfOrganizingMap**. This class is implemented like the other training methods; it goes through a series of iterations until the error is sufficiently small. The training iteration is discussed in the next section.

Training Iteration

To perform one **Iteration** of training, the **Iteration** method of the **TrainSelfOrganizingMap** class is called. The signature for the **Iteration** method is shown here:

```
public void Iteration()
{
```

First, **EvaluateErrors** is called to determine the current error level. The **totalError** variable, which was just calculated, is saved to the **globalError** variable.

```
EvaluateErrors();
this.totalError = this.globalError;
```

The current error is evaluated to see if it is better than the best error encountered thus far. If so, the weights are copied over the previous best weight matrix.

```
if (this.totalError < this.bestError)
{
  this.bestError = this.totalError;
  CopyWeights(this.som, this.bestnet);
}
```

The number of neurons that have won, since the last time the errors were calculated, is determined.

```
int winners = 0;
for (int i = 0; i < this.won.Length; i++)
{
  if (this.won[i] != 0)
  {
    winners++;
  }
}
```

If there have been too few winners, one is forced.

```
if ((winners < this.outputNeuronCount) && (winners < this.train.
Length))
{
  ForceWin();
  return;
}
```

The weights are adjusted based on the training from this iteration.

```
AdjustWeights();
```

The learning rate is gradually decreased down to 0.01.

```
if (this.learnRate > 0.01)
{
  this.learnRate *= this.reduction;
}
```

The weights are then copied from the best network.

```
private void CopyWeights(SelfOrganizingMap source,
SelfOrganizingMap target)
```

Finally, these weights are copied.

```
MatrixMath.Copy(source.OutputWeights, target
```

```
.OutputWeights);
```

This completes one training iteration.

Evaluating Errors

Error evaluation is an important part of the training process. It involves determining how many neurons win for a given training pattern. The neuron that has the greatest response to a given training pattern is adjusted to strengthen that win. The errors are calculated using the **EvaluateErrors** method. The signature for this method is shown here:

```
public void EvaluateErrors()
```

First, the correction matrix is cleared. The correction matrix will hold the training corrections. These corrections will be applied to the actual neural network later when the **AdjustWeights** method is called. The **AdjustWeights** method is covered in the next section.

```
this.correc.Clear();

for (int i = 0; i < this.won.Length; i++)
{
   this.won[i] = 0;
}

this.globalError = 0.0;
```

Next, we loop through all the training sets.

```
for (int tset = 0; tset < this.train.Length; tset++)
{
```

The input is normalized and presented to the neural network.

```
  NormalizeInput input = new NormalizeInput(this.train[tset],
this.som.NormalizationType);
```

The variable **best** will hold the winning neuron.

```
  int best = this.som.Winner(input);
```

The number of times each neuron wins is recorded.

```
  this.won[best]++;
```

The weights for the winning neuron are then obtained.

```
  Matrix.Matrix wptr = this.som.OutputWeights.GetRow(best);
```

The length will be calculated and placed in the **length** variable.

```
  double length = 0.0;
```

```
double diff;
```

We now loop over all of the input neurons.

```
for (int i = 0; i < this.inputNeuronCount; i++)
{
```

The difference between the training set and the corresponding weight matrix entry are calculated.

```
diff = this.train[tset][i] * input.Normfac
                    - wptr[0, i];
            length += diff * diff;
```

The length is calculated by squaring the difference. A length is the square root of the sum of the squares.

```
length += diff * diff;
```

What is done next depends upon the learning method.

```
if (this.learnMethod == LearningMethod.SUBTRACTIVE)
{
```

For the subtractive method, the difference is added to the winning neuron.

```
this.correc.Add(best, i, diff);
}
else
{
```

For the additive method, a work matrix is used. The work matrix is a temporary matrix used to hold the values to be added. The work matrix is a single column with a number of rows equal to the input neurons. The training set multiplied by the corresponding weight value is added and scaled by the learning rate.

```
this.work[0, i] = this.learnRate * this.train[tset][i]
        * input.Normfac + wptr[0, i];
}
}
```

Finally, the synthetic input is addressed. The difference between the synthetic input and the corresponding weight matrix value is determined.

```
diff = input.Synth - wptr[0, this.inputNeuronCount];
```

This difference is added to the length.

```
length += diff * diff;
```

If the learning method is additive, then the synthetic difference is simply added.

```
if (this.learnMethod == LearningMethod.SUBTRACTIVE)
{
```

```
        this.correc.Add(best, this.inputNeuronCount, diff);
    }
    else
    {
```

The work matrix value for this input neuron is set to the synthetic input added to the corresponding weight matrix value scaled by the learning rate.

```
        this.work[0, this.inputNeuronCount] =  this.learnRate
                                        * input.Synth
                                        + wptr[0,
        this.inputNeuronCount];
    }
```

The calculated length of the differences is the error. We then determine if this beats the current error.

```
    if (length > this.globalError)
    {
        this.globalError = length;
    }
```

So far, the additive method has not been modifying the correction matrix; rather it has been modifying the work matrix. The correction matrix must now be updated with any changes to be reflected when the **AdjustWeights** method is called.

```
if (this.learnMethod == LearningMethod.ADDITIVE)
{
  NormalizeWeight(this.work, 0);
  for (int i = 0; i <= this.inputNeuronCount; i++)
  {
    this.correc.Add(best, i, this.work[0, i]
      - wptr[0, i]);
  }
}
```

The error calculation is now complete.

```
this.globalError = Math.Sqrt(this.globalError);
```

Finally, the length is determined by performing the square root of the error, which is the sum of the differences squared.

Force a Winner

There are times when certain neurons will not win for any training pattern. These neurons are dead weight and should be adjusted to win for a few patterns. The **ForceWin** method is used to adjust these neurons. This method is called when too few neurons have been winning. The signature for the **ForceWin** method is shown here.

```
protected void ForceWin()
```

The variable **best** will hold the winning neuron for each training set iteration. The variable **which** will hold the training set that has the lowest winning neuron.

```
int best, which = 0;
```

First, the output weights and the last output from the self-organizing map to be trained are obtained.

```
Matrix.Matrix outputWeights = this.som.OutputWeights;
```

We then loop over all training sets and see which output neuron has the smallest response. We initialize **dist** to a large value, and continue to lower it as we find increasingly small output values.

```
double dist = Double.MaxValue;
```

Next, we loop over all of the training sets.

```
for (int tset = 0; tset < this.train.Length; tset++)
{
```

The winning neuron from each training set is obtained.

```
best = this.som.Winner(this.train[tset]);
double[] output = this.som.Output;
```

The neuron is evaluated to see if it has a lower output than any previous neuron encountered. If so, this is the new lowest neuron.

```
if (output[best] < dist)
{
  dist = output[best];
  which = tset;
}
```

We then reprocess the neuron with the lowest output. The training set is normalized so it can be presented to the neural network.

```
NormalizeInput input = new NormalizeInput(this.train[which],
this.som.NormalizationType);

best = this.som.Winner(input);
double[] output2 = this.som.Output;
```

The neuron with the greatest output for the training set that produced the lowest winner is then identified.

```
dist = Double.MinValue;
int i = this.outputNeuronCount;
while ((i--) > 0)
{
  if (this.won[i] != 0)
  {
    continue;
  }
```

If this neuron is lower, then it is chosen.

```
  if (output2[i] > dist)
  {
    dist = output2[i];
    which = i;
  }
}
```

The weights for the lowest neuron are adjusted so that the neuron will respond to this training pattern.

```
  for (int j = 0; j < input.InputMatrix.Cols; j++)
  {
    outputWeights[which, j] =  input.InputMatrix[0, j];
  }
```

```
  NormalizeWeight(outputWeights, which);
}
```

Finally, the weights are normalized.

Adjust Weights

After the errors have been calculated, the **AdjustWeights** method is called. The **AdjustWeights** method applies the correction matrix to the actual matrix. The signature for the **AdjustWeights** method is shown here.

```
protected void AdjustWeights()
```

We loop over all of the output neurons.

```
for (int i = 0; i < this.outputNeuronCount; i++)
{
```

If this output neuron has never won, then continue; there is nothing to be done. The **ForceWin** method will likely assist this neuron later.

```
  if (this.won[i] == 0)
```

```
{
  continue;
}
```

The reciprocal of the number of times this output neuron has won is calculated.

```
double f = 1.0 / this.won[i];
```

If using the subtractive method, then this reciprocal is scaled by the learning rate.

```
if (this.learnMethod == LearningMethod.SUBTRACTIVE)
{
  f *= this.learnRate;
}
```

The vector length of the input weights multiplied by their correction matrix values is calculated.

```
double length = 0.0;

for (int j = 0; j <= this.inputNeuronCount; j++)
{
  double corr = f * this.correc[i, j];
  this.som.OutputWeights.Add(i, j, corr);
  length += corr * corr;
}
```

The weights have been adjusted.

Using the Self-organizing Map

We will now examine a simple program that trains a self-organizing map. As the network is trained, you will be shown a graphical display of the weights. The output from this program is shown in Figure 11.2.

Figure 11.2: Training a self-organizing map.

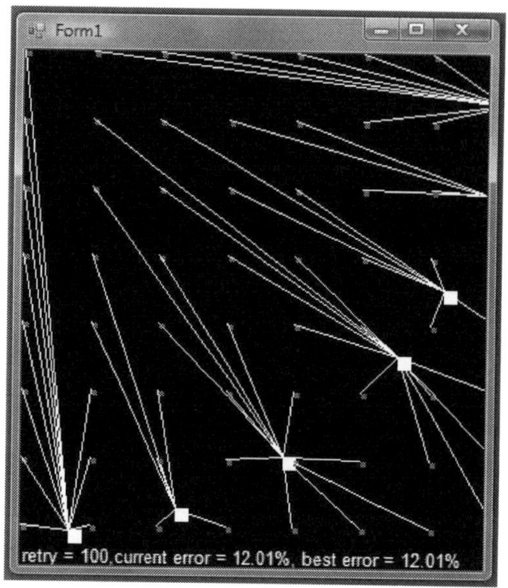

This program contains two input neurons and seven output neurons. Each of the seven output neurons are plotted as white squares. The x-dimension shows the weights between them and the first input neuron and the y-dimension shows the weights between them and the second input neuron. You will see the boxes move as training progresses.

You will also see lines from select points on the grid drawn to each of the squares. These identify which output neuron is winning for the x and y coordinates of that point. Points with similar x and y coordinates are shown as being recognized by the same output neuron.

We will now examine the program, as shown in Listing 11.1.

Listing 11.1: The SOM Training Example (TestSOMForm.cs)

```
using System;
using System.Collections.Generic;
using System.ComponentModel;
using System.Data;
using System.Drawing;
using System.Linq;
using System.Text;
using System.Windows.Forms;
using System.Threading;
```

```csharp
using HeatonResearchNeural.SOM;
using HeatonResearchNeural.Matrix;

namespace Chapter11TestSOM
{
    public partial class TestSOMForm : Form
    {


        /// <summary>
        /// How many input neurons to use.
        /// </summary>
        public const int INPUT_COUNT = 2;

        /// <summary>
        /// How many output neurons to use.
        /// </summary>
        public const int OUTPUT_COUNT = 7;

        /// <summary>
        /// How many random samples to generate.
        /// </summary>
        public const int SAMPLE_COUNT = 100;

        /// <summary>
        /// The unit length in pixels, which is the max
        /// of the height and width of
        /// the window.
        /// </summary>

        protected int unitLength;

        /// <summary>
        /// How many retries so far.
        /// </summary>
        protected int retry = 1;

        /// <summary>
        /// The current error percent.
        /// </summary>
        protected double totalError = 0;

        /// <summary>
        /// The best error percent.
        /// </summary>
        protected double bestError = 0;
```

```csharp
/// <summary>
/// The neural network.
/// </summary>
protected SelfOrganizingMap net;

/// <summary>
/// Input to the neural network.
/// </summary>
protected double[][] input;


public TestSOMForm()
{
    InitializeComponent();
    Start();
}


private void TestSOMForm_Paint(object sender,
    PaintEventArgs e)
{
    Graphics g = e.Graphics;

    if (this.net == null)
    {
        return;
    }

    int width = this.Width;
    int height = this.Height;
    this.unitLength = Math.Min(width, height);
    SolidBrush blackBrush = new SolidBrush(Color.Black);
    SolidBrush whiteBrush = new SolidBrush(Color.White);
    SolidBrush greenBrush = new SolidBrush(Color.Green);
    Pen whitePen = new Pen(Color.White);
    g.FillRectangle(blackBrush, 0, 0, width, height);

    // plot the weights of the output neurons
    Matrix outputWeights = this.net.OutputWeights;

    for (int y = 0; y < outputWeights.Rows; y++)
    {

        g.FillRectangle(whiteBrush,
    (int)(outputWeights[y, 0] * this.unitLength),
            (int)(outputWeights[y, 1] *
```

```csharp
        this.unitLength), 10, 10);

    }

    // plot a grid of samples to test the net with
    for (int y = 0; y < this.unitLength; y += 50)
    {
        for (int x = 0; x < this.unitLength; x += 50)
        {
            g.FillEllipse(greenBrush, x, y, 5, 5);
            double[] d = new double[2];
            d[0] = x;
            d[1] = y;

            int c = this.net.Winner(d);

            int x2 = (int)(outputWeights[c, 0]
                * this.unitLength);
            int y2 = (int)(outputWeights[c, 1]
                * this.unitLength);

            g.DrawLine(whitePen, x, y, x2, y2);
        }

    }

    // display the status info
    string status = "retry = " + this.retry + ",
        current error = "
        + (this.totalError * 100).ToString("N2")
        + "%, best error = "
        + (this.bestError * 100).ToString("N2") + "%";

Font drawFont = new Font("Arial", 10);
SolidBrush drawBrush = new SolidBrush(Color.White);
StringFormat drawFormat = new StringFormat();
e.Graphics.DrawString(status, drawFont, drawBrush,
0, this.Height - drawFont.Height - 35, drawFormat);


}

public void Start()
{
    ThreadStart ts = new ThreadStart(ThreadProc);
    Thread thread = new Thread(ts);
```

```csharp
        thread.Start();
    }


    void ThreadProc()
    {
        Random rand = new Random();
        // build the training set
        this.input = new double[SAMPLE_COUNT][];

        for (int i = 0; i < SAMPLE_COUNT; i++)
        {
            this.input[i] = new double[INPUT_COUNT];
            for (int j = 0; j < INPUT_COUNT; j++)
            {
                this.input[i][j] = rand.NextDouble();
            }
        }


        // build and train the neural network
        this.net = new SelfOrganizingMap(INPUT_COUNT,
                OUTPUT_COUNT,
                    NormalizationType.MULTIPLICATIVE);
        TrainSelfOrganizingMap train =
                new TrainSelfOrganizingMap(
                this.net, this.input,
    TrainSelfOrganizingMap.LearningMethod.SUBTRACTIVE, 0.5);
        train.Initialize();
        double lastError = Double.MaxValue;
        int errorCount = 0;

        while (errorCount < 10)
        {
            train.Iteration();
            this.retry++;
            this.totalError = train.TotalError;
            this.bestError = train.BestError;
            this.Invalidate();

            if (this.bestError < lastError)
            {
                lastError = this.bestError;
                errorCount = 0;
            }
            else
            {
                errorCount++;
```

```
            }
          }
        }
      }
    }
```

There are several constants that govern the way the SOM training example works. These constants are summarized in Table 11.4.

Table 11.4: TestSOM Constants

Constant	Value	Purpose
INPUT_COUNT	2	How many input neurons to use.
OUTPUT_COUNT	7	How many output neurons to use.
SAMPLE_COUNT	100	How many random samples to generate.

There are two major components to this program. The first is the **ThreadProc** method, which implements the background thread. The background thread processes the training of the SOM. The second is the **Paint** event, which graphically displays the progress being made by the training process. These two methods will be discussed in the next two sections.

Background Thread

A background thread is used to process the SOM while the application runs. This allows you to see the training progress graphically. The background thread is handled by the **ThreadProc** method. The signature for the **ThreadProc** method is shown here:

```
void ThreadProc()
```

First, the training set is created using random numbers. These are random points on a grid to which the program will train.

```
Random rand = new Random();

this.input = new double[SAMPLE_COUNT][];

for (int i = 0; i < SAMPLE_COUNT; i++)
{
  this.input[i] = new double[INPUT_COUNT];
  for (int j = 0; j < INPUT_COUNT; j++)
  {
    this.input[i][j] = rand.NextDouble();
  }
```

```
}
```

The neural network is then created.

```
this.net = new SelfOrganizingMap(INPUT_COUNT, OUTPUT_COUNT,
NormalizationType.MULTIPLICATIVE);
```

A training class is then created to train the SOM.

```
TrainSelfOrganizingMap train = new TrainSelfOrganizingMap(
this.net, this.input, TrainSelfOrganizingMap.LearningMethod.SUB-
TRACTIVE, 0.5);
```

The trainer is initialized.

```
train.Initialize();
```

The **lastError** variable is initialized to a very high value and the **errorCount** is set to zero.

```
double lastError = Double.MaxValue;
int errorCount = 0;
```

We then loop until the error has not improved for ten iterations.

```
while (errorCount < 10)
{
```

One training iteration is processed and the best error is maintained.

```
    train.Iteration();
    this.retry++;
    this.totalError = train.TotalError;
    this.bestError = train.BestError;
```

The window is updated with the current grid using the **Paint** method described in the next section. The **Paint** event is called by calling the Invalidate method.

```
    this.Invalidate();
```

The best error is evaluated to determine if there has been an improvement. If there was no improvement, then **errorCount** is increased by one.

```
    if (this.bestError < lastError)
    {
      lastError = this.bestError;
      errorCount = 0;
    }
    else
    {
      errorCount++;
    }
```

The looping continues until there has been no improvement in the error level for ten iterations.

Displaying the Progress

The current state of the neural network's weight matrix and training is displayed by calling the **Paint** event. The signature for the **Paint** event is shown here:

```
private void TestSOMForm_Paint(object sender, PaintEventArgs e)
```

If there is no network defined, then there is nothing to draw, so we return.

```
Graphics g = e.Graphics;

if (this.net == null)
{
   return;
}
```

The following lines of code create several brushes that are needed to draw. The dimensions of the window are determined.

```
int width = this.Width;
int height = this.Height;
this.unitLength = Math.Min(width, height);
SolidBrush blackBrush = new SolidBrush(Color.Black);
SolidBrush whiteBrush = new SolidBrush(Color.White);
SolidBrush greenBrush = new SolidBrush(Color.Green);
Pen whitePen = new Pen(Color.White);
```

Create a black background to draw upon.

```
g.FillRectangle(blackBrush, 0, 0, width, height);

// plot the weights of the output neurons
Matrix outputWeights = this.net.OutputWeights;
```

Then we loop through and display the output neurons. These will correspond to the random training data generated in the previous section.

```
for (int y = 0; y < outputWeights.Rows; y++)
{
```

Filled rectangles are drawn that correspond to all of the output neurons.

```
   g.FillRectangle(whiteBrush, (int)(outputWeights[y, 0]
      * this.unitLength),
      (int)(outputWeights[y, 1] *
      this.unitLength), 10, 10);
}
```

A grid is then plotted of the samples with which to test the net. We then determine into which of the output neurons each training point is grouped.

```
for (int y = 0; y < this.unitLength; y += 50)
{
  for (int x = 0; x < this.unitLength; x += 50)
  {
```

An oval is drawn at each of the training points.

```
    g.FillEllipse(greenBrush, x, y, 5, 5);
    double[] d = new double[2];
```

The training point is presented to the SOM.

```
    d[0] = x;
    d[1] = y;
```

The winning neuron is then obtained.

```
    int c = this.net.Winner(d);
```

The weights for the winning neuron are determined.

```
    int x2 = (int)(outputWeights[c, 0] * this.unitLength);
    int y2 = (int)(outputWeights[c, 1] * this.unitLength);
```

A line is then drawn from the sample to the winning neuron.

```
    g.DrawLine(whitePen, x, y, x2, y2);
  }
}
```

As training progresses, status information is obtained and the output numbers are properly formatted. A text string is displayed.

```
string status = "retry = " + this.retry + ",current error = "
   + (this.totalError * 100).ToString("N2") + "%, best error = "
   + (this.bestError * 100).ToString("N2") + "%";

Font drawFont = new Font("Arial", 10);
SolidBrush drawBrush = new SolidBrush(Color.White);
StringFormat drawFormat = new StringFormat();
e.Graphics.DrawString(status, drawFont, drawBrush, 0, this.Height
 - drawFont.Height - 35, drawFormat);

g.drawString("retry = "
  + this.retry
  + ",current error = "
  + nf.format(this.totalError * 100)
  + "%, best error = "
  + nf.format(this.bestError * 100)
```

```
+ "%", 0,
(int)getContentPane().getBounds().getHeight());
```

The training progress is now visible to the user.

Chapter Summary

In this chapter we learned about the self-organizing map. The self-organizing map differs from the feedforward backpropagation network in several ways. The self-organizing map uses unsupervised training. This means that it receives input data, but no anticipated output data. It then maps the training samples to each of its output neurons.

A self-organizing map contains only two layers. The network is presented with an input pattern that is passed to the input layer. This input pattern must be normalized to numbers between −1 and 1. The output from this neural network will be one single winning output neuron. The output neurons can be thought of as groups that the self-organizing map has classified.

To train the self-organizing map, we present it with the training elements and see which output neuron "wins." This winning neuron's weights are then modified so that it will respond even more strongly to the pattern that caused it to win the next time the pattern is encountered.

There may also be a case in which one or more neurons fail to ever win. Such neurons are dead weight on the neural network. We must identify such neurons and adjust them so they will recognize patterns that are already recognized by other more "overworked" neurons. This will allow the burden of recognition to fall more evenly over the output neurons.

This chapter presented only a simple example of the self-organizing map. In the next chapter we will apply the self-organizing map to a real-world application. We will see how to use the self-organizing map to recognize handwriting.

Vocabulary

Additive Weight Adjustment

Competitive Learning

Input Normalization

Multiplicative Normalization

Self-Organizing Map

Subtractive Weight Adjustment

Z-Axis Normalization

Questions for Review

1.   How many hidden layers are normally used with a self-organizing map? What are their roles?

2.   For what types of problems are self-organizing maps normally used?

3.   How is competitive learning different from the learning presented earlier in this book, such as backpropagation or genetic algorithms?

4.   What output does a self-organizing map produce, and what does this output represent?

5.   What is the main advantage of z-axis normalization over multiplicative normalization? When might multiplicative normalization be more useful?

Chapter 12: OCR with the Self-Organizing Map

- What is OCR?
- Cropping an Image
- Downsampling an Image
- Training the Neural Network to Recognize Characters
- Recalling Characters
- A "Commercial-Grade" OCR Application

In the previous chapter, you learned how to construct a self-organizing map (SOM). You learned that an SOM can be used to classify samples into several groups. In this chapter, we will examine a specific SOM application; we will apply an SOM to Optical Character Recognition (OCR).

OCR programs are capable of reading printed text. This may be text scanned from a document or handwritten text drawn on a hand-held device, such as a personal digital assistant (PDA). OCR programs are used widely in many industries. One of the largest users of OCR systems is the United States Postal Service.

In the 1970s and 1980s, the US Postal Service had many letter-sorting machines (LSMs). These machines were manned by human clerks, who keyed the zip codes of 60 letters per minute. Human letter-sorters have now been replaced by computerized letter-sorting machines. These new letter-sorting machines rely on OCR technology; they scan incoming letters, read their zip codes, and route them to their correct destinations.

In this chapter, a program will be presented to demonstrate how a self-organizing map can be trained to recognize human handwriting. We will not create a program that can scan pages of text; rather, this program will read individual characters as they are drawn by the user. This function is similar to the handwriting recognition techniques employed by many PDA's.

The OCR Application

When the OCR application is launched, it displays a simple GUI interface. Through this interface, the user can both train and use the neural network. The GUI interface is shown in Figure 12.1.

Figure 12.1: The OCR application.

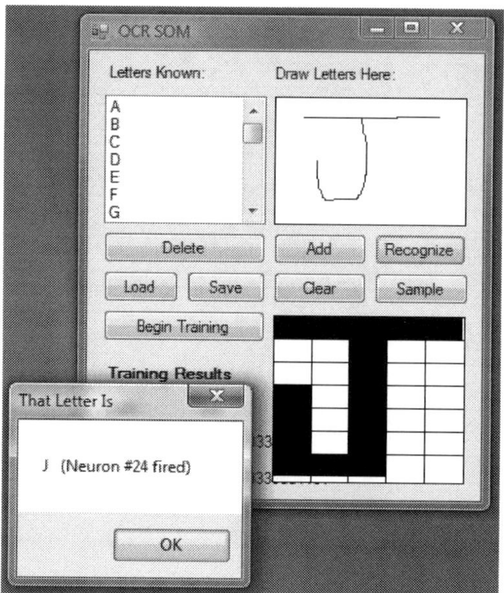

The program is not immediately ready to recognize letters upon startup. It must first be trained using letters that have actually been drawn. Training files are stored in the same directory as the OCR application. The name of the training sample is "sample.dat".

If you downloaded the "sample.dat" file from Heaton Research, you will see it contains handwriting samples I produced. If you use this file to train the program and then attempt to recognize your own handwriting, you may not experience the results you would achieve with a training file based on your own handwriting. Creating a sample based on your own handwriting will be covered in the next section. For now, we will focus on how the program recognizes handwriting using the sample file provided.

You should begin by clicking the "Load" button on the OCR application. The program will then attempt to load the training file. A small message box should be displayed indicating that the file was loaded successfully. Once the file has been loaded, the program will display all of the letters for which it will be trained. The training file provided only contains entries for the 26 capital letters of the Latin alphabet.

Now that the letters have been loaded, the neural network must be trained. By clicking the "Train" button, the application will begin the training process. The training process may take anywhere from a few seconds to several minutes, depending on the speed of your computer. A small message box will be displayed once training is complete.

Using the Sample Program to Recognize Letters

Now that the training set has been loaded and the neural network has been trained, you are ready to recognize characters. The user interface makes this process very easy. You simply draw the character that you would like to have the program recognize in the large rectangular region containing the instruction "Draw Letters Here". Once you have drawn a letter, you can select several different options.

The letters that you draw are downsampled before they are recognized, meaning the image is mapped to a small grid that is five pixels wide and seven pixels high. The advantage of downsampling to such a size is twofold. First, the lower-resolution image requires fewer input neurons for processing than a full-sized image. Second, by downsampling everything to the same size, the size of a character is neutralized; it does not matter if you draw a large character or a small character. If you click the "Downsample" button, you can see the downsampled version of your letter. Clicking the "Clear" button will cause the drawing and downsampled regions to be cleared.

You will notice that a box is drawn around your letter when you display the downsampled version. This is a cropping box. The purpose of the cropping box is to remove any non-essential white space in the image. This also has the desirable effect of eliminating the need to have the program consider a letter's position. A letter can be drawn in the center of the drawing region, near the top, or in some other location, and the program will still recognize it.

When you are ready to recognize a letter, you should click the "Recognize" button. This will cause the application to downsample your letter and then attempt to recognize it using the self-organizing map. The exact process for downsampling an image will be discussed in the next section. The pattern is then presented to the self-organizing map and the winning neuron is selected.

If you recall from chapter 11, a self-organizing map has several output neurons. One output neuron is selected as the winner for each input pattern. The self-organizing map used by this sample program has 26 output neurons to match the 26 letters in the sample set. The program will respond to the letter you enter by telling you both which neuron fired, and which letter it believes you have drawn. In matching my own handwriting, I have found this program generally achieves a success rate of approximately 80–90%. If you are having trouble getting the program to recognize your letters, ensure that you are writing clear capital letters. You may also try training the neural network to recognize your own handwriting, as covered in the next section.

Training the Sample Program to Recognize Letters

You may find that the program does not recognize your handwriting as well as you think it should. This may be because the program was trained using my handwriting, which may not be representative of the handwriting of the entire population. (My grade school teachers would surely argue that this is indeed the case.) In this section, I will explain how you can train the network using your own handwriting.

There are two approaches from which you can choose: you can start from a blank training set and enter all 26 letters yourself, or you can start with my training set and replace individual letters. The latter is a good approach if the network is recognizing most of your characters, and failing on only a small set. In this case, you can just retrain the neural network for the letters that the program is failing to recognize.

To delete a letter that the training set already has listed, you should select that letter and press the "Delete" button on the OCR application. Note that this is the GUI's "Delete" button and not the delete button on your computer's keyboard.

To add a new letter to the training set, you should draw your letter in the drawing input area. Once your letter is drawn, click the "Add" button. You will be prompted for the actual letter that you just drew. The character you type in response to this prompt will be displayed to you when the OCR application recognizes the letter.

Once your training set is complete you should save it. This is accomplished by clicking the application's "Save" button. This will save the training set to the file "sample.dat". If you already have a file named "sample.dat", it will be overwritten; therefore, it is important to make a copy of your previous training file if you would like to keep it. If you exit the OCR application without saving your training data, it will be lost. When you launch the OCR application again, you can click "Load" to retrieve the data you stored in the "sample.dat" file.

In the previous two sections you learned how to use the OCR application. As you have seen, the program is adept at recognizing characters that you have entered and demonstrates a good use of the self-organizing map.

Implementing the OCR Program

We will now see how the OCR program was implemented. There are several classes that make up the OCR application. The purpose of each class in the application is summarized in Table 12.1.

Table 12.1: Classes for the OCR Application

Class	Purpose
DownSample	Downsamples what the user draws..
OCRForm	The form that allows the user to draw characters.
Program	Does little more than start the main form.

We will now examine each section of the program. We will begin by examining how a user draws an image.

Drawing Images

Though not directly related to neural networks, the process by which a user is able to draw characters is an important part of the OCR application. We will examine the process in this section. The code for this process is contained in the **OCRForm** class.

Most of the actual drawing is handled by the **MouseMove**. A line is drawn when a user drags the mouse from the last mouse position to the current mouse position. The mouse moves faster than the program can accept new values; thus, by drawing the line, we cover missed pixels as best we can. The line is drawn to the off-screen image, and then updated to the user's screen. This is accomplished with the following lines of code.

```
if (entry.Capture == true)
{
  entryGraphics.DrawLine(blackPen, entryLastX, entryLastY,
      e.X, e.Y);
  entry.Invalidate();
  entryLastX = e.X;
  entryLastY = e.Y;
}
```

This method is called repeatedly as the program runs, and whatever the user is drawing is saved to the off-screen image. In the next section, you will learn how to downsample an image. You will then see that the off-screen image from this section is accessed as an array of integers, which allows the image data to be directly manipulated.

Downsampling the Image

Every time a letter is drawn for either training or recognition, it must be downsampled. In this section, we will examine the process by which downsampling is achieved. However, before we discuss the downsampling process, we should discuss how downsampled images are stored. All downsampling is done by the **DownSample** class. This class is shown in Listing 12.1.

Listing 12.1: Downsampling Images (DownSample.cs)

```csharp
using System;
using System.Collections.Generic;
using System.Linq;
using System.Text;
using System.Drawing;

namespace Chapter12OCR
{
    public class DownSample
    {
        private Bitmap image;
        private int downSampleTop;
        private int downSampleBottom;
        private int downSampleLeft;
        private int downSampleRight;
        private double ratioX;
        private double ratioY;

        public DownSample(Bitmap image)
        {
            this.image = image;
        }

        public bool[] PerformDownSample(int downSampleWidth,
            int downSampleHeight)
        {
            int size = downSampleWidth * downSampleHeight;
            bool[] result = new bool[size];

            FindBounds();

            // now downsample

            this.ratioX = (double)(this.downSampleRight
                    - this.downSampleLeft)
                    / (double)downSampleWidth;
            this.ratioY = (double)(this.downSampleBottom
                    - this.downSampleTop)
                    / (double)downSampleHeight;

            int index = 0;
            for (int y = 0; y < downSampleHeight; y++)
            {
                for (int x = 0; x < downSampleWidth; x++)
                {
```

```csharp
                result[index++] = DownSampleRegion(x, y);
            }
        }

        return result;
    }


    /// <summary>
    /// Called to downsample a quadrant of the image.
    /// </summary>
    /// <param name="x">The x coordinate of the
    /// resulting downsample.</param>
    /// <param name="y">The y coordinate of the
    /// resulting downsample.</param>
    /// <returns>Returns true if there were ANY pixels in
    /// the specified quadrant.</returns>
    protected bool DownSampleRegion(int x, int y)
    {
        int startX = (int)(this.downSampleLeft
                + (x * this.ratioX));
        int startY = (int)(this.downSampleTop
                + (y * this.ratioY));
        int endX = (int)(startX + this.ratioX);
        int endY = (int)(startY + this.ratioY);

        for (int yy = startY; yy <= endY; yy++)
        {
            for (int xx = startX; xx <= endX; xx++)
            {

                Color pixel = this.image.GetPixel(xx, yy);
                if (IsBlack(pixel))
                {
                    return true;
                }
            }
        }

        return false;
    }


    /// <summary>
    /// This method is called to automatically crop
    /// the image so that whitespace
    /// is removed.
```

```csharp
/// </summary>
protected void FindBounds()
{
    int h = image.Height;
    int w = image.Width;

    // top line
    for (int y = 0; y < h; y++)
    {
        if (!HLineClear(y))
        {
            this.downSampleTop = y;
            break;
        }

    }
    // bottom line
    for (int y = h - 1; y >= 0; y--)
    {
        if (!HLineClear(y))
        {
            this.downSampleBottom = y;
            break;
        }
    }
    // left line
    for (int x = 0; x < w; x++)
    {
        if (!VLineClear(x))
        {
            this.downSampleLeft = x;
            break;
        }
    }

    // right line
    for (int x = w - 1; x >= 0; x--)
    {
        if (!VLineClear(x))
        {
            this.downSampleRight = x;
            break;
        }
    }
}
```

```csharp
/// <summary>
/// This method is called internally to see if
/// there are any pixels in the
/// given scan line. This method is used to perform
/// autocropping.
/// </summary>
/// <param name="y">The horizontal line to scan.</param>
/// <returns>True if there were any pixels in
/// this horizontal line.</returns>
protected bool HLineClear(int y)
{
    int w = this.image.Width;
    for (int i = 0; i < w; i++)
    {
        Color pixel = this.image.GetPixel(i, y);
        if (IsBlack(pixel))
        {
            return false;
        }
    }
    return true;
}


/// <summary>
/// This method is called to determine if a vertical
/// line is clear.
/// </summary>
/// <param name="x">The vertical line to scan.</param>
/// <returns>True if there are any pixels in the
/// specified vertical line.</returns>
protected bool VLineClear(int x)
{
    int w = this.image.Width;
    int h = this.image.Height;
    for (int i = 0; i < h; i++)
    {
        Color pixel = this.image.GetPixel(x, i);
        if (IsBlack(pixel))
        {
            return false;
        }
    }
    return true;
}
```

```
    protected bool IsBlack(Color pixel)
    {
        return (pixel.R != 255 || pixel.G != 255 || pixel.B !=
255);
    }


  }
}
```

The next sections will explain how the image is downsampled.

Negating Size and Position

As mentioned earlier, all images are downsampled before being used. This facilitates the processing of images by the neural network, since size and position do not have to be considered. This is particularly important, since the drawing area is large enough to allow a user to draw letters of different sizes. Downsampling results in images of consistent size. In this section, I will explain how this is done.

When you draw an image, the first thing the program does is draw a box around the boundaries of your letter. This allows the program to eliminate all of the white space. The process is performed inside the **FindBounds** method of the **DownSample** class. This is done to crop the image and remove any white space. Cropping is accomplished by dragging four imaginary lines, one from the top, one from the left, one from the bottom, and one from the right side of the image. These lines stop as soon as they encounter a pixel containing part of the image.

The four lines then snap to the outer edges of the image. The **HLineClear** and **VLineClear** methods both accept a parameter that indicates the line to scan, and return **true** if that line is clear. The program works by calling **HLineClear** and **VLineClear** until they cross the outer edges of the image. The horizontal line method (**HLineClear**) is shown here:

```
protected bool HLineClear(int y)
{
  int w = this.image.Width;
  for (int i = 0; i < w; i++)
  {
    Color pixel = this.image.GetPixel(i, y);
    if (IsBlack(pixel))
    {
      return false;
    }
  }
return true;
}
```

As you can see, the horizontal line method accepts a y coordinate that specifies the horizontal line to be checked. The program then loops through each x coordinate on this row, checking to see if there are any pixel values. The value of -1 indicates white and is ignored. The **FindBounds** method uses **HLineClear** and **VLineClear** to calculate the four edges. The beginning of this method is shown here:

```
protected void FindBounds()
{
  int h = image.Height;
  int w = image.Width;

  // top line
  for (int y = 0; y < h; y++)
  {
    if (!HLineClear(y))
    {
      this.downSampleTop = y;
      break;
    }
  }
  // bottom line
  for (int y = h - 1; y >= 0; y--)
  {
    if (!HLineClear(y))
    {
      this.downSampleBottom = y;
      break;
    }
  }
}
```

To calculate the top line of the cropping rectangle, the program starts at 0 and continues to the bottom of the image. The first non-clear line encountered is established as the top of the cropping rectangle. The same process, is carried out in reverse to determine the bottom of the image. The processes to determine the left and right boundaries are carried out in the same way.

Performing the Downsampling

Once the cropping has taken place, the image must be downsampled. This involves reducing the image to a 5 X 7 resolution. To understand how to reduce an image to 5 X 7, begin by thinking of an imaginary grid being drawn on top of the high-resolution image. The grid divides the image into regions, five across and seven down. If any pixel in a region is filled, then the corresponding pixel in the 5 X 7 downsampled image is also filled in. Most of the work done by this process is accomplished inside the **DownSampleRegion** method, as shown here:

```
protected bool DownSampleRegion(int x, int y)
{
```

```csharp
int startX = (int)(this.downSampleLeft + (x * this.ratioX));
int startY = (int)(this.downSampleTop + (y * this.ratioY));
int endX = (int)(startX + this.ratioX);
int endY = (int)(startY + this.ratioY);

for (int yy = startY; yy <= endY; yy++)
{
  for (int xx = startX; xx <= endX; xx++)
  {
    Color pixel = this.image.GetPixel(xx, yy);
    if (IsBlack(pixel))
    {
      return true;
    }
  }
}
return false;
}
```

The **DownSampleRegion** method accepts the number of the region to be calculated. The starting and ending **x** and **y** coordinates are then calculated. The **DownSampleLeft** method is used to calculate the first **x** coordinate for the region specified. This is the left side of the cropping rectangle. Then **x** is multiplied by **ratioX**, which is the ratio used to indicate the number of pixels that make up each region. It allows us to determine where to place **startX**. The starting **y** position, **startY**, is calculated in the same way. Next, the program loops through every **x** and **y** in the specified region. If even one pixel in the region is filled, the method returns **true**. The **DownSampleRegion** method is called for each region in the image. The final result is a reduced copy of the image, stored in an array.

Using the Self-Organizing Map

The downsampled character pattern that is drawn by the user is now fed to the input neurons of the self-organizing map. There is one input neuron for every pixel in the downsampled image. Because the downsampled image is a 5 X 7 grid, there are 35 input neurons.

The neural network communicates which letter it thinks the user drew through the output neurons. The number of output neurons always matches the number of unique letter samples provided. Since 26 letters were provided in the sample, there are 26 output neurons. If this program were modified to support multiple samples per individual letter, there would still be 26 output neurons.

In addition to input and output neurons, there are also connections between the individual neurons. These connections are not all equal. Each connection is assigned a weight. The weights are ultimately the only factors that determine what the network will output for a given input pattern. In order to determine the total number of connections, you must multiply the number of input neurons by the number of output neurons. A neural network with 26 output neurons and 35 input neurons will have a total of 910 connection weights. The training process is dedicated to finding the correct values for these weights.

The recognition process begins when the user draws a character and then clicks the "Recognize" button. First, the letter is downsampled to a 5 X 7 image. This downsampled image must be copied from its 2-dimensional array to an array of doubles that will be fed to the input neurons, as seen here:

```
private void btnRecognize_Click(object sender, EventArgs e)
{
  DownSample ds = new DownSample(this.entryImage);
  this.downsampled = ds.PerformDownSample(OCRForm.DOWNSAMPLE_
WIDTH, OCRForm.DOWNSAMPLE_HEIGHT);

  this.sample.Invalidate();
```

Make sure that the neural network was trained.

```
if (this.network == null)
{
  MessageBox.Show("I need to be trained first!");
  return;
}
```

Prepare and present the data.

```
int sampleSize = OCRForm.DOWNSAMPLE_HEIGHT *
    OCRForm.DOWNSAMPLE_WIDTH;
double[] input = new double[sampleSize];

for (int i = 0; i < sampleSize; i++)
{
  input[i] = this.downsampled[i] ? 0.5 : -0.5;
}
```

The above code does the conversion. Neurons require floating point input; therefore, the program uses the value of 0.5 to represent a black pixel and -0.5 to represent a white pixel. The 5 X 7 array of 35 values is fed to the input neurons. This is accomplished by passing the input array to the neural network's **Winner** method. This method will identify which of the 35 neurons won, and will store this information in the **best** integer.

```
int best = this.network.Winner(input);
```

```
char[] map = MapNeurons();
MessageBox.Show("  " + map[best] + "    (Neuron #"
   + best + " fired)", "That Letter Is");
ClearEntry();
}
```

Knowing the winning neuron is not very helpful, because it does not show you which letter was actually recognized. To determine which neuron is associated with each letter, the network must be fed each letter to see which neuron wins. For example, if you were to feed the training image for "J" into the neural network, and neuron #4 was returned as the winner, you would know that neuron #4 is the neuron that was trained to recognize J's pattern. This process is accomplished by calling the **MapNeurons** method. The **MapNeurons** method returns an array of characters. The index of each array element corresponds to the neuron number that recognizes the particular character.

Training the Neural Network

Learning is the process of selecting a neuron weight matrix that will correctly recognize input patterns. A self-organizing map learns by constantly evaluating and optimizing its weight matrix. To do this, a starting weight matrix must be established. This is accomplished by selecting random numbers. This weight matrix will likely do a poor job of recognizing letters, but it will provide a starting point.

Once the initial random weight matrix is created, the training can begin. First, the weight matrix is evaluated to determine its current error level. The error is determined by evaluating how well the training inputs (the letters you created) map to the output neurons. The error is calculated by the **EvaluateErrors** method of the **TrainSelfOrganizingMap** class. When the error level is low, say below 10%, the process is complete.

The training process begins when the user clicks the "Begin Training" button. This begins the training and the number of input and output neurons are calculated. First, the number of input neurons is determined from the size of the downsampled image. Since the height is seven and the width is five for this example, the number of input neurons is 35. The number of output neurons matches the number of characters the program has been given.

This part of the program can be modified if you want to train it with more than one sample per letter. For example, if you want to use 4 samples per letter, you will have to make sure that the output neuron count remains 26, even though 104 input samples will be provided for training—4 for each of the 26 letters.

The training runs in a background thread as a C#**btnBeginTraining_Click** method. The signature for the **btnBeginTraining_Click** method is shown here:

```
private void btnBeginTraining_Click(object sender, EventArgs e)
{
```

First, we calculate the number of input neurons needed. This is the product of the downsampled image's height and width.

```
int inputCount = OCRForm.DOWNSAMPLE_HEIGHT * OCRForm.DOWNSAMPLE_
WIDTH;
int letterCount = this.letters.Items.Count;
this.trainingSet = new double[letterCount][];
```

We then loop through all of the letter samples.

```
int index = 0;
foreach (char ch in this.letterData.Keys)
{
```

A letter's sample data is obtained.

```
this.trainingSet[index] = new double[inputCount];
bool[] data = this.letterData[ch];
```

The data is transferred into the network and the Boolean **true** and **false** are transformed to 0.5 and -0.5.

```
for (int i = 0; i < inputCount; i++)
{
    this.trainingSet[index][i] = data[i] ? 0.5 : -0.5;
}
index++;
}
```

The training data has been created, so the new **SelfOrganizingMap** object is now created. This object will use multiplicative normalization, which was discussed in chapter 11.

```
network = new SelfOrganizingMap(inputCount, letterCount,
NormalizationType.Z_AXIS);
```

A **TrainSelfOrganizingMap** object is now created to train the self-organizing map just created. This trainer uses the subtractive training method, which was also discussed in chapter 11.

```
TrainSelfOrganizingMap train = new TrainSelfOrganizingMap(
    this.network, this.trainingSet, TrainSelfOrganizingMap.Learning-
Method.SUBTRACTIVE, 0.5);
```

The number of training **tries** is tracked.

```
int tries = 1;
```

The number of tries and the error information are updated on the window for each training iteration.

```
do
{
  train.Iteration();
  this.txtTries.Text = "" + tries;
  this.txtBestError.Text = "" + train.BestError;
  this.txtLastError.Text = "" + train.TotalError;
  tries++;
  Application.DoEvents();
} while (train.TotalError > 0.01 && (tries <= 100));
MessageBox.Show("Training complete.");
}
```

When the training error has reached an acceptable level, the final training numbers are displayed. The neural network is now ready to use.

Beyond This Example

The program presented here is only capable of recognizing individual letters, one at a time. In addition, the sample data provided only includes support for the upper-case letters of the Latin alphabet. There is nothing in this program that would prevent you from using both upper and lowercase characters, as well as digits. If you train the program for two sets of 26 letters each and 10 digits, the program will require 62 training sets.

You can quickly run into problems with such a scenario. The program will have a very hard time differentiating between a lowercase "o", an uppercase "O, and the digit zero (0). The problem of discerning between them cannot be handled by the neural network. Instead, you will have to examine the context in which the letters and digits appear.

Many layers of complexity will be added if the program is expanded to process an entire page of writing at one time. Even if the page is only text, it will be necessary for the program to determine where each line begins and ends. Additionally, spaces between letters will need to be located so that the individual characters can be fed to the self-organizing map for processing.

If the image being scanned is not pure text, then the job becomes even more complex. It will be necessary for the program to scan around the borders of the text and graphics. Some lines may be in different fonts, and thus be of different sizes. All of these issues will need to be considered to extend this program to a commercial grade OCR application.

Another limitation of this sample program is that only one drawing can be defined per character. You might want to use three different handwriting samples for a letter, rather than just one. The underlying neural network classes will easily support this feature. This change can be implemented by adding a few more classes to the user interface. To do so, you will have to modify the program to accept more training data than the number of output neurons.

As you can see, there are many considerations that will have to be made to expand this application into a commercial-grade application. In addition, you will not be able to use just a single neural network. It is likely several different types of neural networks will be required to accomplish the tasks mentioned.

Chapter Summary

This chapter presented a practical application of the self-organizing map. You were introduced to the concept of OCR and the uses of this technology. The example presented mimics the OCR capabilities of a PDA. Characters are input when a user draws on a high-resolution box. Unfortunately, this resolution is too high to be directly presented to the neural network. To resolve this problem, we use the techniques of cropping and downsampling to transform the image into a second image that has a much lower resolution.

Once the image has been entered, it must be cropped. Cropping is the process by which extra white space is removed. The program automatically calculates the size of any white space around the image. A rectangle is then plotted around the boundary between the image and the white space. Using cropping has the effect of removing position dependence. It does not matter where the letter is drawn, since cropping eliminates all non-essential areas.

Once the image has been cropped, it must be downsampled. Downsampling is the process by which a high-resolution image is transformed into a lower resolution image. A high-resolution image is downsampled by breaking it up into a number of regions that are equal to the number of pixels in the downsampled image. Each pixel in the downsampled image is assigned the average color of the corresponding region in the high-resolution image. The resulting downsampled image is then fed to either the training or recollection process of the neural network.

The next chapter will present another application of neural networks, bots. Bots are computer programs that can access web sites and perform automated tasks. In doing so, a bot may encounter a wide range of data. Additionally, this data may not be uniformly formatted. A neural network is ideal for use in understanding this data.

Vocabulary

Downsample

Optical character recognition (OCR)

Questions for Review

1. Describe how an image is downsampled.

2. Why is downsampling necessary?

3. How do the dimensions of the downsampled image relate to the input neurons of the self-organizing map?

4. What would be the advantages and disadvantages of using a larger number of input neurons for the self-organizing map used for OCR in this chapter?

5. The OCR application in this chapter drew four imaginary lines over the drawn character. These lines formed a square that fit exactly around the character the user drew. What is the purpose of the imaginary lines?

CHAPTER 13: BOT PROGRAMMING AND NEURAL NETWORKS

- Creating a Simple Bot
- Analyzing Text
- Training a Neural Bot
- Using a Neural Bot

Bots are computer programs that are designed to use the Internet in much the same way as humans use it. Neural networks can be useful in developing bots. In this chapter you will see how a neural network can be used to assist a bot in finding desired information on the Internet.

A discussion exploring the creation of bots could easily fill a book. If you would like to learn more about bot programming, you may find the book HTTP Programming Recipes for C# Bots (ISBN: 0977320677) helpful. This book presents many algorithms commonly used to create bots. The bots created in this chapter will use some of the code from HTTP Programming Recipes for C# Bots.

A Simple Bot

A bot is generally used to retrieve information from a website. Before we create a complex bot that makes use of neural networks, it will be useful to see how a simple bot is created. The simple bot will get the current time for the city of St. Louis, Missouri from a website. The site that has the data we are seeking is located at the following URL:

`http://www.httprecipes.com/1/3/time.php`

If you point a browser to the above URL, the page shown in Figure 13.1 will be displayed.

Figure 13.1: Local time in St. Louis, MO.

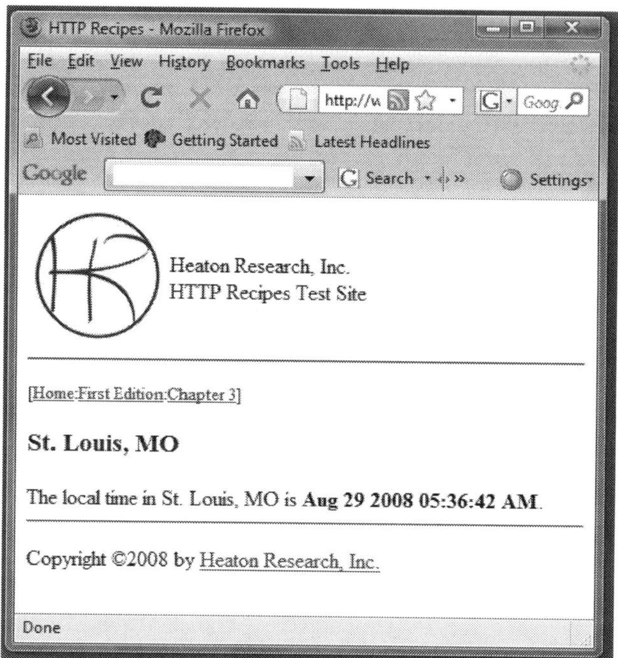

The source code for the simple bot is shown in Listing 13.1.

Listing 13.1: A Simple Bot (SimpleBot.cs)

```
using System;
using System.Net;
using System.IO;

namespace Chapter13SimpleBot
{
    class SimpleBot
    {
        /// <summary>
        /// This method is very useful for grabbing
        /// information from a
        /// HTML page.
        /// </summary>
        /// <param name="str">The string to parse.</param>
        /// <param name="token1">The text, or tag, that
        /// comes before the desired text</param>
        /// <param name="token2">The text, or tag, that
        /// comes after the desired text</param>
        /// <param name="count">Which occurrence of token1
```

```csharp
/// to use, 1 for the first</param>
/// <returns>The contents of the URL that was
/// downloaded.</returns>
public String Extract(String str, String token1,
    String token2, int count)
{
    int location1, location2;

    location1 = location2 = 0;
    do
    {
        location1 = str.IndexOf(token1, location1 + 1);

        if (location1 == -1)
            return null;

        count--;
    } while (count > 0);

    location2 = str.IndexOf(token2, location1 + 1);
    if (location2 == -1)
        return null;

    location1 += token1.Length;
    return str.Substring(location1,
          location2 - location1);
}


/// <summary>
/// This method downloads the specified URL into a C#
/// String. This is a very simple method, that you can
/// reused anytime you need to quickly grab all data from
/// a specific URL.
/// </summary>
/// <param name="url">The URL to download.</param>
/// <returns>The contents of the URL that was
/// downloaded.</returns>
public String DownloadPage(Uri url)
{
    WebRequest http = HttpWebRequest.Create(url);
    HttpWebResponse response =
          (HttpWebResponse)http.GetResponse();
    StreamReader stream =
          new StreamReader(response.
GetResponseStream(), System.Text.Encoding.ASCII);
```

```csharp
            String result = stream.ReadToEnd();

            response.Close();
            stream.Close();
            return result;
        }


        /// <summary>
        /// Run the example.
        /// </summary>
        public void Go()
        {
            Uri u = new Uri(
                    "http://www.httprecipes.com/1/3/time.php");
            String str = DownloadPage(u);

            Console.WriteLine(Extract(str, "<b>", "</b>", 1));
        }


        /// <summary>
        /// The main entry point for the application.
        /// </summary>
        [STAThread]
        static void Main(string[] args)
        {
            SimpleBot module = new SimpleBot();
            module.Go();
        }
    }
}
```

The bot begins by creating a new **Uri** object for the desired web page.

```csharp
Uri u = new Uri("http://www.httprecipes.com/1/3/time.php");
```

The contents of the page are then downloaded into a **String** object. The **DownloadPage** method performs this operation.

```csharp
String str = DownloadPage(u);
```

Finally, the time is extracted from the HTML. This is done using the **Extract** method. The beginning and ending tags that enclose the desired data are provided to the **Extract** method. The third parameter specifies the instance of the **<b>** tag to be found. The number one means that we are seeking the first instance of the **<b>** tag.

```csharp
Console.WriteLine(Extract(str, "<b>", "</b>", 1));
```

The HTML data from the target web page must be examined to see which HTML tags enclose the desired data. The HTML located at the website shown in Figure 13.1 is shown in Listing 13.2.

Listing 13.2: HTML Data Encountered by the Bot

```
<!DOCTYPE HTML PUBLIC "-//W3C//DTD HTML 4.01 Transitional//EN">


<HTML>
<HEAD>
      <TITLE>HTTP Recipes</TITLE>
      <meta http-equiv="Content-Type" content="text/html;
charset=UTF-8">
      <meta http-equiv="Cache-Control" content="no-cache">
      <meta http-equiv="Content-Style-Type" content="text/css">
<link rel="alternate" type="application/rss+xml" title="RSS"
href="http://www.httprecipes.com/1/12/rss2.xml">
</HEAD>


<BODY>


<table border="0"><tr><td>
<a href="http://www.httprecipes.com/"><img src="/images/logo.gif"
alt="Heaton Research Logo" border="0" width="100" height="100">
</a>
</td><td valign="middle">Heaton Research, Inc.<br>
HTTP Recipes Test Site
</td></tr>
</table>
<hr><p><small>[<a href="/">Home</a>:<a href="/1/">First Edition
</a>:
<a href="/1/3/">Chapter 3</a>]</small></p>


<h3>St. Louis, MO</h3>
The local time in St. Louis, MO is <b>Jun 09 2008 10:27:46 PM</b>.


<hr>
<p>Copyright &copy;2008 by <a href="http://www.heatonresearch.
com/">
Heaton Research, Inc.</a></p>
</BODY>
</HTML>
```

As you can see from the above listing, the data the bot seeks is located between a beginning **** tag and an ending **** tag. The bot made use of two methods to download and then extract the data. These two methods will be covered in the following two sections.

Downloading the Page

The contents of a web page are downloaded to a **String** object using the **DownloadPage** method. The signature for the **DownloadPage** method is shown here:

```
public String DownloadPage(Uri url)
```

The **WebRequest** class is used to access the web page.

```
WebRequest http = HttpWebRequest.Create(url);

HttpWebResponse response = (HttpWebResponse)http.GetResponse();

StreamReader stream = new StreamReader(response.GetResponseS-
tream(), System.Text.Encoding.ASCII);
```

Read the contents of the web page.

```
String result = stream.ReadToEnd();                response.Close();
stream.Close();


return result;
```

The **DownloadPage** method is very useful for obtaining a web page as a single **String** object. Once the page has been downloaded, the **Extract** method is used to extract data from the page. The **Extract** method is covered in the next section.

Extracting the Data

Web pages can be thought of as one large **String** object. The process of breaking the string up into useable data is called string parsing. The signature for the **Extract** method is shown below. The first parameter contains the string to be parsed; the second and third parameters specify the beginning and end tokens being sought. Finally, the fourth parameter specifies for which instance of the first token you are looking.

```
public String Extract(String str, String token1, String token2,
int count)
{
```

Two variables are created to hold the locations of the two tokens. They are both initialized to zero.

```
int location1, location2;
location1 = location2 = 0;
```

The location of the first token is then found.

```
do
{
    location1 = str.IndexOf(token1, location1 + 1);
```

If the first token cannot be found, then **null** is returned to indicate that we failed to find anything.

```
if (location1 == -1)
  return null;
```

If the first token is found, then the count variable is decreased and we continue to search as long as there are more instances to find.

```
    count--;
} while (count > 0);
```

We then attempt to locate the second token. If the second token is located, then its index is stored in the **location2** variable. If the **Extract** method fails to find the second token, then null is returned to indicate failure.

```
location2 = str.IndexOf(token2, location1 + 1);

if (location2 == -1)
  return null;
```

Finally, the characters located between the two tokens are returned.

```
location1 += token1.Length;

return str.Substring(location1, location2 - location1);
```

While this bot is very simple, it demonstrates the principles of bot programming. The remaining sections of this chapter will show how to create a much more complex, neural network-based bot.

Introducing the Neural Bot

The neural network-based bot detailed below is provided with the name of a famous person. It uses this information to perform a Yahoo search and obtain information on the person. The bot "reads" all of the information found on the person and attempts to determine the individual's correct birth year.

There are three distinct modes in which this program runs. These modes are summarized in Table 13.1.

Table 13.1: When Born Neural Bot Modes

Mode	Purpose
Gather	In this mode, the bot gathers articles on famous people. It performs a Yahoo search to obtain a number of articles on each. Depending on your Internet speed, this process can take from fifteen minutes to several hours.
Train	Using the data gathered in the first mode, a neural network is built and trained. Once the acceptable error level is reached, this neural network is saved.
Born	After the neural network has been trained, new famous people can be entered. The bot will then attempt to discover their birth year.

The program must run in the **Gather** mode before it can be trained. Likewise, the program must be trained before it can perform the **Born** operation.

There are several configuration constants that can be modified for this bot. These items are shown in Listing 13.3.

Listing 13.3: Configuring the Neural Bot (Config.cs)

```
using System;
using System.Collections.Generic;
using System.Linq;
using System.Text;

namespace Chapter13Bot
{
    public class Config
    {
        public const int INPUT_SIZE = 10;
        public const int OUTPUT_SIZE = 1;
        public const int NEURONS_HIDDEN_1 = 20;
        public const int NEURONS_HIDDEN_2 = 0;
        public const double ACCEPTABLE_ERROR = 0.01;
        public const int MINIMUM_WORDS_PRESENT = 3;

        public const String FILENAME_GOOD_TRAINING_TEXT =
                "bornTrainingGood.txt";
        public const String FILENAME_BAD_TRAINING_TEXT =
                "bornTrainingBad.txt";
        public const String FILENAME_COMMON_WORDS = "common.csv";
        public const String FILENAME_WHENBORN_NET = "whenborn.net";
        public const String FILENAME_HISTOGRAM = "whenborn.hst";
    }
}
```

The configuration constants are defined in Table 13.2.

Table 13.2: Configuring the Neural Bot

Constant	Default	Purpose
INPUT_SIZE	10	Number of input neurons.
OUTPUT_SIZE	1	Number of output neurons.
NEURONS_HIDDEN_1	20	Number of neurons in the first hidden layer.
NEURONS_HIDDEN_2	0	Number of neurons in the second hidden layer.
ACCEPTABLE_ERROR	0.01	The maximum acceptable error level.
MINIMUM_WORDS_PRESENT	3	Minimum number of words for a sentence.
FILENAME_GOOD_TRAINING_TEXT	bornTrainingGood.txt	Good sentences gathered.
FILENAME_BAD_TRAINING_TEXT	bornTrainingBad.txt	Bad sentences gathered.
FILENAME_COMMON_WORDS	common.csv	Common English words.
FILENAME_WHENBORN_NET	whenborn.net	The saved trained neural network.
FILENAME_HISTOGRAM	whenborn.hst	The saved histogram of common words.

We will now examine each mode of operation for the neural bot.

Gathering Training Data for the Neural Bot

The neural-based bot works by performing a Yahoo search on a person of interest. All articles returned from Yahoo are decomposed into sentences and scanned for the correct birth year. A list containing famous people and their birth years is used as training data. This list is stored in a file named "famous.csv". A sampling of the data is shown in Listing 13.4.

Listing 13.4: Famous People

```
Person,Year
Abdullah bin Abdul Aziz Al Saud,1924
Al Gore,1948
Alber Elbaz,1961
America Ferrera,1984
Amr Khaled,1967
Angela Merkel,1954
Anna Netrebko,1971
Arnold Schwarzenegger,1947
Ayatullah Ali Khamenei,1939
Barack Obama,1961
Bernard Arnault,1949
Bill Gates,1955
Brad Pitt,1963
...
Warren Buffett,1930
Wesley Autrey,1956
William Jefferson Clinton,1946
Youssou N'Dour,1959
Zeng Jinyan,1983
```

Using this list, a Yahoo search will be performed to gather information for each of these people.

Gathering the Data

To gather data for the training, the **GatherForTrain** class is executed. The **GatherForTrain** class begins performing Yahoo searches and gathering data for all of the famous people. The **GatherForTrain** class is built to be multithreaded. This speeds the processing, even on a single-processor computer. Because the program must often wait for the many websites it visits to respond, it improves efficiency to access several websites at once. The source code for the **GatherForTrain** class is shown in Listing 13.5.

Listing 13.5: Gathering Training Data (GatherForTrain.cs)

```
using System;
using System.Collections.Generic;
using System.Linq;
using System.Text;
using System.Threading;
using System.IO;


using HeatonResearchNeural.Util;


namespace Chapter13Bot.Gather
```

```csharp
{
    public class GatherForTrain : ScanReportable
    {
        public const bool LOG = true;
        public const int THREAD_POOL_SIZE = 20;

        private ICollection<String> trainingDataGood =
            new List<String>();
        private ICollection<String> trainingDataBad =
            new List<String>();
        private int currentTask;

        private int totalTasks;

        public void Run()
        {


            ReadCSV famous = new ReadCSV("famous.csv");
            Report(
            "Building training data from list of famous people.");
            DateTime started = new DateTime();

            ThreadPool.SetMaxThreads(10, 10);

            List<ManualResetEvent> events =
                new List<ManualResetEvent>();
            this.totalTasks = 0;
            while (famous.Next())
            {
                String name = famous.Get("Person");
                int year = famous.GetInt("Year");

                CollectionWorker worker
                  = new CollectionWorker(this, name,
                        year);
                this.totalTasks++;

                ThreadPool.QueueUserWorkItem(
                  worker.ThreadPoolCallback);
            }

            // wait to finish
            while (this.totalTasks > this.currentTask)
            {
                Thread.Sleep(1000);
```

```
        }


        long length = (DateTime.Now - started).Ticks;
        length /= 1000L;
        length /= 60;
        Console.WriteLine("Took " + length
+ " minutes to collect training data from the Internet.");
        Console.WriteLine("Writing training file");
        WriteTrainingFile();

    }


    public void ReceiveBadSentence(String sentence)
    {
        this.trainingDataBad.Add(sentence);

    }


    public void ReceiveGoodSentence(String sentence)
    {
        this.trainingDataGood.Add(sentence);

    }


    public void Report(String str)
    {
        Console.WriteLine(str);
    }


    public void ReportDone(String str)
    {
        Report((this.currentTask+1) + "/"
        + this.totalTasks + ":" + str);
        this.currentTask++;
    }


    private void WriteTrainingFile()
    {
        TextWriter o = new StreamWriter(
            Config.FILENAME_GOOD_TRAINING_TEXT);

        foreach (String str in this.trainingDataGood)
        {
            o.WriteLine(str.Trim());
```

```
            }

            o.Close();

            o = new StreamWriter(
                    Config.FILENAME_BAD_TRAINING_TEXT);

            foreach (String str in this.trainingDataBad)
            {
                o.WriteLine(str.Trim());
            }

            o.Close();
        }
    }
}
```

The **Run** method performs almost all of the work in the **GatherForTrain** class. The signature for the **Run** method is shown here:

```
public void Run()
{
```

First, the **ReadCSV** class is used to read the comma separated value list of famous people. Comma separated files were introduced in chapter 10.

```
ReadCSV famous = new ReadCSV("famous.csv");
Report("Building training data from list of famous people.");
DateTime started = new DateTime();
```

Set the thread pool to use 20 threads. This is an arbitrary number.

```
ThreadPool.SetMaxThreads(20, 20);
```

While there is still data to be read, we continue to loop through the list of famous people.

```
this.totalTasks = 0;
while (famous.Next())
{
```

The famous person and their birth year are obtained from the CSV file.

```
    String name = famous.Get("Person");
    int year = famous.GetInt("Year");
```

A **CollectionWorker** object is created to actually process this person, and it is added to the thread pool.

```
CollectionWorker worker = new CollectionWorker(this, name,
year);
```

```
this.totalTasks++;
                ThreadPool.QueueUserWorkItem(worker.ThreadPoolCal-
lback);
```

We must now wait for the pool to finish.

```
while (this.totalTasks > this.currentTask)
{
  Thread.Sleep(1000);
}
```

Once the thread pool terminates, the processing is complete and the amount of time the processing took is displayed.

```
long length = (DateTime.Now - started).Ticks;
length /= 1000L;
length /= 60;
Console.WriteLine("Took " + length
+ " minutes to collect training data from the Internet.");
Console.WriteLine("Writing training file");
WriteTrainingFile();
```

Finally, the data is written to the training file.

Support for Multithreading

Multithreading for the gathering mode is provided by the **CollectionWorker** class. The **CollectionWorker** class is shown in Listing 13.6.

Listing 13.6: Collection Worker (CollectionWorker.cs)

```
using System;
using System.Collections.Generic;
using System.Linq;
using System.Text;
using System.IO;

using System.Threading;
using System.Net;

namespace Chapter13Bot.Gather
{
    public class CollectionWorker
    {
        private GatherForTrain bot;


        /// <summary>
```

```
/// The search object to use.
/// </summary>
private YahooSearch search;

private String name;
private int year;

public CollectionWorker(GatherForTrain bot, String name,
        int year)
{
    this.bot = bot;
    this.name = name;
    this.year = year;
    this.search = new YahooSearch();
}


public void ThreadPoolCallback(Object threadContext)
{
    try
    {
        ScanPerson(this.name, this.year);
        this.bot.ReportDone(this.name + ",
          done scanning.");
    }
    catch (Exception e)
    {
        this.bot.ReportDone(this.name
          + ", error encountered.");
        Console.WriteLine(e);
    }
}

private void ScanPerson(String name, int year)
{
    ICollection<Uri> c = this.search.Search(name);
    int i = 0;

    foreach (Uri u in c)
    {
        try
        {
            //Console.WriteLine(i + ":" + name + ":" + u);
            i++;
            Text.CheckURL(this.bot, u, year);
        }
        catch (WebException)
```

```
                {
                }
              }
            }
          }
        }
```

The thread pool initiates the worker by calling the **ThreadPoolCallback** method. As you can see from the listing of the **ThreadPoolCallback** method above, it does little more than call the **ScanPerson** method. The signature for the **ScanPerson** method is shown here:

```
private void ScanPerson(String name, int year)
{
```

First, a collection of URLs is obtained from Yahoo for the specified famous person.

```
ICollection<Uri> c = this.search.Search(name);
int i = 0;
```

For each URL that is obtained, the **CheckURL** method of the **Text** class is called. The **Text** class will be covered in the next section.

```
foreach (Uri u in c)
{
  try
  {
    Console.WriteLine(i + ":" + name + ":" + u);
    i++;
    Text.CheckURL(this.bot, u, year);
  }
  catch (WebException)
  {
  }
```

If an error is encountered, it is likely an invalid URL was obtained from Yahoo. This is not an unusual occurrence; such URLs are simply ignored.

Parsing Websites

As you saw in the last section, websites are parsed using the class named **Text**. The **Text** class is shown in Listing 13.7.

Listing 13.7: Parsing Websites (Text.cs)

```
using System;
using System.Collections.Generic;
using System.Linq;
using System.Text;
```

```
using System.IO;
using System.Net;

using HeatonResearch.Spider.HTML;

namespace Chapter13Bot
{
    public class Text
    {
        /// <summary>
        /// Check the specified URL for a birth year. This will
        /// occur if one sentence
        /// is found that has the word born, and a numeric
        /// value less than 3000.
        /// </summary>
        /// <param name="report">What to report to.</param>
        /// <param name="url">The URL to check.</param>
        /// <param name="desiredYear">The desired year.</param>
        public static void CheckURL(ScanReportable report,
            Uri url, int desiredYear)
        {


            WebRequest http = HttpWebRequest.Create(url);
            http.Timeout = 1000;
            HttpWebResponse response =
                (HttpWebResponse)http.GetResponse();

            using(Stream istream = response.GetResponseStream() )
            {
                ParseHTML html = new ParseHTML(istream);
                ParseURL(html, report, desiredYear);
            }

            response.Close();

        }

        private static void ParseURL(ParseHTML html,
            ScanReportable report, int desiredYear)
        {
            int ch;
            StringBuilder sentence = new StringBuilder();
            String ignoreUntil = null;

            do
```

```csharp
{
    ch = html.Read();
    if ((ch != -1) && (ch != 0)
      && (ignoreUntil == null))
    {
        if (".?!".IndexOf((char)ch) != -1)
        {
            String str = sentence.ToString();
            int year = Text.ExtractYear(str);

            if (desiredYear == -1)
            {
                // looking for any year
                if (year != -1)
                {
                    //report.ReceiveGoodSentence(str);
                }
            }
            else
            {
                // looking for a specific year
                if (year == desiredYear)
                {
                    //report.ReceiveGoodSentence(str);
                }
                else if (year != -1)
                {
                    //report.ReceiveBadSentence(str);
                }
            }
            sentence.Length = 0;
        }
        else if (ch == ' ')
        {
            string str = sentence.ToString();
            if ((sentence.Length > 0)
                    && (str[str.Length - 1] != ' '))
            {
                //sentence.Append(' ');

            }
        }
        else if ((ch != '\n') && (ch != '\t')
            && (ch != '\r'))
        {
            if ((ch) < 128)
```

```
                {
                        //sentence.Append((char)ch);
                }
            }
        }
        else if (ch == 0)
        {
                // clear anything before a body tag
                if (html.Tag.Name.Equals("body",
StringComparison.CurrentCultureIgnoreCase)
                        || html.Tag.Name.Equals("br",
StringComparison.CurrentCultureIgnoreCase)
                        || html.Tag.Name.Equals("li",
StringComparison.CurrentCultureIgnoreCase)
                        || html.Tag.Name.Equals("p",
StringComparison.CurrentCultureIgnoreCase)
                        || html.Tag.Name.Equals("h1",
StringComparison.CurrentCultureIgnoreCase)
                        || html.Tag.Name.Equals("h2",
StringComparison.CurrentCultureIgnoreCase)
                        || html.Tag.Name.Equals("h3",
StringComparison.CurrentCultureIgnoreCase)
                        || html.Tag.Name.Equals("td",
StringComparison.CurrentCultureIgnoreCase)
                        || html.Tag.Name.Equals("th",
StringComparison.CurrentCultureIgnoreCase))
                    {
                        sentence.Length = 0;
                    }
                // ignore everything between script
                // and style tags
                if (ignoreUntil == null)
                {
                    if (html.Tag.Name.Equals("script",
                StringComparison.CurrentCultureIgnoreCase))
                        {
                            ignoreUntil = "/script";
                        }
                    else if (html.Tag.Name
                            .Equals("style",
                StringComparison.CurrentCultureIgnoreCase))
                        {
                            ignoreUntil = "/style";
                        }
                }
                else
```

```csharp
                {
                    if (html.Tag.Name.Equals(
ignoreUntil, StringComparison.CurrentCultureIgnoreCase))
                    {
                        ignoreUntil = null;
                    }
                }

                // add a space after the tag
                if (sentence.Length > 0)
                {
                    string str = sentence.ToString();
                    if (str[str.Length - 1] != ' ')
                    {
                        sentence.Append(' ');
                    }
                }
            }
        } while (ch != -1);
    }

    /// <summary>
    /// Examine a sentence and see if it contains the
    /// word born and a number.
    /// </summary>
    /// <param name="sentence">The sentence to search.</param>
    /// <returns>The number that was found.</returns>
    public static int ExtractYear(String sentence)
    {
        int result = -1;

        string[] tok = sentence.Split(' ');
        for (int i = 0; i < tok.Length; i++)
        {
            String word = tok[i];

            try
            {
                result = int.Parse(word);

                if ((result < 1600) || (result > 2100))
                {
                    result = -1;
                }
            }
```

```
            catch (FormatException)
            {
            }
        }

        return result;
    }

  }
}
```

The **CheckURL** method of the **Text** class is called to scan a web page and look for sentences. These sentences are then divided into two categories: good and bad. If a sentence contains a year, and it is the year of the famous person's birth, then this sentence is a good sentence; otherwise, it is a bad sentence. The two lists created as a result of this sorting are then used to train the neural network. The signature for the **CheckURL** method is shown here:

```
public static void CheckURL(
  ScanReportable report,
  Uri url,
  int desiredYear)
{
```

As you can see, three parameters are passed to this method. The first, named **report**, specifies the object that will receive the good and bad sentence lists that this method will produce. The second, named **url**, specifies the **Uri** of the website to be scanned. The third, named **desiredYear**, specifies the year that the person was actually born.

First, variable **ch** is declared to hold the current character. Variable **sentence** is declared to hold the current sentence, and **ignoreUntil** is declared to hold an HTML tag that we will rely on to indicate when we should begin processing data again. For example, if we encounter the HTML tag **<script>**, we will set **ignoreUntil** to **</script>** and will not process any of the code between **<script>** and the **</script>** tag. The data between these tags is Javascript and will not be useful in determining a birth year.

```
int ch;
StringBuilder sentence = new StringBuilder();
String ignoreUntil = null;
```

An HTTP connection is opened to the specified URL. Timeouts of 1,000 milliseconds, or one second, are specified. We will be processing a large number of pages and we do not want to wait too long for one to return an error. If data is not ready in a second, we move on to the next page.

```
WebRequest http = HttpWebRequest.Create(url);
http.Timeout = 1000;
```

```
HttpWebResponse response = (HttpWebResponse)http.GetResponse();
Stream istream = response.GetResponseStream();
ParseHTML html = new ParseHTML(istream);
```

With the connection established, we begin reading from the HTML page. This method uses the HTML parser provided in the book HTTP Programming Recipes for C# Bots (ISBN: 0977320677).

```
do
{
  ch = html.Read();
```

If the value of **ch** is -1, then an HTML tag has been encountered. Otherwise, **ch** will be the next character of text. If the character is a period, question mark, or exclamation point, then we know we have reached the end of a sentence, unless we are ignoring data until we reach a tag, in which case **ignoreUntil** will not be **null**.

```
if ((ch != -1) && (ch != 0) && (ignoreUntil == null))
{
    if (".?!".IndexOf((char)ch) != -1)
    {
```

When we have accumulated a complete sentence, we convert the **sentence StringBuilder** into a **String** and determine whether or not the sentence contains a year. The **Text** class is used to accomplish this. The **Text** class does nothing more than use a **StringTokenizer** to split the sentence at each blank space and search for a year.

```
        String str = sentence.ToString();
        int year = Text.ExtractYear(str);
```

We then determine if a particular year has been specified.

```
        if (desiredYear == -1)
        {
```

If not, then the year found is reported and the user is told this a "good sentence." If no year was found, then the **year** variable is -1.

```
          if (year != -1)
          {
            report.ReceiveGoodSentence(str);
          }
        }
        else
        {
```

If we are looking for a specific year, then we determine if the year found matches the **desiredYear** variable and report it as either a "good" or "bad" sentence. If no year was found, then we do not report anything.

```
    if (year == desiredYear)
    {
      report.ReceiveGoodSentence(str);
    }
    else if (year != -1)
    {
      report.ReceiveBadSentence(str);
    }
  }
```

The **sentence StringBuilder** is then cleared to make way for the next sentence.

```
        sentence.Length = 0;
```

If multiple spaces occur together, they are trimmed to a single space.

```
  }
  else if (ch == ' ')
  {
    string str = sentence.ToString();
    if ((sentence.Length > 0)
       && (str[str.Length - 1] != ' '))
    {
      sentence.Append(' ');
    }
  }
```

The following formatting characters and any characters above 128 are not processed.

```
    else if ((ch != '\n') && (ch != '\t') && (ch != '\r'))
    {
      if ((ch) < 128)
      {
        sentence.Append((char)ch);
      }
    }
  }
```

The following tags begin new sections. The **sentence** is cleared if one is encountered and we start over.

```
  else if (ch == 0)
  {
    // clear anything before a body tag
    if (html.Tag.Name.Equals("body",
StringComparison.CurrentCultureIgnoreCase)
        || html.Tag.Name.Equals("br",
StringComparison.CurrentCultureIgnoreCase)
```

```
        || html.Tag.Name.Equals("li",
StringComparison.CurrentCultureIgnoreCase)
        || html.Tag.Name.Equals("p",
StringComparison.CurrentCultureIgnoreCase)
        || html.Tag.Name.Equals("h1",
StringComparison.CurrentCultureIgnoreCase)
        || html.Tag.Name.Equals("h2",
StringComparison.CurrentCultureIgnoreCase)
        || html.Tag.Name.Equals("h3",
StringComparison.CurrentCultureIgnoreCase)
        || html.Tag.Name.Equals("td",
StringComparison.CurrentCultureIgnoreCase)
        || html.Tag.Name.Equals("th",
StringComparison.CurrentCultureIgnoreCase))
  {
    sentence.Length = 0;
  }
```

If we are not already in the "ignore until" mode, then we determine if we should now switch to this mode.

```
// ignore everything between script and style tags
if (ignoreUntil == null)
{
  // ignore everything between script and style tags
  if (ignoreUntil == null)
  {
```

If the tag encountered is a **<script>** tag, then we ignore all text until an ending **</script>** tag is found.

```
    if (html.Tag.Name.Equals("script", StringComparison.Current-
CultureIgnoreCase))
    {
      ignoreUntil = "/script";
    }
    else if (html.Tag.Name
    .Equals("style", StringComparison.CurrentCultureIgnoreCase))
    {
      ignoreUntil = "/style";
    }
  }
  else
  {
```

If we encounter the tag that we have been looking for, then we clear the **ignoreUntil** variable and begin processing characters again.

```
      if (html.getTag().getName().equalsIgnoreCase(ignoreUntil))
```

```
{
            ignoreUntil = null;
        }
      }
```

A space is added after any tag is encountered.

```
    if (html.Tag.Name.Equals(ignoreUntil,
StringComparison.CurrentCultureIgnoreCase))
    {
      ignoreUntil = null;
    }
  }


  // add a space after the tag
  if (sentence.Length > 0)
  {
    string str = sentence.ToString();
    if (str[str.Length - 1] != ' ')
    {
      sentence.Append(' ');
    }
  }
 }
} while (ch != -1);
```

Processing continues until the end is reached. At the end of this process, the sentences are sorted into good and bad. Only those sentences that contained a valid year are considered.

Training the Neural Bot

The **TrainBot** class is executed to train the neural bot. This class makes use of several other classes in the **train** package. The **TrainBot** class is shown in Listing 13.8.

Listing 13.8: Training the Bot (TrainBot.cs)

```
using System;
using System.Collections.Generic;
using System.Linq;
using System.Text;

using HeatonResearchNeural.Feedforward;
using Chapter13Bot;
using HeatonResearchNeural.Util;
using HeatonResearchNeural.Feedforward.Train.Backpropagation;
```

```
namespace Chapter13Bot.Train
{
    public class TrainBot
    {

        private int sampleCount;
        private CommonWords common;
        private double[][] input;
        private double[][] ideal;
        private FeedforwardNetwork network;
        private AnalyzeSentences goodAnalysis;
        private AnalyzeSentences badAnalysis;
        WordHistogram histogramGood;
        WordHistogram histogramBad;

        private TrainingSet trainingSet;

        public TrainBot()
        {
            this.common = new CommonWords(
                Config.FILENAME_COMMON_WORDS);
            this.trainingSet = new TrainingSet();
        }

        private void AllocateTrainingSets()
        {
            this.input = new double[this.sampleCount][];
            this.ideal = new double[this.sampleCount][];
        }

        private void CopyTrainingSets()
        {
            int index = 0;
            // first the input
            foreach (double[] array in
                this.trainingSet.GetInput())
            {
                this.input[index] = new double[array.Length];
                for (int i = 0; i < array.Length; i++)
                {
                    this.input[index][i] = array[i];
                }
                index++;
            }
            index = 0;
            // second the ideal
```

```
    foreach (double[] array in
        this.trainingSet.GetIdeal())
    {
        this.ideal[index] = new double[array.Length];
        for (int i = 0; i < array.Length; i++)
        {
            this.ideal[index][i] = array[i];
        }
        index++;
    }


}


public void Process()
{
    this.network = NetworkUtil.CreateNetwork();
    Console.WriteLine("Preparing training sets...");
    this.common = new CommonWords(
        Config.FILENAME_COMMON_WORDS);
    this.histogramGood = new WordHistogram(this.common);
    this.histogramBad = new WordHistogram(this.common);

    // load the good words
    this.histogramGood.BuildFromFile(
        Config.FILENAME_GOOD_TRAINING_TEXT);
    this.histogramGood.BuildComplete();

    // load the bad words
    this.histogramBad.BuildFromFile(
        Config.FILENAME_BAD_TRAINING_TEXT);
    this.histogramBad.BuildComplete();

    // remove low scoring words
    this.histogramGood
            .RemoveBelow((int)this.histogramGood.
        CalculateMean());
    this.histogramBad.RemovePercent(0.99);

    // remove common words
    this.histogramGood.RemoveCommon(this.histogramBad);

    this.histogramGood.Trim(Config.INPUT_SIZE);

    this.goodAnalysis = new AnalyzeSentences(
        this.histogramGood,
        Config.INPUT_SIZE);
```

```
            this.badAnalysis = new AnalyzeSentences(
                    this.histogramGood,
                Config.INPUT_SIZE);

            this.goodAnalysis.Process(this.trainingSet, 0.9,
                    Config.FILENAME_GOOD_TRAINING_TEXT);
            this.badAnalysis.Process(this.trainingSet, 0.1,
                    Config.FILENAME_BAD_TRAINING_TEXT);

            this.sampleCount = this.trainingSet.GetIdeal().Count ;
            Console.WriteLine("Processing " +
            this.sampleCount + " training sets.");

            AllocateTrainingSets();

            CopyTrainingSets();

            TrainNetworkBackpropBackprop();
            SerializeObject.Save(
                    Config.FILENAME_WHENBORN_NET, this.network);
            SerializeObject.Save(
                    Config.FILENAME_HISTOGRAM, this.histogramGood);
            Console.WriteLine("Training complete.");

        }


        private void TrainNetworkBackpropBackprop()
        {
            Backpropagation train = new Backpropagation(
                this.network, this.input,
                    this.ideal, 0.01, 0.00);

            int epoch = 1;

            do
            {
                train.Iteration();
                Console.WriteLine(
                  "Backprop:Iteration #" + epoch + " Error:"
                        + train.Error);
                epoch++;
            } while ((train.Error > Config.ACCEPTABLE_ERROR));
        }

    }
}
```

The **Process** method is the first method that is called by the **Main** method of the **Program** class. The **Process** method will be discussed in the next section.

Processing the Training Sets

The **Process** method begins by creating a neural network and reporting that the training sets are being prepared.

```
this.network = NetworkUtil.CreateNetwork();
Console.WriteLine("Preparing training sets...");
```

Only the top 1,000 most common English words are allowed to influence the neural network. Occurrences of these common words in both the good and bad sentence sets will be analyzed. Histograms, which will be covered later in this chapter, keep track of the number of occurrences of each of the common words in both the good and bad sentences.

```
this.common = new CommonWords(Config.FILENAME_COMMON_WORDS);
this.histogramGood = new WordHistogram(this.common);
this.histogramBad = new WordHistogram(this.common);
```

First, the good words are loaded into their histogram.

```
this.histogramGood.BuildFromFile(Config.FILENAME_GOOD_TRAINING_
TEXT);
this.histogramGood.BuildComplete();
```

Next, the bad words are loaded into their histogram.

```
this.histogramBad.BuildFromFile(Config.FILENAME_BAD_TRAINING_TEXT);
this.histogramBad.BuildComplete();
```

We would like to remove any words that occur in both the good and bad training lists. The occurrence counts are used to trim the lists; there is likely to be considerable overlap. To overcome this overlap, we remove any words from the good histogram that are below the average number of occurrences. We then remove the lowest 99% of bad words.

```
this.histogramGood
                .RemoveBelow((int)this.histogramGood.Calcu-
lateMean());
this.histogramBad.RemovePercent(0.99);
```

Next, we remove the words that appear in both the good and bad histograms.

```
this.histogramGood.RemoveCommon(this.histogramBad);
```

Finally, we trim the good histogram to the number of inputs.

```
this.histogramGood.Trim(Config.INPUT_SIZE);
```

We then analyze the good and bad sentences. This will allow us to create both an input array and an ideal array based on each sentence. The input array reflects how many of the good words were present in each sentence. The output array reflects whether this sentence contains the birth year or not. We begin by allocating two **AnalyzeSentence** objects.

```
this.goodAnalysis = new AnalyzeSentences(this.histogramGood,
  Config.INPUT_SIZE);
this.badAnalysis = new AnalyzeSentences(
  this.histogramGood,
  Config.INPUT_SIZE);
```

We then process both the good and bad sentences. They will all be added to the **TrainingSet** collection that is passed to the method.

```
this.goodAnalysis.Process(this.trainingSet, 0.9,
  Config.FILENAME_GOOD_TRAINING_TEXT);
this.badAnalysis.Process(this.trainingSet, 0.1,
  Config.FILENAME_BAD_TRAINING_TEXT);
```

Notice the values of 0.9 and 0.1 above. These are the ideal output values. The closer the value of the output neuron is to 0.9, the more likely that the sentence contains the birth year of the famous person. The closer it is to 0.1, the less likely.

Next, we report the number of training sets that were collected.

```
this.sampleCount = this.trainingSet.GetIdeal().Count ;
Console.WriteLine("Processing " + this.sampleCount + " training
sets.");
```

To allow the training sets to grow easily, they are stored as a collection. In order to use them to train the neural network, they must be converted into the usual 2-dimensional array, as were the samples used to train previous neural networks in this book. We begin by allocating the training sets.

```
AllocateTrainingSets();
```

Next, the **trainingSet** collection is copied into the actual training sets.

```
CopyTrainingSets();
```

The neural network is now trained using backpropagation.

```
TrainNetworkBackpropBackprop();
```

The neural network and the histogram are then saved.

```
SerializeObject.Save(Config.FILENAME_WHENBORN_NET, this.network);
SerializeObject.Save(Config.FILENAME_HISTOGRAM, this.histogram-
Good);
Console.WriteLine("Training complete.");
```

The training is now complete.

Analyzing Sentence Histograms

A histogram is a linear progression of frequencies. The histograms in this application are managed by the **WordHistogram** class. They are used to store the frequency with which each common word occurs in a sentence. The **WordHistogram** class is shown in Listing 13.9.

Listing 13.9: Managing Histograms (WordHistogram.cs)

```csharp
using System;
using System.Collections.Generic;
using System.Linq;
using System.Text;

using System.Diagnostics.Eventing;
using System.IO;

namespace Chapter13Bot.Train
{

    [Serializable]
    public class WordHistogram
    {
        private CommonWords common;
        private Dictionary<String, HistogramElement>
      histogram = new Dictionary<String, HistogramElement>();

        private SortedList<HistogramElement, HistogramElement>
sorted = new SortedList<HistogramElement, HistogramElement>();

        public WordHistogram(CommonWords common)
        {
            this.common = common;
        }

        public void BuildComplete()
        {
            this.sorted.Clear();
            foreach (HistogramElement e in this.histogram.Values)
            {
                this.sorted.Add(e, null);
            }

        }

        public void BuildFromFile(TextReader istream)
```

```csharp
{
    string line;

    while ((line = istream.ReadLine()) != null)
    {
        BuildFromLine(line);
    }
    istream.Close();
}


public void BuildFromFile(String filename)
{
    TextReader fis = new StreamReader(filename);
    BuildFromFile(fis);
    fis.Close();
}


public void BuildFromLine(String line)
{
    string[] tok = line.Split();

    for (int i = 0; i < tok.Length; i++)
    {
        String word = tok[i];
        BuildFromWord(word);
    }
}


public void BuildFromWord(String word)
{
    word = word.Trim().ToLower();
    if (this.common.IsCommonWord(word))
    {
        HistogramElement element = null;
        if (this.histogram.ContainsKey(word))
        {
            element = this.histogram[word];
        }
        else
        {
            element = new HistogramElement(word, 0);
            this.histogram.Add(word, element);
        }

        element.Increase();
    }
```

```
}

public double CalculateMean()
{
    int total = 0;
    foreach (HistogramElement element in this.sorted.Keys)
    {
        total += element.GetCount();
    }
    return (double)total / (double)this.sorted.Count;
}

public double[] Compact(string line)
{
    double[] result = new double[this.sorted.Count];

    string[] tok = line.Split();

    for(int i=0;i<tok.Length;i++)
    {
        String word = tok[i].ToLower();
        int rank = GetRank(word);
        if (rank != -1)
        {
            result[rank] = 0.9;
        }
    }
    return result;
}

public int Count(string line)
{
    int result = 0;

    string[] tok = line.Split();

    for(int i=0;i<tok.Length;i++)
      {
        String word = tok[i].ToLower();
        int rank = GetRank(word);
        if (rank != -1)
        {
            result++;
        }
    }
    return result;
```

```csharp
    }

    public HistogramElement Get(String word)
    {
        return this.histogram[word.ToLower()];
    }


    public CommonWords GetCommon()
    {
        return this.common;
    }


    public int GetRank(String word)
    {
        int result = 0;

        foreach (HistogramElement element in this.sorted.Keys)
        {
            if (string.Compare(
              element.GetWord(),word,true)==0)
            {
                return result;
            }
            result++;
        }
        return -1;
    }


    public SortedList<HistogramElement, HistogramElement>
        GetSorted()
    {
        return this.sorted;
    }


    public void RemoveBelow(int value)
    {
        Object[] elements = this.sorted.Keys.ToArray();
        for (int i = 0; i < elements.Length; i++)
        {
            HistogramElement element =
                (HistogramElement)elements[i];
            if (element.GetCount() < value)
            {
                this.histogram.Remove(element.GetWord());
                this.sorted.Remove(element);
            }
```

```
    }
}

public void RemoveCommon(WordHistogram other)
{
    foreach (HistogramElement element in
            other.GetSorted().Keys)
    {
        HistogramElement e = this.Get(element.GetWord());
        if (e == null)
        {
            continue;
        }
        this.sorted.Remove(e);
        this.histogram.Remove(element.GetWord());

    }
}

public void RemovePercent(double percent)
{
    int countdown = (int)(this.sorted.Count * (1 -
            percent));

    Object[] elements = this.sorted.Keys.ToArray();
    for (int i = 0; i < elements.Length; i++)
    {
        countdown--;
        if (countdown < 0)
        {
            HistogramElement element =
                    (HistogramElement)elements[i];
            this.histogram.Remove(element.GetWord());
            this.sorted.Remove(element);
        }
    }
}

public void Trim(int size)
{

    Object[] elements = this.sorted.Keys.ToArray();
    for (int i = 0; i < elements.Length; i++)
    {
        if (i >= size)
        {
            {
```

```
                        HistogramElement element =
                            (HistogramElement)elements[i];
                        this.histogram.Remove(element.GetWord());
                        this.sorted.Remove(element);
                }
            }
        }
    }
}
```

The individual words in the histogram are stored in the **HistogramElement** class.   A   collection   of   **HistogramElement**   objects   is   stored   inside   the **WordHistogram** class. The **HistogramElement** class is shown in Listing 13.10.

Listing 13.10: Histogram Elements (HistogramElement.cs)

```
using System;
using System.Collections.Generic;
using System.Linq;
using System.Text;

namespace Chapter13Bot.Train
{
    [Serializable]
    public class HistogramElement : IComparable<HistogramElement>
    {
        private string word;
        private int count;

        public HistogramElement(string word, int count)
        {
            this.word = word.ToLower();
            this.count = count;
        }

        public int CompareTo(HistogramElement o)
        {
            int result = o.GetCount() - GetCount();
            if (result == 0)
            {
                return this.GetWord().CompareTo(o.GetWord());
            }
            else
            {
                return result;
            }
        }
```

```
public int GetCount()
{
    return this.count;
}

public String GetWord()
{
    return this.word;
}

public void Increase()
{
    this.count++;
}

public void SetCount(int count)
{
    this.count = count;
}

public void SetWord(string word)
{
    this.word = word.ToLower();
}

}

}
```

The **HistogramElement** class is very simple. It stores a word and the number of times the word occurs. You can see both of these values in the above listing. Additionally, the **HistogramElement** class implements the **IComparable** interface, which it uses for sorting. If you examine the above listing, you will see that the **CompareTo** method causes the sorting to occur first by the number of times a word occurs, and then alphabetically by the word itself.

The **WordHistogram** class, as seen in Listing 13.9, provides many services. These are used by the neural bot in all three modes of operation. These services include the following:

- Count the number of times words occur to build a histogram
- Compact a sentence to an input pattern
- Remove common words that also appear in another histogram
- Remove the bottom percentage of words
- Calculate the average number of occurrences of the words in the histogram

One of the most important functions of the **WordHistogram** class is to compact a sentence into an input pattern for the neural network. The input pattern for the neural network is simply a relative count of the number of occurrences of the most common "good words" in the sentence. The number of good words expressed in the input pattern is the number of input neurons. The single output neuron specifies the degree to which the neural network believes the sentence contains a birth year.

The input pattern is built inside the **Compact** method of the **WordHistogram** class. The signature for the **Compact** method is shown here:

```
public double[] Compact(string line)
```

The result is the same size as the number of words in this histogram. This size is the same as the number of input neurons in the neural network.

```
double[] result = new double[this.sorted.Count];
```

The **Split** method is used to parse the sentence into words.

```
string[] tok = line.Split();
```

We continue to loop as long as there are more words to read.

```
for(int i=0;i<tok.Length;i++)
{
```

The next word is then obtained and converted to lowercase.

```
String word = tok[i].ToLower();
```

The rank for the word is then given. If the word is present, the input neuron is set to a relatively high 0.9.

```
int rank = GetRank(word);
if (rank != -1)
{
  result[rank] = 0.9;
}
}
```

This process continues while there are more words.

```
return result;
}
```

Once the process is complete, the resulting input array for the neural network is returned. This input array will be used to build training sets or to actually query the neural network, once it has been trained.

Building the Training Sets

The training sets for the neural network are managed by the **TrainingSet** class. The **TrainingSet** class is shown in Listing 13.11.

Listing 13.11: Traning Set Management (TrainingSet.cs)

```csharp
using System;
using System.Collections.Generic;
using System.Linq;
using System.Text;

namespace Chapter13Bot.Train
{
    public class TrainingSet
    {
        private List<double[]> input = new List<double[]>();
        private List<double[]> ideal = new List<double[]>();

        public void AddTrainingSet(double[] addInput,
            double addIdeal)
        {
            // does the training set already exist
            foreach (double[] element in this.input)
            {
                if (Compare(addInput, element))
                {
                    return;
                }
            }

            // add it
            double[] array = new double[1];
            array[0] = addIdeal;
            this.input.Add(addInput);
            this.ideal.Add(array);

        }

        private bool Compare(double[] d1, double[] d2)
        {
            bool result = true;

            for (int i = 0; i < d1.Length; i++)
            {
                if (Math.Abs(d1[i] - d2[i]) > 0.000001)
                {
```

```
                            result = false;
                    }
            }

            return result;
        }

        public List<double[]> GetIdeal()
        {
            return this.ideal;
        }

        public List<double[]> GetInput()
        {
            return this.input;
        }

        public void SetIdeal(List<double[]> ideal)
        {
            this.ideal = ideal;
        }

        public void SetInput(List<double[]> input)
        {
            this.input = input;
        }
    }
}
```

Like any other supervised training set in this book, the neural bot training set uses an input array and an ideal array. The most important job of the **TrainingSet** class is to allow new training sets to be added without introducing duplicates. It accomplishes this using the **AddTrainingSet** method. The signature for the **AddTrainingSet** method is shown here:

```
public void AddTrainingSet(double[] addInput, double addIdeal)
{
```

Two arguments are passed to the **AddTrainingSet** method. The first, **AddInput**, specifies the input array. The second, **AddIdeal**, specifies the ideal values for the specified input pattern.

We begin by checking to see if the training set already exists. To do this, we loop over all of the elements.

```
// does the training set already exist
foreach (double[] element in this.input)
{
```

If the training set is already present, then we simply return and ignore it.

```
if (Compare(addInput, element))
{
  return;
}
```

If it does not exist, we add it to the list of sets we have already accumulated.

```
// add it
double[] array = new double[1];
array[0] = addIdeal;
this.input.Add(addInput);
this.ideal.Add(array);
}
```

Once all of the training sets have been added, the neural network can be trained.

Training the Neural Network

Backpropagation is used to train the neural network. This procedure is essentially the same as all other examples of backpropagation in this book. The training occurs in the **TrainNetworkBackprop** method of the **TrainBot** class. The signature for the **TrainNetworkBackprop** method is shown here:

```
private void TrainNetworkBackpropBackprop()
```

First, a training object is created. Because this neural network uses a sigmoidal activation function, a relatively high learning rate and high momentum can be specified. For more information on learning rate and momentum refer to chapter 5.

```
Backpropagation train = new Backpropagation(this.network, this.in-
put, this.ideal, 0.01, 0.00);
```

The starting epoch is 1.

```
int epoch = 1;
```

We begin a training loop.

```
do {
```

Each epoch of the training is performed and the error at each epoch is reported.

```
train.Iteration();
Console.WriteLine("Backprop:Iteration #" + epoch + " Error:"
+ train.Error);

epoch++;
} while ((train.Error > Config.ACCEPTABLE_ERROR));
```

Looping continues as long as we are above the acceptable error level. Once the training is complete, the neural network is saved, as covered earlier in this chapter.

Querying the Neural Bot

Once the bot has been trained, it can be used to lookup the birth year for a famous person. The main bot for performing this function is contained in the package named **born**. To execute the bot, the class **YearBornBot** is executed. The **YearBornBot** class is shown in Listing 13.12.

Listing 13.12: WhenBornBot Class (WhenBornBot.cs)

```csharp
using System;
using System.Collections.Generic;
using System.Linq;
using System.Text;
using System.IO;

using Chapter13Bot;
using Chapter13Bot.Train;
using HeatonResearchNeural.Feedforward;
using HeatonResearchNeural.Util;

namespace Chapter13Bot.Born
{
    public class YearBornBot : ScanReportable
    {
        public const bool LOG = true;

        /// <summary>
        /// The search object to use.
        /// </summary>
        static YahooSearch search;



        private FeedforwardNetwork network;

        private WordHistogram histogram;



        /// <summary>
        /// This map stores a mapping between a year, and how
        /// many times that year
        /// has come up as a potential birth year.
        /// </summary>
        private Dictionary<int, int> results =
```

```csharp
        new Dictionary<int, int>();

public YearBornBot()
{
    this.network = (FeedforwardNetwork)SerializeObject
            .Load(Config.FILENAME_WHENBORN_NET);
    this.histogram = (WordHistogram)SerializeObject
            .Load(Config.FILENAME_HISTOGRAM);
}


/// <summary>
/// Get birth year that occurred the largest
/// number of times.
/// </summary>
/// <returns>The birth year that occurred the largest
/// number of times.</returns>
public int GetResult()
{
    int result = -1;
    int maxCount = 0;

    foreach (int year in this.results.Keys)
    {
        int count = this.results[year];
        if (count > maxCount)
        {
            result = year;
            maxCount = count;
        }
    }


    return result;
}


private void IncreaseYear(int year)
{
    int count = this.results[year];
    if (count == 0)
    {
        count = 1;
    }
    else
    {
        count++;
    }
```

```csharp
            this.results.Add(year, count);
    }

    /// <summary>
    /// This method is called to determine the birth year
    /// for a person. It
    /// obtains 100 web pages that Yahoo returns for that
    /// person. Each of these
    /// pages is then searched for the birth year of
    /// that person. Which ever year
    /// is selected the largest number of times
    /// is selected as the birth year.
    /// </summary>
    /// <param name="name"></param>
    public void Process(String name)
    {
        search = new YahooSearch();

        if (YearBornBot.LOG)
        {
            Console.WriteLine(
              "Getting search results form Yahoo.");
        }
        ICollection<Uri> c = search.Search(name);
        int i = 0;

        if (YearBornBot.LOG)
        {
            Console.WriteLine("Scanning URL's from Yahoo.");
        }
        foreach (Uri u in c)
        {
            try
            {
                i++;
                Text.CheckURL(this, u, 0);
            }
            catch (IOException )
            {

            }
        }

        int resultYear = GetResult();
        if (resultYear == -1)
        {
```

```
            Console.WriteLine("Could not determine when "
                    + name
                    + " was born.");
        }
        else
        {
            Console.WriteLine(name + " was born in "
                    + resultYear);
        }


    }

    public void ReceiveBadSentence(String sentence)
    {



    }

    public void ReceiveGoodSentence(String sentence)
    {
        if (this.histogram.Count(sentence) >=
            Config.MINIMUM_WORDS_PRESENT)
        {
            double[] compact =
              this.histogram.Compact(sentence);
            int year = Text.ExtractYear(sentence);

            double[] output =
              this.network.ComputeOutputs(compact);

            if (output[0] > 0.8)
            {
                IncreaseYear(year);
                Console.WriteLine(year + "-" + output[0]
                    + ":" + sentence);
            }
        }


    }

}
}
```

The first method called by the **Main** method is the **Process** method. This method processes the request to determine the birth year of the famous person. The **Process** method is covered in the next section. Other prmethods called by the **Process** method are covered in later sections of this chapter.

Processing the Request

The **Process** method accepts the name of the famous person and attempts to determine the birth year for that famous person. The signature for the **Process** method is shown here:

```
public void Process(String name)
```

The **Process** method begins by performing a Yahoo search on the **name** specified.

```
search = new YahooSearch();

if (YearBornBot.LOG)
{
  Console.WriteLine("Getting search results form Yahoo.");
}
```

The results of the Yahoo search are stored in the **c** object.

```
ICollection<Uri> c = search.Search(name);
int i = 0;

if (YearBornBot.LOG)
{
  Console.WriteLine("Scanning URL's from Yahoo.");
}
```

We loop through the entire list and process each URL. As each URL is processed, the sentences that contain birth years are returned to the **ReceiveGoodSentence** method. The **ReceiveGoodSentence** method will be covered in the next section.

```
foreach (Uri u in c)
{
  try
  {
    i++;
    Text.CheckURL(this, u, 0);
```

All errors are ignored. We hit a large number of websites and some are sure to be down.

```
  }
  catch (IOException )
  {
  }
}
```

As we find years with a high probability of being the birth year, we count the number of times they occur. The **GetResult** method returns the birth year that is the most likely candidate. The **GetResult** method is covered later in this chapter.

```
int resultYear = GetResult();
```

Negative one is returned if no likely birth year is found.

```
if (resultYear == -1)
{
  Console.WriteLine("Could not determine when " + name
  + " was born.");
```

Otherwise, the most likely birth year is found.

```
}
else
{
  Console.WriteLine(name + " was born in " + resultYear);
}
```

The **Process** method made use of several other methods as it executed. The next two sections will cover these methods.

Receiving Sentences

Just as the gathering process used the **Text** class to parse individual sentences, so does the query process. As the **Text** class parses the data, the **ReceiveGoodSentence** method is called each time a sentence is identified. The signature for the **ReceiveGoodSentence** is shown here:

```
public void ReceiveGoodSentence(String sentence)
```

First, we check to see if the sentence found has the minimum number of recognized words. If it does not, then the sentence is ignore.

```
if (this.histogram.Count(sentence) >= Config.MINIMUM_WORDS_PRESENT)
{
```

The sentence is compacted into an input array for the neural network.

```
  double[] compact = this.histogram.Compact(sentence);
```

The potential birth year is obtained from the **Text** class.

```
  int year = Text.ExtractYear(sentence);
```

The output from the neural network is returned using the input array generated from the current sentence.

```
  double[] output = this.network.ComputeOutputs(compact);
```

If the specified sentence causes an output greater than 0.8, then there is a decent chance that this is a birth year. The count is increased for this year and the year is reported.

```
if (output[0] > 0.8)
{

  IncreaseYear(year);
  Console.WriteLine(year + "-" + output[0] + ":" + sentence);
}
}
```

Finding the Best Birth Year Candidate

Once all of the year counts have been updated, the **GetResult** method is called to determine which year has the highest count. This is the year that will be proposed as the birth year for this person. The signature for the **GetResult** method is shown here:

```
public int GetResult()
```

The **result** is set to a default of -1. If no potential birth years are found, then this -1 value is returned. The **maxCount** variable is used to track which year has the maximum count.

```
int result = -1;
int maxCount = 0;
```

All of the years identified as potential birth years are reviewed.

```
foreach (int year in this.results.Keys)
{
```

The count for the specified year is obtained.

```
  int count = this.results[year];
  if (count > maxCount)
  {
    result = year;
    maxCount = count;
  }
}
```

We continue to loop and update the result as better candidates are found.

```
  return result;
}
```

This process continues until the best candidate has been selected.

Chapter Summary

Bots are computer programs that perform repetitive tasks. Often, a bot makes use of an HTTP protocol to access websites in much the same way as do humans. Because a bot generally accesses a very large amount of data, neural networks can be useful in helping the bot understand the incoming data.

This chapter presented a neural network that attempts to determine the birth year for a famous person. This neural network is divided into three distinct modes of operation. The first mode uses a threaded bot to gather lots of information on the birth year of specified famous people. Using these famous people and their birth years, the bot is trained in the second mode. The final mode allows the user to query the network and determine the birth years of other famous people.

This book has covered a number of different types of neural networks and methods for using them. Despite all they are able to do, neural networks still fall considerably short of achieving the ability to reason like a human brain. The next chapter will look at the current state of neural network research and where neural networks are headed in the future.

Vocabulary

Bot

Histogram

HTTP Protocol

Parsing

Questions for Review

1. How does this chapter suggest to transform a sentence into an input pattern for the neural network?

2. Other than the method discussed in this chapter, how else might a sentence be transformed into input for a neural network? Is it necessary for every sentence to produce the same number of inputs for the neural network?

3. Why was the sigmoidal activation function a good choice for an activation function for the neural bot?

4.   What is text parsing, and how is it useful?

5.   If you wanted to expand this bot to also locate the name of the famous person's spouse, how might this be done?

CHAPTER 14: THE FUTURE OF NEURAL NETWORKS

- Where are Neural Networks Today?
- To Emulate the Human Brain or the Human Mind
- Understanding Quantum Computing

Neural networks have existed since the 1950s. They have come a long way since the early perceptrons that were easily defeated by problems as simple as the XOR operator; however, they still have a long way to go. This chapter will examine the state of neural networks today, and consider directions they may go in the future.

Neural Networks Today

Many people think the purpose of neural networks is to attempt to emulate the human mind or pass the Turing Test. The turing test is covered later in this chapter. While neural networks are used to accomplish a wide variety of tasks, most fill far less glamorous roles than those filled by systems in science fiction.

Speech and handwriting recognition are two common uses for today's neural networks. Neural networks tend to work well for these tasks, because programs such as these can be trained to an individual user. Chapter 12 presented an example of a neural network used in handwriting recognition.

Data mining is another task for which neural networks are often employed. Data mining is a process in which large volumes of data are "mined" to establish trends and other statistics that might otherwise be overlooked. Often, a programmer involved in data mining is not certain of the final outcome being sought. Neural networks are employed for this task because of their trainability.

Perhaps the most common form of neural network used by modern applications is the feedforward backpropagation neural network. This network processes input by feeding it forward from one layer to the next. Backpropagation refers to the way in which neurons are trained in this sort of neural network. Chapter 5 introduced the feedforward backpropagation neural network.

A Fixed Wing Neural Network

The ultimate goal of AI is to produce a thinking machine and we are still a long way from achieving this goal. Some researchers suggest that perhaps the concept of the neural network itself is flawed. Perhaps other methods of modeling human intelligence must be explored. Does this mean that such a machine will have to be constructed exactly like a human brain? To solve the AI puzzle, must we imitate nature? Imitating nature has not always led mankind to the optimal solution—consider the airplane.

Man has been fascinated with the idea of flight since the beginnings of civilization. Many inventors in history worked towards the development of the "Flying Machine." To create a flying machine, most inventors looked to nature. In nature, they found the only working model of a flying machine, the bird. Most inventors who aspired to create a flying machine, developed various forms of ornithopters.

Ornithopters are flying machines that work by flapping their wings. This is how a bird flies, so it seemed logical that this would be the way to create a flying machine. However, no ornithopters were ever successful. Many designs were attempted, but they simply could not generate sufficient lift to overcome their weight. Figure 14.1 shows one such design that was patented in the late 1800s.

Figure 14.1: An ornithopter.

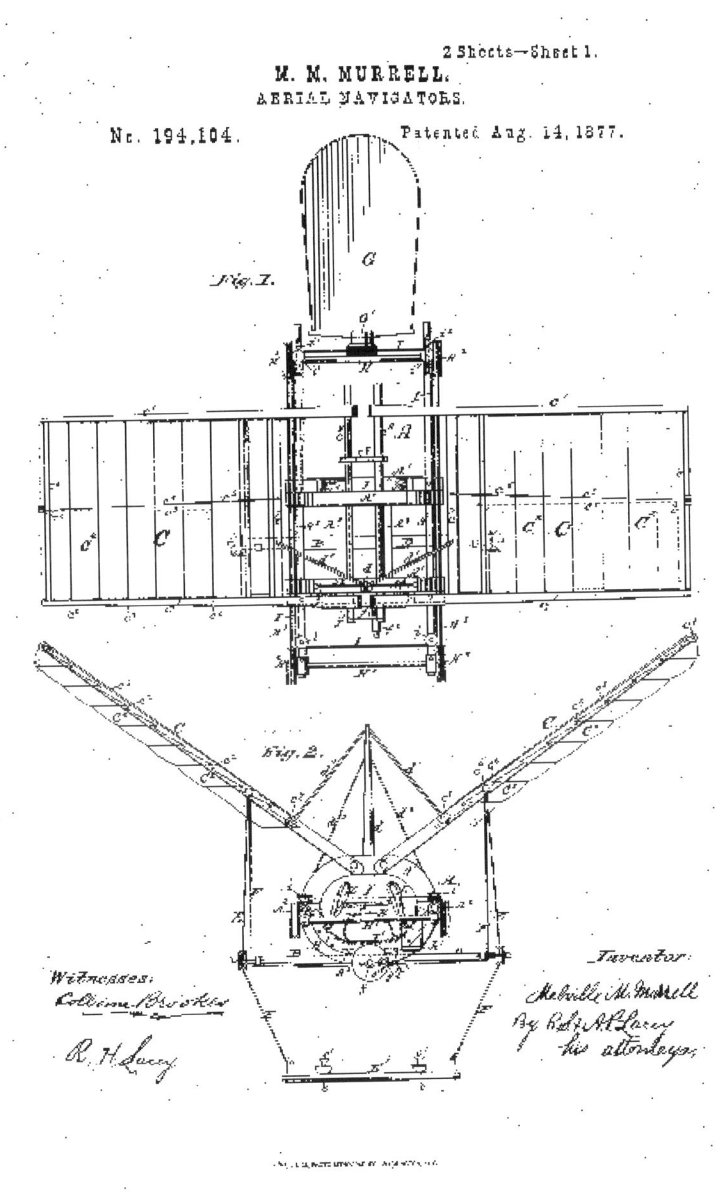

It was not until Wilbur and Orville Wright decided to use a fixed wing design that airplane technology began to truly advance. For years, the paradigm of modeling a bird was pursued. Once the two brothers broke with tradition, this area of science began to move forward. Perhaps AI is no different. Perhaps it will take a new paradigm, different from the neural network, to usher in the next era of AI.

Quantum Computing

One of the most promising areas of future computer research is quantum computing. Quantum computing has the potential to change every aspect of how computers are designed. To understand quantum computers, we must first examine how they are different from computer systems that are in use today.

Von Neumann and Turing Machines

Practically every computer in use today is built upon the Von Neumann principle. A Von Neumann computer works by following simple discrete instructions, which are chip-level machine language codes. This type of machine is implemented using finite state units of data known as "bits," and logic gates that perform operations on the bits. In addition, the output produced is completely predictable and serial. This classic model of computation is essentially the same as Babbage's analytical engine developed in 1834. The computers of today have not strayed from this classic architecture; they have simply become faster and have gained more "bits." The Church-Turing thesis sums up this idea.

The Church-Turing thesis is not a mathematical theorem in the sense that it can be proven. It simply seems correct and applicable. Alonzo Church and Alan Turing created this idea independently. According to the Church-Turing thesis, all mechanisms for computing algorithms are inherently the same. Any method used can be expressed as a computer program. This seems to be a valid thesis. Consider the case in which you are asked to add two numbers. You likely follow a simple algorithm that can easily be implemented as a computer program. If you are asked to multiply two numbers, you follow another approach that could be implemented as a computer program. The basis of the Church-Turing thesis is that there seems to be no algorithmic problem that a computer cannot solve, so long as a solution exists.

The embodiment of the Church-Turing thesis is the Turing machine. The Turing machine is an abstract computing device that illustrates the Church-Turing thesis. The Turing machine is the ancestor from which all existing computers have descended. The Turing computer consists of a read/write head and a long piece of tape. The head can read and write symbols to and from the tape. At each step, the Turing machine must decide its next action by following a very simple algorithm consisting of conditional statements, read/write commands, and tape shifts. The tape can be of any length necessary to solve a particular problem, but the tape cannot be infinite in length. If a problem has a solution, that problem can be solved using a Turing machine and some finite length of tape.

Quantum Computing

Practically every neural network developed thus far has been implemented using a Von Neumann computer. But it is possible that the successor to the Von Neumann computer, quantum computing, may take neural networks to a near human level. A quantum computer is constructed very differently than a Von Neumann computer.

Quantum computers use small particles to represent data. For example, a pebble is a quantum computer for calculating the constant-position function. A quantum computer would also use small particles to represent the neurons of a neural network. Before we consider how a quantum neural network is constructed, we must first consider how a quantum computer is constructed.

The most basic level of a Von Neumann computer is the bit. Similarly, the most basic level of the quantum computer is the "qubit." A qubit, or quantum bit, differs from a normal bit in one very important way. Where a normal bit can only have a value of 0 or 1, a qubit can have a value of 0, 1, or both simultaneously. To demonstrate how this is possible, first you will be shown how a qubit is constructed.

A qubit is constructed with an atom of some element. Hydrogen makes a good example. The hydrogen atom consists of a nucleus and one orbiting electron. For the purposes of quantum computing, only the orbiting electron is important. This electron can exist in different energy levels, or orbits about the nucleus. The different energy levels are used to represent the binary 0 and 1. When the atom is in its lowest orbit, the ground state, the qubit might have a value of 0. The next highest orbit could be represented by the value 1. The electron can be moved to different orbits by subjecting it to a pulse of polarized laser light. This has the effect of adding photons to the system. To flip a qubit from 0 to 1, enough light is added to move the electron up one orbit. To flip from 1 to 0, we do the same thing, since overloading the electron will cause the it to return to its ground state. Logically, this is equivalent to a NOT gate. Using similar ideas, other gates can be constructed, such as AND and OR.

Thus far, there is no qualitative difference between qubits and regular bits. Both are capable of storing the values 0 and 1. What is different is the concept of a superposition. If only half of the light necessary to move an electron is added, the electron will occupy both orbits simultaneously. A superposition allows two possibilities to be computed at once. Further, if you have one "qubyte," that is, 8 qubits, then 256 numbers can be represented simultaneously. bers can be represented simultaneously.

Calculations with superpositions can have certain advantages. For example, to perform a calculation with the superpositional property, a number of qubits are raised to their superpositions. The calculation is then performed on these qubits. When the algorithm is complete, the superposition is collapsed. This results in the true answer being revealed. You can think of the algorithm as being run on all possible combinations of the definite qubit states (i.e., 0 and 1) in parallel. This is called quantum parallelism.

Quantum computers clearly process information differently than their Von Neumann counterparts. But does quantum computing offer anything not already provided by classical computers? The answer is yes. Quantum computing provides tremendous speed advantages over the Von Neumann architecture.

To see this difference in speed, consider a problem that takes an extremely long time to compute on a classical computer, such as factoring a 250-digit number. It is estimated that this would take approximately 800,000 years to compute with 1400 present-day Von Neumann computers working in parallel. Even as Von Neumann computers improve in speed, and methods of large-scale parallelism improve, the problem is still exponentially expensive to compute. This same problem presented to a quantum computer would not take nearly as long. A quantum computer is able to factor a 250-digit number in just a few million steps. The key is that by using the parallel properties of superposition, all possibilities can be computed simultaneously.

It is not yet clear whether or not the Church-Turing thesis is true for all quantum computers. The quantum computer previously mentioned processes algorithms much the way Von Neumann computers do, using bits and logic gates; however, we could use other types of quantum computer models that are more powerful. One such model may be a quantum neural network, or QNN. A QNN could be constructed using qubits. This would be analogous to constructing an ordinary neural network on a Von Neumann computer. The result would only offer increased speed, not computability advantages over Von Neumann-based neural networks. To construct a QNN that is not restrained by Church-Turing, a radically different approach to qubits and logic gates must be sought. As of yet, there does not seem to be any clear way of doing this.

Quantum Neural Networks

How might a QNN be constructed? Currently, there are several research institutes around the world working on QNNs. Two examples are Georgia Tech and Oxford University. Most research groups are reluctant to publish details of their work. This is likely because building a QNN is potentially much easier than building an actual quantum computer; thus, a quantum race may be underway.

A QNN would likely gain exponentially over classic neural networks through superposition of values entering and exiting a neuron. Another advantage might be a reduction in the number of neuron layers required. This is because neurons can be used to calculate many possibilities, using superposition. The model would therefore require fewer neurons to learn. This would result in networks with fewer neurons and greater efficiency.

Reusable Neural Network Frameworks

This book introduced many classes that implement many aspects of neural networks. These classes can be reused in other applications; however, they have been designed to serve primarily as educational tools. They do not attempt to hide the nature of neural networks, as the purpose of this book is to teach the reader about neural networks, not simply how to use a neural network framework. As a result, this book did not use any third-party neural frameworks.

Unfortunately, there is not much available in terms of free open-source software (FOSS) for neural network processing in C#. One project that once held a great deal of potential was the Java Object Oriented Neural Engine (JOONE), which can be found at **http://www.jooneworld.com**. There is a C# version of JOONE. However, the project appears to be dying. As of the writing of this book, the latest version was a release candidate for version 2.0. There have been no updates beyond RC1 for over a year. Additionally, RC1 seems to have several serious bugs and architectural issues. Support requests go unanswered.

The first edition of this book used JOONE for many of the examples. However, JOONE was removed from the second edition, because it no longer seems to be a supported project.

Another option for a third-party neural framework is Encog. Encog is a free open-source project I have organized. Encog is based on classes used to create this book. It is essentially the classes provided by the books Introduction to Neural Networks with C# and HTTP Programming Recipes for C# Bots. Encog provides a neural network-based framework that has the ability to access web data for processing. If the project does not call for web access, the HTTP classes do not need to be used.

Encog is a new project. The classes presented in this book will evolve beyond the learning examples provided. Specifically, Encog will be extended in the following areas:

- Advanced hybrid training
- Consolidation of classes for all types of neural architectures
- Improved support for multicore and grid computing
- More efficient, but somewhat less readable code
- Integration of the pruning and training processes

Adding all of these elements into the instructional classes provided in this book would have only obscured the key neural network topics this book presents. This book provided an introduction to how neural networks are constructed and trained. If you require more advanced training and capabilities, I encourage you to take a look at the Encog project. More information on the Encog project can be found at the Heaton Research website:

`http://www.heatonresearch.com/`

As you will see, Encog is available in both Java and C#. Because Encog is an open-source project, we are always looking for additional contributions. If you would like to contribute to a growing open-source neural network project, I encourage you to take a look. Sub-projects are available for all levels of neural network experience.

Chapter Summary

Computers can process information considerably faster than human beings. Yet, a computer is incapable of performing many of the tasks that a human can easily perform. For processes that cannot easily be broken into a finite number of steps, a neural network can be an ideal solution.

The term neural network usually refers to an artificial neural network. An artificial neural network attempts to simulate the real neural networks contained in the brains of all animals. Neural networks were introduced in the 1950s and have experienced numerous setbacks; they have yet to deliver on the promise of simulating human thought.

The future of artificial intelligence programming may reside with quantum computers or perhaps a framework other than neural networks. Quantum computing promises to speed computing to levels that are unimaginable with today's computer platforms.

Early attempts at flying machines model birds. This was done because birds were the only working models of flight. It was not until Wilbur and Orville Wright broke from the model of nature and created the first fixed wing aircraft that success in flight was finally achieved. Perhaps modeling AI programs after nature is analogous to modeling airplanes after birds; a model that is much better than the neural network may exist, but only time will tell.

There are not many open-source neural network frameworks available. One early and very promising project was the Java Object Oriented Neural Engine. Unfortunately, the project seems to be unsupported and somewhat unstable at this time. A project called Encog is underway based on the classes developed in this book. Encog has added advanced features that were beyond the scope of this introductory book. If you would like to evaluate the Encog framework, more information can be found at the Heaton Research website at **http://www.heatonresearch.com**.

Neural networks are a fascinating topic. This book has provided an introduction. To continue learning about neural networks I encourage you to look at the Encog project and look for additional books and articles from Heaton Research.

I hope you have found this book enjoyable and informative. I would love to hear your comments, suggestions, and criticisms of this book. You can contact me at **support@heatonresearch.com**. There is also a forum at **http://www.heatonresearch.com,** where all of our books and software can be discussed.

Vocabulary

Ornithopter

Perceptron

Quantum Computer

Quantum Neural Network

Qubit

Turing Machines

Von Neumann Machine

APPENDIX A: DOWNLOADING EXAMPLES

This book contains many source code examples. You do not need to retype any of these examples; they can all be downloaded from the Internet.

Simply go to: http://www.heatonresearch.com/download/

There you will find additional information on how to download the sample programs.

APPENDIX B: MATHEMATICAL BACKGROUND

Neural networks are mathematical structures. This book touches on several mathematical concepts related to neural networks. Provided below is a brief overview of these concepts.

Matrix Operations

The weights and thresholds of neural networks are stored in matrixes. A matrix is a grid of numbers that can have any number of rows and columns. A typical matrix is shown in Equation B.1.

Equation B.1: A typical matrix.

$$\begin{bmatrix} 1 & 2 & 3 \\ 4 & 5 & 6 \\ 7 & 8 & 9 \end{bmatrix}$$

Neural networks use many concepts from matrix mathematics. Operations such as matrix multiplication, dot products, identities, and others contribute to neural network processing. Because matrixes are so important to neural networks, an entire chapter of this book is dedicated to them. For a review of matrix mathematics, refer to chapter 2.

Sigma Notation

Summation is also a very important concept in neural networks. Frequently, a sequence of numbers will need to be summed. Sigma notation is used in several parts of this book to denote this operation. Sigma notation is very similar to a 'for' loop. For example, Equation B.2 shows the very simple sigma notation used to represent the summation of numbers between 1 and 10.

Equation B.2: Sum the Numbers Between 1 and 10

$$f = \sum_{i=1}^{10} i$$

The above equation could easily be written as the following C# program:

```
int total = 0;
for(int i=1;i<=10;i++)
{
   count = count + i;
}
Console.WriteLine( "Result: " + count );
```

In equation B.2, you can see that variable **i** starts at 1 and ends at 10. These numbers are below and above the sigma, respectively. The value to the right of the sigma specifies the amount to add with each iteration. For this simple equation, the summation is only being performed on **i**; however, variable **i** could be replaced with a more complex equation. Consider Equation B.3.

Equation B.3: Sum the Values Between 1 and 10

$$f = \sum_{i=1}^{10} 2i+1$$

The above equation could easily be written as the following C# program:

```
int total = 0;
for(int i=1;i<=10;i++)
{
   count = count + (i*2)+1;
}
Console.WriteLine( "Result: " + count );
```

As you can see, the sigma notation indicates that the value of the equation is summed for each value of **i** specified.

Derivatives and Integrals

Derivatives and integrals are concepts from calculus. It is sometimes necessary to take the derivative or the integral of a threshold function. The derivative of a function is a measurement of how a function changes when the values of its inputs change. Equation B.4 shows the derivative of a simple function.

Equation B.4: Taking the Derivative of x2

$$\frac{d}{dx}x^2 = 2x$$

The integral of a function is equal to the area of a region in the xy-plane bounded by the graph of f, the x-axis, and the vertical lines x = a and x = b, with areas below the x-axis being subtracted. Equation B.5 shows how to calculate the integral of the sigmoid function.

Equation B.5: Calculating the Integral of the Sigmoid Function

$$\int \frac{1}{1+e^{-x}}\,dx = x + \ln\left(1+e^{-x}\right) = \ln\left(1+e^{x}\right)$$

If you are unfamiliar with derivatives and integrals, an introductory calculus book may be helpful. Fortunately, you do not need an in-depth understanding of calculus to understand neural networks. Generally, you will need to calculate the integral of a threshold function, and you can easily find the integral of most common threshold functions on the Internet. The integrals for two activation functions are provided in chapter 5 of this book.

APPENDIX C: COMMON THRESHOLD FUNCTIONS

Threshold functions are very important to neural networks. Threshold functions keep the numbers processed by neural networks within acceptable ranges. Your choice of which threshold function to use is very important to the operation of the neural network, since it will limit the numbers that can be accepted and output by the network.

Linear Threshold Function

The linear threshold function is the simplest of the threshold functions. In fact, it is not really a threshold function at all, as whatever number is passed to it is returned unchanged. The equation for the linear threshold function is shown here:

Equation C.1: The Linear Threshold Function

$$f(x) = x$$

Generally speaking, you should never use the linear threshold function, because it does not keep the input or output of the neuron within any sort of range. Further, because there is no useful integral for Equation C.1, the backpropagation training algorithm cannot be used with the linear threshold function.

A graph of the linear threshold function is shown in Figure C.1.

Figure C.1: Graph of the Linear Threshold Function

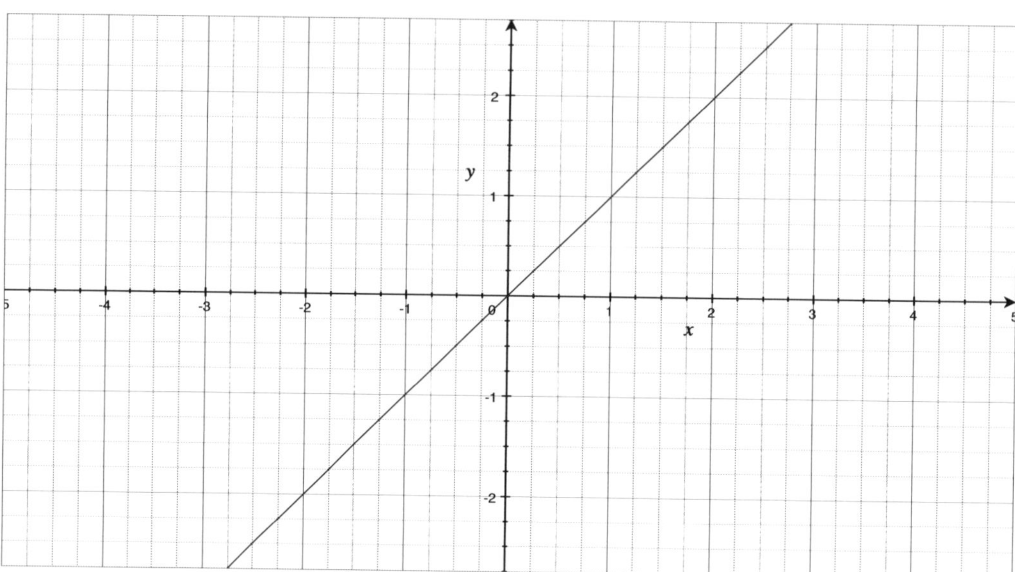

The two most commonly used threshold functions are the sigmoidal and hyperbolic tangent functions. These two threshold functions are covered in the next two sections.

Sigmoidal Threshold Function

The sigmoidal threshold function is useful when you will only be inputting positive numbers into the neural network. The equation for the sigmoidal function is shown in Equation C.2.

Equation C.2: The Sigmoidal Threshold Function

$$f(x) = \frac{1}{1 + e^{-x}}$$

A graph of the sigmoidal threshold function is shown in Figure C.2.

Figure C.2: Graph of the Sigmoidal Threshold Function

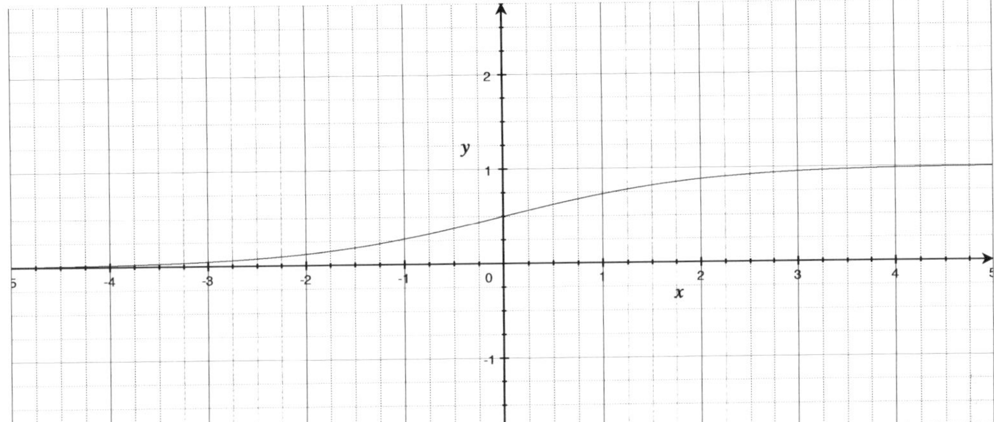

The backpropagation algorithm requires the integral of the threshold function. The integral of the sigmoidal threshold function is shown in Equation C.3.

Equation C.3: The Integral of the Sigmoidal Threshold Function

$$f(x) = \frac{e^x}{(1+e^x)^2}$$

One of the most significant limitations of the sigmoidal threshold function is that it is only capable of producing positive output. If negative output is required, then the hyperbolic tangent threshold function should be considered.

Hyperbolic Tangent Threshold Function

The hyperbolic tangent threshold function allows for both positive and negative output. The equation for the hyperbolic tangent threshold function is shown in Equation C.4.

Equation C.4: The Hyperbolic Tangent Threshold Function

$$f(x) = \frac{e^{2x} - 1}{e^{2x} + 1}$$

A graph of the hyperbolic tangent threshold function is shown in Figure C.3. As you can see, the hyperbolic tangent threshold function produces positive and negative numbers.

Figure C.3: Graph of the hyperbolic tangent threshold function.

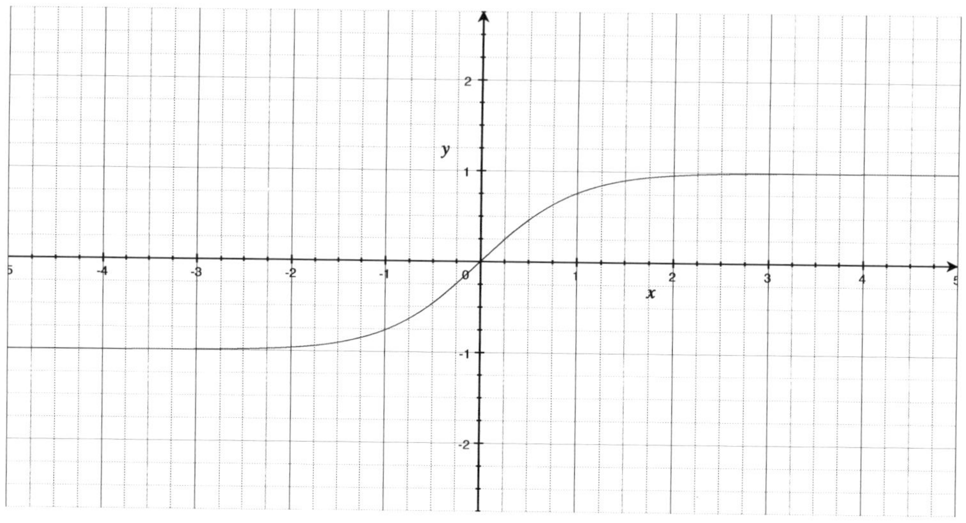

The integral for the hyperbolic tangent threshold function is also easy to obtain. Equation C.5 shows this integral.

Equation C.5: The Integral of the Hyperbolic Tangent Threshold Function

$$f(x) = 1 - e^{\left(\frac{e^{2x}-1}{e^{2x}+1}\right)}$$

APPENDIX D: EXECUTING EXAMPLES

All of the examples in this book have been compiled and tested with Microsoft Visual C# 2008, using version 3.5 of the .NET CLR. The examples should work with later versions of C# just fine. We tested with both the regular and express edition of C#. You can obtain a free version of C# Express at the following URL.

`http://www.microsoft.com/express/`

Using Visual Studio

The examples are packaged as individual projects in one solution. Once you download and uncompress the examples, use Visual Studio to open the solution file. You can do this simply by double clicking the solution file in Windows Explorer. Figure D.1 shows the solution file.

Figure D.1: Visual Studio Solution File

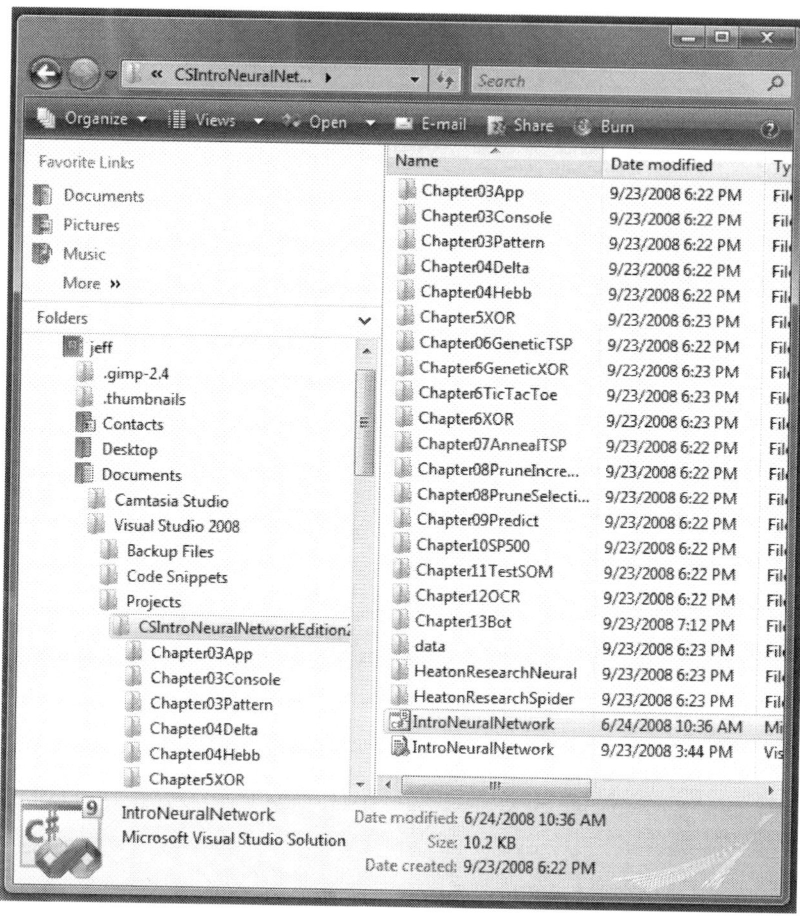

Figure D.2 shows the examples opened in Visual Studio.

Figure D.2: Neural Network Examples in Visual Studio

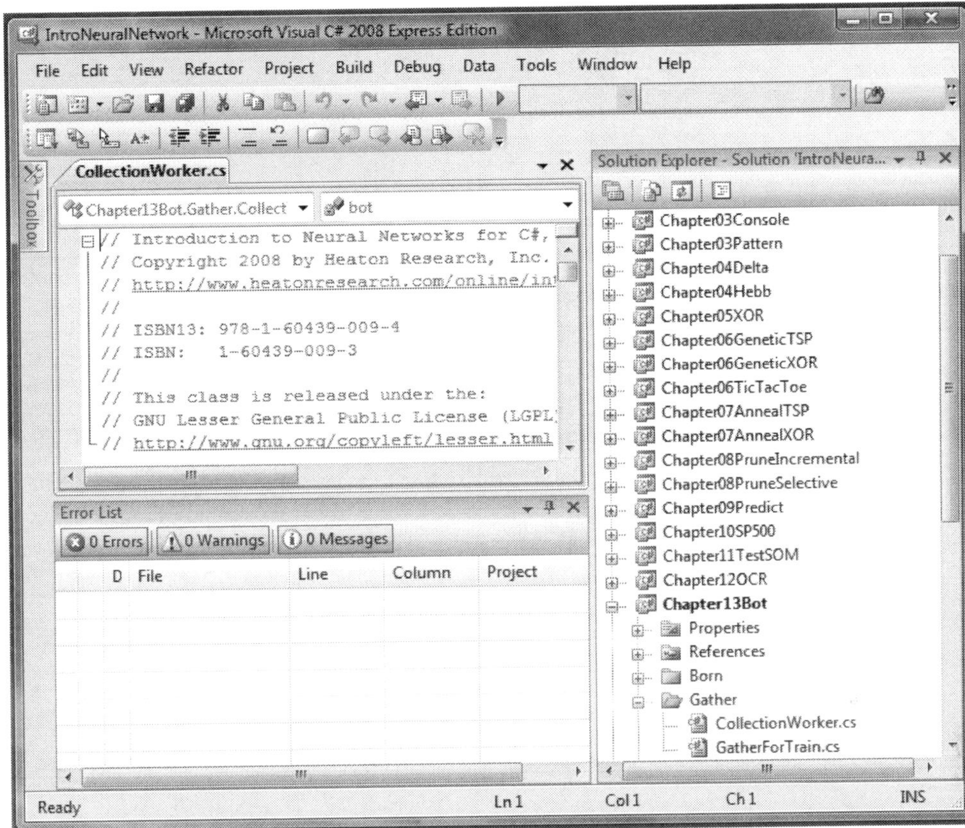

To pick which example to run, you must right-click the project and choose it as the startup project. Then when you select run, that project will start. Figure D.3 shows a project about to be selected.

Figure D.3: Selecting the Startup Project

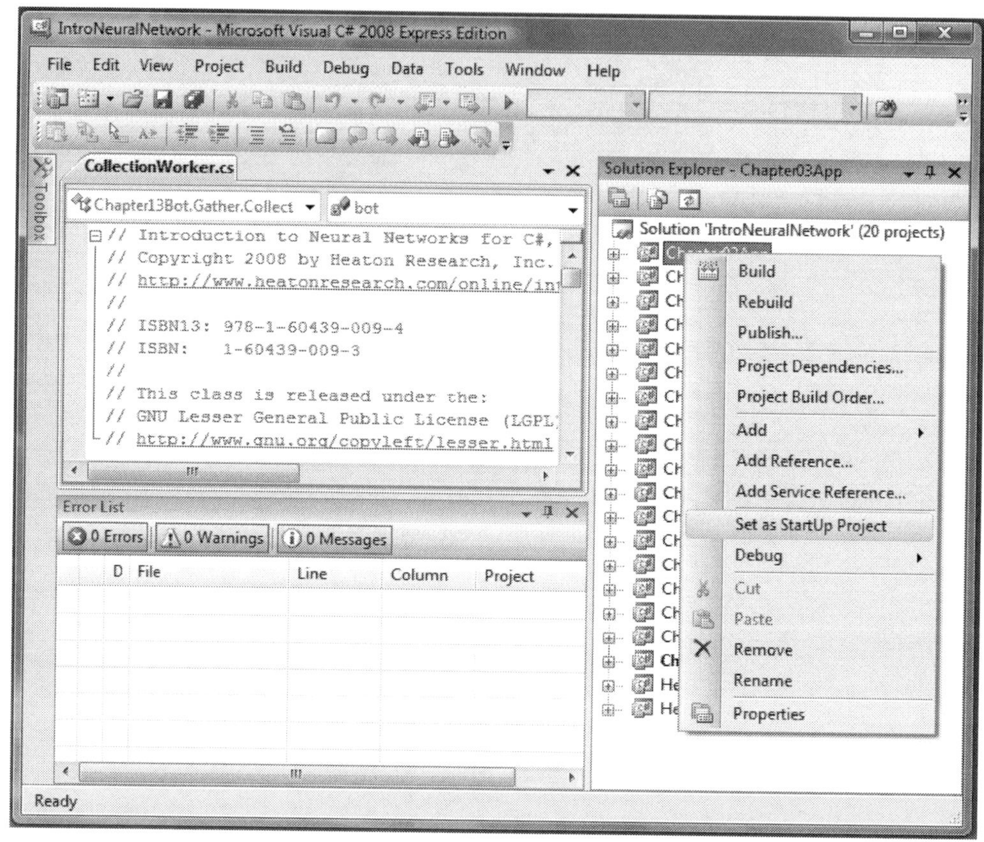

Some of the examples make use of external files that must be loaded. For example, the S&P 500 prediction example must load historic market data. These examples need to know where to find these files. This is set under the debug tab, of the properties. You must specify the location of the "data" directory contained with the downloaded files. Figure D.4 shows this property being set.

Figure D.4: Locate the Data Files

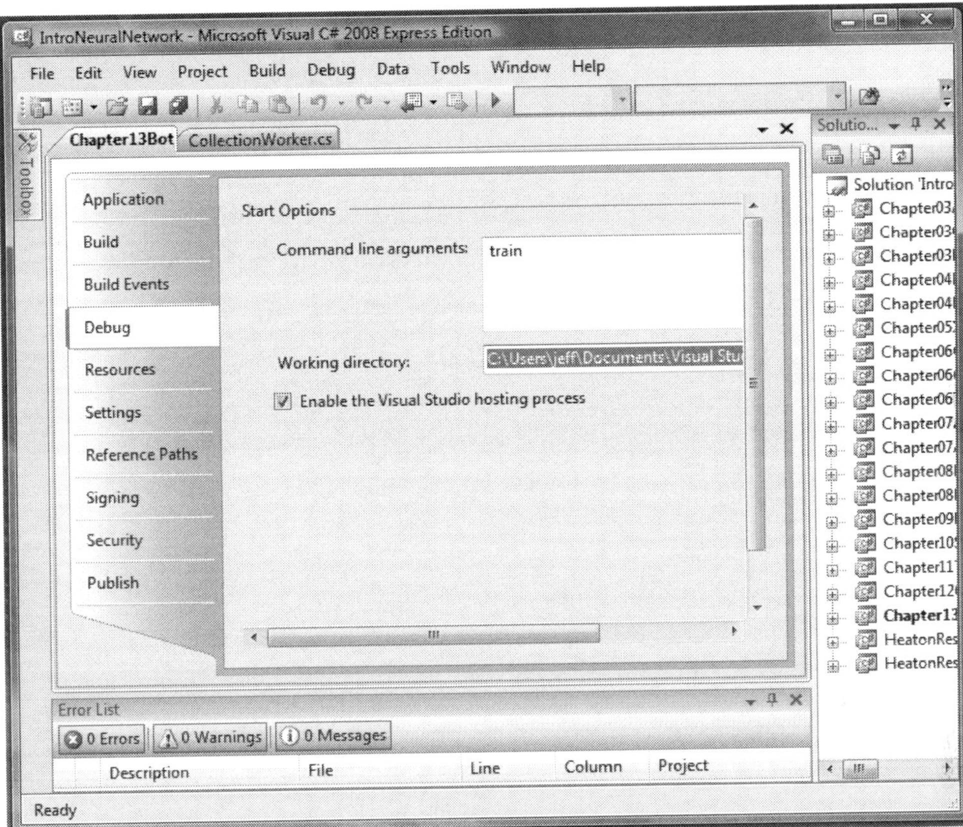

GLOSSARY

Activation Function – A mathematical function that the output of a neuron layer is passed through. The activation function ensures that the output is in the correct range. Common choices for activation functions include the hyperbolic tangent and the sigmoid function. (3)

Activation Level – Also called the threshold. The activation level is the input value a neuron requires to fire. (1)

Actual Data – Actual data is provided to the neural network, not provided by the neural network. If the accuracy of the actual data is acceptable, then it can be used to evaluate the accuracy of the neural network. (9)

Additive Weight Adjustment – A training technique used to train self-organizing maps. The calculated weight matrix deltas are added together. See also subtractive weight adjustment. (11)

Analog Computer – An analog computer processes information by varying the levels of voltage flowing through the computer. A digital computer uses only two voltage levels that represent either on or off. Most modern computers are not analog. See also digital computer or quantum computer. (1)

Annealing – A metallurgical process whereby molten metal is slowly cooled. This slow cooling produces a metal with a uniform molecular structure, which results in greater strength. A process modeled after annealing, called simulated annealing, is often used to train neural networks. (7)

Annealing Cycle – The period in which the temperature starts high and slowly decreases over an annealing. (7)

Artificial Intelligence – A broad field of study in the domain of computer science that attempts to simulate human thought processes using computer programs. (1)

Artificial Neural Network – A neural network composed of artificial neurons; generally simulated with a computer program. An artificial neural network attempts to simulate a biological neural network. (1)

Autoassociative – An autoassociative neural network echoes an input pattern back when the neural network recognizes it. If the pattern is not recognized, the neural network outputs the pattern that most closely matches the input data from those with which it was trained. (3)

Axon – An axon is a long, slender projection of a nerve cell, or neuron, that conducts electrical impulses away from the neuron's cell body or soma. (1)

Backpropagation – A method for training neural networks. Backpropagation works by analyzing the output layer and evaluating the contribution to the error of each of the previous layer's neurons. The previous layer is adjusted to attempt to minimize its contribution to the error. This process continues until the program has worked its way back to the input layer. (5)

Binary – A base-2 number system that uses only zeros and ones. Information in a digital computer is stored in binary. A value of 'true' is represented by 1 and a value of 'false' is represented by 0. Binary numbers appear as long strings of 1s and 0s. (1)

Biological Neural Network – A series of biological neurons inside a human or animal. Artificial neural networks attempt to emulate a biological neural network. (1)

Bipolar – A system for representing Boolean numbers where false is -1 and true is 1. The self-organizing map (SOM) and Hopfield Neural Network both use bipolar numbers. (2)

Boolean – A variable type that is either true or false. (2)

Bot – A computer program that performs repetitive tasks in place of a human. Bots often work directly with web sites or chat networks. (13)

Chromosome – A unit of genetic code in a life form. Chromosomes are made up of genes. The complete DNA sequence for a life form is made up of one or more chromosomes. See genetic algorithm. (6)

Classification – A technique used by neural networks to organize input into groups. (1)

Column Matrix – A matrix with only one column, and one or more rows. See row matrix. (2)

Comma Separated Value (CSV) File – A file format commonly used by Microsoft Excel and other spreadsheets. CSV files are often used as input to neural networks. (10)

Competitive Learning – A type of neural network training that returns output from one neuron, which is considered the winner, as opposed to returning output from each neuron. (11)

Connection Significance – The amount one connection contributes to desirable output from the neural network. A neuron that has connections of generally low connection significance can often be pruned from the neural network without having a sizable impact on the suitability of the neural network. (8)

Delta Rule – A gradient descent training technique that adjusts a network's weights based on differences between output and the ideal output. Backpropagation is a form of the delta rule. (4)

Dendrite – A branched projection of a neuron that conducts the electrical stimulation received from other neural cells to the cell body, or soma, of the neuron from which it projects. (1)

Derivative – A derivative is a measurement of how a function changes when the values of its inputs change. (5)

Digital Computer – A computer that processes information using digital signals. Most modern computers are digital. See also analog computer and quantum computer. (1)

Dot Product – A real number that is the product of the lengths of two vectors and the cosine of the angle between them. (2)

Downsample – The process of lowering the resolution of an image. Downsampling can be used to prepare an image for presentation to a neural network. (12)

Epoch – One training interval; synonymous with iteration. (4)

Evolution – The process by which an organism adapts itself to its surroundings. A genetic algorithm evolves towards an optimal solution. (6)

Excite – As temperature in a simulated annealing algorithm increases, the values of the weight matrix are increasingly excited, or changed slightly using random values. (7)

Feedforward – A neural network in which values only flow forward. The feedforward network is one of the most common neural network architectures. (5)

Fire – When a neuron fires, it sends output to the next layer. (1)

Gene – A unit of genetic material. One or more genes make up a chromosome. (6)

Genetic Algorithm – A training technique that attempts to emulate the natural process of evolution. Solutions are viewed as organisms that compete for the ability to mate. The best solutions mate and produce solutions that, ideally, are better than the parent solutions. (6)

Global Minimum – The smallest error for which a neural network can be trained. It is the goal of every training algorithm to reach the global minimum. See local minima. (10)

Hebb's Rule – An unsupervised type of training that reinforces what a neural network already knows. (4)

Hidden Layer – One or more layers of a neural network that occur between the input and output layers. (1)

Histogram – In statistics, a histogram is a graphical display of tabulated frequencies. It shows the proportion of cases that fall into each of several categories. (13)

Hopfield Neural Network – A Hopfield net, invented by John Hopfield, is a form of recurrent artificial neural network. Hopfield nets serve as content-addressable memory systems with binary threshold units. (3)

HTTP Protocol – The protocol that the World Wide Web (WWW) is built upon. Bots usually access web sites by using the HTTP protocol directly. (13)

Hybrid Training – A training method that utilizes one or more traditional training methods. A hybrid training method will often use backpropagation to train the neural network and then simulated annealing to move beyond local minima. (10)

Hyperbolic Tangent Activation Function – An activation function based on the hyperbolic tangent function. The hyperbolic tangent activation function outputs both positive and negative numbers. See activation function. (5)

Identity Matrix – A matrix that when multiplied by matrix X results in a product that is the same as matrix X. (2)

Incremental Pruning – A pruning method that gradually adds neurons to a neural network until the network can be trained to an acceptable level. See selective pruning. (8)

Input Layer – The layer of the neural network that accepts input. (1)

Input Normalization – A process for normalizing the input to a neural network into a specific range. This is a very common technique used with self-organizing maps (SOM). (11)

Iteration – One cycle through the training process. Synonymous with epoch. (1)

Kohonen Neural Network – A neural network developed by Dr. Teuvo Kohonen. Usually called a self-organizing map (SOM). See self-organizing map. (4)

Layer – A set of related neurons in a neural network. (1)

Learning Rate – A concept in many neural network training algorithms that specifies how radically the weight matrix should be updated based on training results. Properly setting the learning rate can have a profound impact on the speed with which the neural network learns. Setting it too low will impede performance; too high may cause the neural network to behave randomly and never converge on a solution. (4)

Linear Activation Function – A very simple activation function that always returns exactly what was provided. A linear activation function is rarely used, as it has no real effect. (5)

Local Minima – The low points of error for a neural network. It can often be challenging for neural network training to escape local minima on the way to the global minimum. (10)

Mate – A biological process whereby a male organism and a female organism produce an offspring that shares DNA with each parent. A genetic algorithm produces offspring solutions from two superior parent solutions. Ideally, the offspring has a good chance of being superior to both parent solutions. (6)

Matrix – A rectangular table of numbers that can have a number of operations performed on it. A neural network's memory is stored in a matrix. (1)

Min-Max Algorithm – A brute-force algorithm often used to play games. All possible moves are considered and only a move that might result in a win is chosen. (6)

Momentum – A concept used in many neural network training algorithms that specifies **the** degree to which the previous training iteration should influence the current iteration. (5)

Multicore CPU – A CPU architecture that facilitates the efficient concurrent processing of multiple threads. The CPU has multiple cores, each capable of acting as a traditional CPU. While one core is executing one thread, other cores can execute other threads. Software must be specifically designed to take advantage of a multicore CPU. (6)

Multiplicative Normalization – A simple normalization technique based on vector length that is commonly used with a self-organizing map. In general, you will want to use z-axis normalization, unless many of the values are near zero. If many of the values are near zero, multiplicative normalization may work better. (11)

Mutate – A biological process in which the offspring of two parents does not receive exact copies of the parents' DNA. The DNA undergoes a small degree of change and randomness is introduced. This provides genetic variety that may not have been available from either parent. It will either produce a better solution or a genetically inferior solution. See genetic algorithm. (6)

Neural Network – A computer algorithm that attempts to simulate biological neurons. A neural network can be trained to a variety of problems. (1)

Neuron – A neuron is one component of a neural network. A neuron is a member of one layer of the network and has connections to the next layer. In some neural network architectures, neurons may also have connections to themselves, as well as previous layers. (1)

Optical Character Recognition (OCR) – A process by which a computer turns an image file containing text into a text file. To do this, the computer must recognize each individual character in the image. (12)

Ornithopter – An aircraft that flies by flapping its wings—similar to a bird. Most early attempts at aircraft were ornithopters. (14)

Output Layer – The final layer of a neural network that produces the output for the neural network. (1)

Overfitting – Occurs when the neural network has so much information processing capacity that the limited amount of information contained in the training set is not enough to train all of the neurons in the hidden layers. See underfitting. (5)

Parsing – The process used by a computer to analyze, and to some degree understand, textual input. (13)

Pattern Recognition – Neural networks can be trained to recognize and classify patterns. These neural networks perform pattern recognition. (1)

Perceptron – A type of artificial neural network invented in 1957 at the Cornell Aeronautical Laboratory by Frank Rosenblatt. It can be thought of as the simplest kind of feedforward neural network, a linear classifier. (14)

Population – A group of solutions in a genetic algorithm. The best solutions in the population mate and produce new solutions. See genetic algorithm. (6)

Prediction – An attempt to use current data to predict future data. Neural networks can sometimes be used to make predictions. (1)

Predictive Neural Network – A neural network that is designed to make predictions. A predictive neural network is also called a temporal neural network. (9)

Prime Interest Rate – A term applied in many countries to a reference interest rate used by banks. (10)

Pruning – A process for removing unnecessary neurons from the hidden or input layers of a neural network. (8)

Quantum Computer – A device for computation that makes direct use of quantum mechanical phenomena, such as superposition and entanglement, to perform operations on data. Quantum computers are primarily a theoretical concept and are not currently used. See also digital computer or analog computer. (14)

Quantum Neural Network – A neural network created on a quantum computer. (14)

Qubit – A unit of quantum information in a quantum computer. (14)

Root Mean Square (RMS) – Also known as the quadratic mean, is a statistical measure of the magnitude of a varying quantity. (4)

Row Matrix – A matrix with only one row and one or more columns. See column matrix. (2)

S & P 500 – A collection of 500 US-based companies defined by Standard and Poor. The S & P 500 is often used as a benchmark for the US economy. (10)

Sample – A piece of data obtained at a specific time. (10)

Scalar – A real number. See vector. (2)

Selective Pruning – A pruning technique for removing neurons that have minimal connection relevance. These neurons should not impact the overall effectiveness of the neural network. See incremental pruning. (8)

Self-Organizing Map (SOM) – A type of neural network that is trained using unsupervised learning to produce a low-dimensional (typically two-dimensional), representation of the input space of the training samples, called a map. This map can be used to classify new patterns outside of the training set. (4)

Sigmoid Activation Function – An activation function that has a "c", or sigmoid, shape. The output from the sigmoid activation function does not include negative numbers. See activation function. (5)

Signal – Another name for the input to a neural network. (1)

Simulated Annealing – A training technique that attempts to simulate the metallurgical process of annealing. The neural network is put through several annealing cycles in which the memory of the neural network is excited, or randomized, as the temperature is decreased over the cycles. (7)

Sine Wave – The output from the trigonometric sine function. The sine function produces a distinctive wave pattern. (9)

Single-Layer Neural Network – A neural network that contains a single layer. This single layer acts as both the input and output layer. There are no hidden layers in a single-layer neural network. (3)

Subtractive Weight Adjustment – A training technique used with self-organizing maps in which the weight deltas are subtracted from the weight matrix. (11)

Supervised Training – A training method that provides a neural network with expected outputs. The neural network is then trained to produce these desired outputs. See unsupervised training. (1)

Synapse – Specialized junctions through which neurons signal to each other and to non-neuronal cells, such as those in muscles or glands. (1)

Temperature – The degree to which a neural network's matrix should be randomized. Simulated annealing subjects a neural network to a decreasing temperature. See simulated annealing. (7)

Temporal Neural Network – A neural network that is designed to make predictions. Also called a predictive neural network. (9)

Thread Pool – A series of threads that are used to perform parts of a task. A thread pool allows a program to better utilize a multicore CPU. (6)

Thresholds – Threshold values exist for each neuron in the neural network. These values determine whether or not the neuron's input is sufficient to fire. Threshold values are usually stored in the same matrix as the weights. (1)

Time Slice – An interval at which a sample is taken. (9)

Training – A process used to adjust a neural network to produce more desirable output. (1)

Truth Table – A table that shows the possible inputs and expected outputs for a mathematical operation. (1)

Turing Machine – An abstract concept of a computer that is able to execute any defined algorithm. (14)

Underfitting – Occurs when there are too few neurons in the hidden layers of a network to adequately detect the signals in a complicated data set. (5)

Unsupervised Training – A training method that does not provide the neural network with expected outputs. See supervised training. (1)

Validation – The process of evaluating how well a neural network has been trained. Validation is often performed using actual data that was not made part of the training set. (1)

Vector – A matrix that is composed of a single row or single column. A vector may not have multiple rows and columns. (2)

Von Neumann Machine – A design model for a stored-program digital computer that uses a processing unit and a single separate storage structure to hold both instructions and data. See quantum computer. (14)

Weight Matrix – The weights between the neurons. A layer's weighs are often stored in the same matrix as the threshold values. (1)

XOR – A logical operation, also called exclusive disjunction. It is a type of logical disjunction on two operands that results in a value of "true" if and only if exactly one of the operands has a value of "true." (1)

Z-Axis Normalization – A normalization technique that is based on adding a z-axis component. Z-axis normalization is typically used with a self-organizing map. In general, you will want to use z-axis normalization, unless many of the values are near zero. If many of the values are near zero, multiplicative normalization may work better. (11)

INDEX

32502648R00241